CONTENTS

INTRODUCTION TO THIS EDITION	vii
Preface	xxi

ADVENTURE 1

Intransigence	3
A Preliminary Encounter	11
A Lull	23
Coming To Grips	29
Capitulation	43

ADVENTURE 2

Prologue	49
Coming Events	57
Shatrah	63
The Legacy Of The Turks	69
British Methods	75
The Rumblings Of Rebellion	81
Holding The Fort	89

ADVENTURE 3

On Trek With The Sultan In The Western Batinah	107
On Trek With The Sultan In The Western Batinah	133
A Hold Up— A Camel Journey Across The Oman Peninsula	161
On Trek With The Sultan Through The Shamailiyah	187
Trekking Southwards Home	213

ADVENTURE 4

The Alarm	225
The State Gunboat Al Saidi's Commander	233
In The Land Of The Shuhites	239
The List Of Iniquities	247
A Naval Bombardment	257

ADVENTURE 5

A Thwarted Flirtation	277
With The Bani Bu Ali	287
Southern Borderlands	297
Sharks And Locusts	311
The Unknown Interior	319
Endnotes	329
Images	341
INDEX	343

ALARMS AND EXCURSIONS IN ARABIA

BERTRAM THOMAS IN IRAQ AND OMAN DURING
THE EARLY 20TH CENTURY

BERTRAM THOMAS

Arabesque

TO

HIS HIGHNESS THE SULTAN OF MUSCAT AND OMAN,
SIR SAIYID TAIMUR BIN FAISAL BIN TURKI BIN SAID, K.C.I.E..
C.S.I.

WITH ACKNOWLEDGMENTS
FOR MANY FAVOURS ENJOYED AT HIS HANDS
AND IN TOKEN OF
FIVE HAPPY YEARS SPENT IN THE
SERVICE OF HIS STATE

INTRODUCTION TO THIS EDITION

This edition has been completely retyped, images from the original books were scanned to improve print quality, and place-specific modern photographs included for context. Punctuation and spellings, though occasionally at odds with current usage and often inconsistent within the book have generally been kept as in the Bertram Thomas text. However, where place names have been inconsistent, such as Dabai, Dibai and Dubai – a single choice was made, in this case to the current spelling, Dubai. People's names also required some standardisation, most especially Badr bin Rumaiyidh who also was called Badr ar Rumaiyidh. Badr bin Rumaiyidh has been used, as Gavin Young's book 'Return to the Marshes' included that style of his name, and it avoids confusion with the settlement named Badr ar Rumaiyidh.

Though Bertram Thomas showed a profound understanding of both the people and customs of Iraq and Oman (as described in his book Alarms & Excursions in Arabia), indeed his work in Iraq entailed him acting as judge, Thomas's tone is detached and full of phrases that today are at the least politically incorrect and certainly derogatory. His phrasing may simply be the every-day terminology used 100 years ago, with no meaning to be assumed, much as today's language is full of phrasing that is easy to be offended by. His ability to achieve his aims in Iraq and in Oman show that he, in fact, maintained a very positive relationship with all he met. In Iraq, during 1920 Iraqi revolt against British rule, he used his rapport with the shaikhs of the area he administered to ensure that there was effectively no uprising against Britain by the population he was administrator of. In Oman he needed to negotiate for escorts and camels for transport at several stages on his journey down the east coast of Oman to Salala. Most of that route was in areas only nominally under the administration of Oman's ruler the Sultan Taimur, and neither the Sultan Taimur or Britain would be in a position to offer a lone British traveller any support.

Thomas lived in Iraq from 1916 to 1922, and usually as the only Englishman in town. Perforce, he spoke in Arabic after his appointment as a British Assistant Political Officer and learnt the culture of his region. His subsequent time in Jordan (Trans-Jordan), though shorter and part of a larger British team, must also have reinforced his awareness of the fundamentals of the culture in northern Arabia. Moving to Muscat for 5 years, from 1925, and living and travelling by camel through Oman built on these insights. It's clear that he had an enquiring mind-set, as the pages of his writings are full of either his questions or explanations by his companions about some aspect of a location or culture.

Despite his remarkable life, from working in Iraq then becoming a minister for the Oman government, and the achievement of being the first non-Arab to cross the Rub Al Khali, Bertram Thomas has been eclipsed in fame by his contemporaries. Reading his correspondence with the British Raj bureaucracy, it is quite possible that he resented the restrictions put on him; he wrote sardonically to British officials after their reply to his request to take up part-time employment as a newspaper correspondent, that he regretted causing them a waste of paper, suggest irritation at the least. After his crossing of the Rub Al Khali which was the subject of his book 'Arabia Felix', there was some correspondence about awarding him a knighthood as suggested to the

British Prime Minister Ramsay MacDonald, by an un-named government Minister. In May 1931 the Viceroy of India, the Earl of Willingdon, on the advice of the Persian Gulf Resident (this term and Political Resident were used interchangeably in the region for the same senior British position), advised the Prime Minister that it was to be 'deprecated'. Key reasons given were Thomas's 'deceptive' organisation of the Rub Al Khali crossing; though when planned earlier in the year by Thomas it would have been made during any two month holiday at the end of his 5 year contract and before the start of his hoped for additional 3 years employment. Additionally, his 'lax' handling of the Sultanate's finances was mentioned, noting that 'he has taken little interest in his work'. It's clear that the establishment, after declining offering him any honour, would have been unlikely to enhance his reputation as an explorer at all.

Bertram Thomas was born on 13 June 1892 in a large village Pill, near Bristol the city and port on the River Avon in western England. A rail line, between a new port for Bristol at Portishead west of Pill (on the south bank of the River Avon) and the city to the east, served the village. The adjacent port of Avonmouth on the north side of the Avon made the area of Pill ideal for sailors and workers at these ports, and the village became well known for the mariners living there. Bertram Thomas's father, William, a master mariner who worked as a pilot (as did many of his family), lived at Avon Villa, 5 Springfield Road in Pill, one of a row of modest houses near the village centre.

Thomas's father died, leaving his wife and five children, when Bertram was 16. Enabling his mother, Eliza, and his siblings to remain living in Avon Villa, Thomas started working at the Post Office the same year. As with so many men in Europe, the 1st World War changed his life. Thomas joined the North Somerset Yeomanry serving in Belgium, 1914-15. He then was posted with 4th Battalion Prince Albert's (Somerset Light Infantry) to Mesopotamia, the start of 34 years association with the Arab world.

In origin, this regiment was founded during the reign of King James II in 1685. The rapid increase in the British military in the 1st World War also increased the size of Prince Albert's (Somerset Light Infantry) to 18 battalions. After the Ottoman Empire sided with the German Empire, Britain, through the British Raj in India, invaded Iraq, with large numbers of Indian troops involved. After the major Ottoman victory against Britain in the Siege of Kut in January 1916, and a series of connected British military failures in the country, a wholesale reorganisation of the military in Iraq was undertaken. The military was to be overseen from London, rather than India, with new Generals and, after the death or wounding of 23,000 men and capture of 13,000 at Kut, new forces were required. The 4th Battalion was originally based in India from 1914 and its repositioning into Mesopotamia was when Thomas joined it, where he was one of some 150,000 troops in the country. Britain eventually overwhelmed the Ottoman forces and occupied Baghdad in March 1917. At the end of the 1st World War the number of soldiers were substantially reduced, however Britain then had a new role in Iraq, that of the League of Nations mandatory power.

In spring 1918 Thomas moved into the British Mandate administration of Iraq. Arnold Wilson, who wrote the preface to Alarms and Excursions was the administrator for Iraq and also acting Persian Gulf Resident (the regional governor within the British India Raj). Wilson however had an approach at odds with the growing attitude in London, which was that Iraq should become independent. A revolt in Iraq during 1920, described in Alarms and Excursions, was partly a result of Wilson's methods, following which Wilson was removed from his job. Thomas eventually became Assistant Political Officer at Al Shatrah, an Ottoman-era town in southern Iraq, near the marshes. The town was a key centre for the al-Muntafiq tribe, Iraq's largest and most influential Iraqi Shia tribe. Small numbers from the Jewish and Mandean (monotheistic Gnostic religion) communities also inhabited the area. Thomas was not only the political administrator for the town and its surrounds, but the policeman and judge, an unenviable situation for the only British representative in the area. The previous practice of hearing court cases was in the imperial power's language, previously Turkish. He heard all his cases in Arabic, testimony to his fluency in the language. Remarkably during the 'Iraqi Revolt' between May–October 1920 which was widespread against British rule, his district did not rise against the administration, therefore his official role can be considered a success.

For a time Thomas lived in the same Baghdad compound as Gertrude Bell, attending various events with her and others. Despite Thomas being an official in the country, the book Alarms and Excursions does not cover the next key event in Iraqi history, the installation of King Faisal as King of Iraq in August 1921. Thomas's abilities were however recognised with the award of an O.B.E. He then transferred to Trans-Jordan in 1922 as Assistant British Representative. He was a rising part of the British administration in the Middle East, his next position was confirmation of their confidence in him; it would be life changing for him.

Great Britain's first contact with Oman dates to AD1613 when a ship, the Expedition, anchored off Dhofar with an ambassador to Persia, Sir Thomas Powell. A treaty with the English East India Company was signed in AD1646 by Philip Wylde with Imam Nasir bin Murshid Al Yarubi giving the English exclusive trading rights and religious freedom along with extraterritorial jurisdiction, along with the exclusion of any other Christian nation to have supply rights at Sohar. Further treaties were concluded between Oman and Britain; however the most significant event in the relationship was not directly between Oman & Britain but came with the death of Sultan Said bin Sultan, who ruled Oman and Zanzibar and their various dependencies. An agreement, supported by Britain, between two sons of Sultan Said bin Sultan formalised the separation of these two regions, with one son becoming ruler of Zanzibar and its dependencies and another ruler of Oman and its dependencies that included Gwadar in Pakistan. With the stroke of a pen, Oman was separated from its wealthier former colony. Oman from that date became increasingly reliant on Britain for financial, political and military support.

This reliant relationship between Oman and Britain was thrown into sharp focus in 1920, when the Treaty of Seeb, an agreement between Sultan Taimur and the Imam Salim ibn Rashid al-Kharusi, was signed.

The Imam a religious and political leader, whose supporters controlled the northern mountain region around Al Jabal Al Akhdar, had been leading a revolt against the Sultan's rule for several years, which was noted in The Times 18 September 1913. The 1st World War had impeded any general support Britain might be able to offer to Sultan Taimur. In general, there was a disinclination to become militarily involved in Oman, and this continued after the war. The Treaty of Seeb was directly negotiated between the Imam's representatives and the British Political Agent Ronald Wingate, Sultan Taimur being in India. The treaty agreed that the Imam could rule in the mountain areas under his control and the Sultan in the coastal and others areas under his control and that only the Sultan would conduct foreign relations of either side.

Sultan Taimur bin Faisal Al Said, who Thomas would be working for, became the ruler of Muscat and Oman in 1913 after his father Sultan Faisal bin Turki died. Sultan Faisal had become increasingly reliant on Britain for income, and both internal and external security; a state of affairs that continued after the accession of 27-year-old Sultan Taimur. In 1924, a search of a financial adviser/minister for the Sultanate of Muscat and Oman and Sultan Taimur got underway.

The Persian Gulf Resident at Bushire in Persia, Arthur Prescott Trevor, had noted that the finances of the Sultanate of Muscat and Oman needed an overhaul and modern methods. Reginald Graham Hinde, the British Political Agent (a form of British ambassador but here also power behind the throne) in Muscat, started a search for a financial adviser/minister on 17 March 1924, noting that Sultan Taimur hoped to interview the applicant in Dehra Dun, the north Indian summer resort, during June. A person under 40, who had experience in Egypt or Iraq was preferred and fluency in Arabic was essential. The salary would be Indian Rupees (INR) 1,500 a month, rising by INR100 annually (INR10 – 15 to GBP1 appx), with an annual holiday of one month and furnished accommodation.

Several British people working in Iraq were considered for the financial adviser/minister position; however their poor health or lack of Arabic resulted in Thomas being considered from 24 May. On 21 July, having arrived from Jordan, he was interviewed by Reginald Hinde in Muscat, and they proposed a meeting with Sultan Taimur bin Faisal, with Thomas requesting employment from early September. The Sultan of Muscat and Oman was moving between Bombay, Karachi and Dehra Dun during the second half of 1924 and communication with him was by telegram. On 29 July Thomas, accompanied by Hinde, was interviewed by the Sultan at the Taj Mahal Hotel in Bombay and was accepted for the position. However the Persian Gulf Resident at Bushire in the Persian Gulf also needed to meet Thomas to approve his appointment, so Thomas sailed on the 'Vasna' from Bombay to arrive at Bushire, on the 6 August. These delays meant that the appointment date slipped to 1 April 1925, and a temporary person from India was considered until then. The appointment of Thomas was confirmed by telegram 24 September 1924 and the temporary person from India, Mr Bower, was approved on 10 October 1924. By 31 January 1925 Thomas was in London to organise his arrival into Muscat, having left Trans-Jordan.

Bertram Thomas planned to leave London on 27 February 1925, arriving in Bombay on 23 March and berthing in Muscat on 1 April (he actually arrived on 2 April). His accommodation was to be a 'comparatively', new house, in Muscat about 80 meters behind the British seafront 'embassy' and close to the home of the new British Political Agent Charles Gilbert Crosthwaite. Both embassy and the house, Bait Kharajiyah, were demolished in 2005, and the new guest palace in Muscat lies over their location. The only thing missing from Thomas's home was its furniture. This was purchased in Bombay, the shipment included cutlery and a bed, the allowance was given at INR4,000.

Remarkably, the British Political Agent in Muscat only drew up the details of Thomas's employment contract on 14 April 1926, almost 2 years after the search had started. On 18 April the Council of Ministers of Oman, two members of the royal family and two Omani advisors approved the furniture purchase. On 25 June, the approval for his contract was received from the British Resident at Bushire, with an amendment increasing his leave from one month per year to two months. The agreement was signed on 23 July by Thomas and Sultan Taimur and witnessed by Captain Reginald George Evelyn William Alban, yet another new British Political Agent in Muscat.

Muscat at the time was a coastal town hemmed by arid mountains, one of a series of sea bays including its own and a larger one at the nearby town of Mutrah. The town walls of Muscat secured it and enabled some control over the comings and goings of people. The Sultan's palace and adjacent British Political Agent's building (the embassy) dominated the seafront, and on either side of the harbour two crumbling Portuguese forts offered some semblance of power. Muscat had changed little for a century, indeed there was no road connection between Muscat and Mutrah or any other farther location, though one was constructed in 1927 (it remained unpaved until 1962). In its heyday, 70 years earlier, Muscat was by far the most important port in the north Arabian Sea, however trade had long ago moved to other ports in the Arabian Gulf.

Thomas was clearly unused to the bureaucracy his role in Muscat entailed. He sent a letter to Sir Arnold Wilson the former administrator in Baghdad, now the manager of the Anglo-Persian Oil Company Middle Eastern operation, and Thomas sped up delivery by using the British official delivery service. The letter was returned to Muscat on 12 August 1925 attached to a letter from a secretary at the Persian Gulf Residency in Bushire to Reginald Alban, the Political Agent in Muscat with an official request that all such letters be sent through the Political Agent. A personal covering letter by Charles Crosthwaite, who had worked in Muscat and who was now in Bushire, to Alban was also sent noting that Thomas is 'now apt to forget his own place in the scheme of things'. Wilson subsequently wrote the preface to Alarms and Excursions in Arabia. Later in the year, when Thomas was approached to be a part-time newspaper correspondent in Oman, he asked permission from the Persian Gulf Resident in Bushire to undertake the work. The approval was granted on 17 September 1925, subject to any article being shown to the Political Agent in Muscat. Thomas withdrew his request on 20 October and noted he regretted causing a 'waste of the Political Resident's (Persian Gulf Resident's) time and stationery'.

Thomas, however, did adapt to his place in the scheme of things and adapted them to his ambitions.

Francis Bellville Prideaux, the Persian Gulf Resident wrote, on 24 April 1926, to the Secretary to the Government of India in the Foreign and Political Department. He noted that the Sultan of Muscat wishes Mr B.S. Thomas, at present Financial Adviser to the State, to be recognised as a member of his State Council, and to be referred to in official correspondence as 'Wazir', (not Mr.). In the letter from Prideaux, some consideration was given to the requirement for official gun salutes by British government vessels to members of the State Council, in the absence of the Sultan. It was noted that "Mr Thomas should not be the minister in question can definitely safeguarded against". Prideaux concluded by writing that "In these circumstances I recommend that the Sultan's request be agreed to". A further letter dated 18 June from Prideaux to Secretary to the Government of India in the Foreign and Political Department, said "In my opinion no objection exists at the present time to the Sultan's request about Mr Thomas. This officer understands his positon thoroughly and, so far, has executed his duties to the entire satisfaction of all parties in Muscat". They emphasised the point about gun salutes in an additional letter on 18 July, which concluded by agreeing to the Sultan's request. The British Consulate and Political Agency confirmed this on 22 July, "subject to the condition that in no case should Mr Thomas alone pay an official visit to a British Government vessel". There were no restrictions on his accompanying any other member of the Council of the Muscat State. The issue regarding gun salutes must have arisen as the Sultan received a sovereign's salute of 21 guns, the highest level given to local rulers (Maharajas etc) in the British Raj's sphere. However, the Persian Gulf Resident received a 13 gun salute, and the Political Agent received an 11 gun salute; clearly Thomas could not be allowed to rise above them in the gun salute scheme of things, even while representing the Sultan.

Notwithstanding his role as finance minister, Thomas's focus does seem to have been exploration of the country. In Alarms and Excursions in Arabia he wrote "But the bondage of an office stool …. was less to my liking than the comparatively free life — most of it spent in the saddle —

of a District Political Officer". In 1926, he travelled northwest from Muscat and, from the coast, cut through the mountains to Sharjah, in what was then termed 'Trucial Oman'.

Thomas had planned his Rub Al Khali crossing for several years and made clear his desire to Sultan Taimur by 1926. In winter 1927-28, he travelled from Suwaiah, south of Sur Oman, down the coast to Salalah. He had to negotiate safe passage and include *rabias* (a tribesman of an area to act as protector) along the way and moving south towards Salala obtained replacement fresh camels and their bedouin owners at Bani bu Ali, Khaluf and Wadi Ainain.

In 1928 he had visited Kuwait and met Harold Dickson whom he had known from Iraq and was previously British Agent in Kuwait, but was now working with the Kuwait Oil Company. According to Wilfred Thesiger, Dickson had told Thomas that he (Dickson) planned to cross the Empty Quarter & Thomas replied: "I should consider that a most unfriendly action. I intend to cross the Empty Quarter and live the rest of my life on the proceeds". Thesiger's negative recollection of his own conversation with Dickson may have been coloured by Thomas having achieved the first crossing and Thesiger relying not only the Bedouin who Thomas had recruited but also on Thomas's own maps, which were so detailed that Thesiger could successfully plot a route to a water well in the Rub Al Khali by merely relying on the map.

Visiting Dhofar in January 1930 with Sultan Taimur Al Said, the two now being on very friendly terms, Thomas obtained the Sultan's recommendation of him to key sheikhs. He then left Salala on what was an exploratory journey in Dhofar with 40 camels and a total of 31 people. They included 25 Bedouin from the Bait Kathir, Ar Rashid and Bait Imani tribes who would be a key to his expected travel into the Rub Al Khali later in the year. The party ascended the well-vegetated Jabal Qara before descending through arid foothills to travel north, on the eastern edge of the sands of the Rub Al Khali.

Thomas played a significant, if not critical, role in Musandam, a northern exclave, remaining part of the Sultanate of Muscat and Oman. Following the leader of the main tribe of Musandam sending a letter announcing the region was independent from the Sultan, Thomas sailed in April 1930 from Muscat to Musandam. After unsuccessful negotiation with rebellious inhabitants in Musandam a short naval bombardment was organised, its success detailed in the book 'Alarms and Excursions in Arabia'.

Both Bertram Thomas and Sultan Taimur had wished that Thomas would remain in his position for a further three years after his five-year contract ended (in April 1930) with Sultan Taimur writing to the British Political Agent in Muscat during March 1930 after his Dhofar trip. However, in May the Persian Gulf Resident at Bushire was looking for a replacement for Thomas, the purpose to save INR500, and in July Stuart Hedgcock had applied for the position. Hedgcock had worked in the British political service Iraq for over 12 years, joining as Thomas had done after the 1st World War. Though having obviously staying after April 1930, in anticipation of his employment being extended, Thomas would be unemployed on Hedgcock's arrival. On 3 October 1930 Thomas wrote detailing that he would leave his employment on 1 January 1931. The Persian Gulf Resident in Bushire wrote to the British Political Agent in Muscat that Stuart Hedgcock, who Thomas must have known from Iraq, should arrive in the last week of December. Thomas left Muscat for Salala on the night of 4 October. On 30 November Thomas wrote from Salala, to the Political Agent in Muscat, that the Muscat Council had agreed an unpaid leave of absence from 1-31 December and that "This will bring an easement to the Muscat Treasury of INR2,000 so I hope you will have no objection". The letter arrived in Muscat on 18 December, Thomas by then was approaching Shisur on the edge of the Rub Al Khali.

While crossing the desert with his guides, Thomas made little attempt to reduce the differences between him and the Omani's. He used a Bikaner-pattern saddle, a camel saddle used by soldiers from the British Raj. A heavy piece of equipment, it sat over the camels hump and was far les practical on this journey compared to the light south Arabian style that was placed behind the hump. As he noted, it meant that he rode a different camel almost daily. Under his turban he wore a shallow flying helmet with the brim removed, though unfortunately he gave no indication the benefit of using it. Throughout the journey Thomas was accompanied by his servant Muhammad, this alone must have created a barrier between him and the Bedouin he relied on. Muhammad must however been required as Thomas travelled with what may have been enough scientific equipment to require five pack camels, indeed the expedition seemed to have been partly organised to support Thomas in collecting plant and animal specimens, enabling him to create a report to scientific bodies in London. In this he achieved some success, for a species of lizard, abu qursh, 'the father of the dollar,' was new to science and is now named in his honour Uromastyx thomasi. Possibly the most separating aspect of his behaviour was that he travelled "with head callipers to make and record skull measurements, for such measurements are vital to anthropologists", he was practicing the now obsolete & discredited practice of craniofacial anthropometry. This must have been a degrading experience for the people whose skulls he measured as he also included fairly detailed physical measurement and recording of the subject.

Despite all these separating habits the crossing itself was not only remarkable in itself, it illustrated his ability to maintain the cohesion and loyalty of his group; something Wilfred Thesiger made use of over a decade later. Thomas was travelling with a group of independent people, who hardly acknowledged the authority of the Sultan of Muscat and Oman, let alone being in thrall to a strange Englishman travelling with them.

Thomas travelled with what may have been enough scientific equipment to require five pack camels, indeed the expedition seemed to have been partly organised to support Thomas in collecting plant and animal specimens, enabling him to create a report to scientific bodies in London. In this he achieved some success, for a species of lizard, *abu qursh*, 'the father of the dollar,' was new to science and is now named in his honour *Uromastyx thomasi*.

The route of the journey took the party north from Salala and over the verdant Jabal Qara mountains. They then tracked northwest, over the rocky plain, past Shisur and into the dunes of the Rub Al Khali at Shanna. From there it was a journey north, through the dune-fields until reaching the Sabkhat al Manasir, the water-logged sand-flats which are coated with a salt crust, near the Qatar peninsula.

Thomas succeeded in his attempt to become the first non-Arab to cross the Rub Al Khali on 5 February 1931, and the journey forms a major part of the book ' Arabia Felix'. After time spent in Doha Qatar, Thomas landed in Bahrain on 22 February 1931 and returned to Muscat, arriving 7 March, to then depart Oman forever.

As a postscript to Thomas's departure from Muscat, Hedgcock, the replacement as Financial Advisor to Thomas, resigned in June 1931. Sultan Taimur, after many years of expressing his wish to abdicate did so on 10 February 1932.

Alarms and Excursions, in Arabia, Thomas's first book, was published in 1931; Arabia Felix, the second, was published in 1932 and included a dedication to Sir Arnold Wilson.

After leaving Oman, Thomas gave a number of talks on Arabia in Canada and the U.S.A., as well as Britain and published papers on Arabia. He married Bessie Hoile in London July 1933 with a daughter, Elizabeth, born in September 1934.

Thomas completed a PhD thesis at Cambridge University in 1935 "The Geography and Ethnology of Unknown South Arabia".

After the outbreak of the Second World War, he served for a time as public relations officer in Bahrain (1942-43), and in 1944 became director of the Middle East Centre of Arabic Studies, of which he was the effective founder, first in Palestine and later in Lebanon.

Bertram Thomas died in Cairo, 27 December 1950 and was buried in a churchyard at Pill, not far from his childhood home.

PREFACE

Arabia retains to an extraordinary degree the power of conquering hearts. Those Europeans who live there often find fault for the first few years: they have brought with them watches and evening dress, an acquired or hereditary taste for European meals at stated hours, for cold drinks, newspapers, motor-cars, telephones, and social amenities, including games with various sizes of ball. Yet to most of them whilst on long leave, it they ever get it, there comes a time when they feel that these material pleasures are but conventions, and that it is time to return to simpler ways. When such men think of Arabia, sometimes one point of view, sometimes another, dominates their thoughts. The student reflects with pleasure on the opportunities for research, linguistic and archaeological, that Arabia still offers; the followers of Linnaeus reflect on the unnamed and unidentified birds, beasts, and flowers that the Continent may yet hold. The traveller yearns to traverse and to map a part of the vast areas of Southern Arabia which have hitherto eluded the eye of European explorers. Others again, and they are many, enjoy Arabia because they like Arabs, not on the sentimental grounds, savouring of patronage, which have made Arabs and sandy deserts the theme of innumerable novels in the past ten years, but because they find much in him to admire. They realize that Arabs have evolved, in the course of many centuries, a philosophy and a way of life which is in harmony with their environment, and which makes for bodily health and spiritual contentment. They no longer think of Arabs as "fanatical" or "fatalistic". The amusement, contempt, or even repulsion which human observers, wedded to their own way of life, are apt to feel for a mode of life which differs vitally from their own, gives way, on deeper acquaintance, to a measure of Sympathetic understanding. Such men more often than not begin as students and scholars, and develop into true ambassadors from the West to the East.

The writer of this book was one of the most talented of the younger political officers in Mesopotamia during and after the War, and served in a similar capacity in Trans-Jordan, before being selected to fill the responsible post of Financial Adviser and Wazir to His Highness the Sultan of Muscat and Oman. He showed courage and resource in circumstances of much difficulty and great danger during and after the war in Mesopotamia: the record of his work in Oman, on which the pages of this work incidentally throw but a modest light, is of extraordinary, indeed of unique, interest.

He is, I believe, the first Englishman to hold the position of Prime Minister in an independent Arab State: in this capacity he gained the entire confidence both of the Sultan, my friend Sir Saiyid Taimur bin Faisal, and of the Council of State. His relations with the turbulent leaders of the Arab tribes of the Oman littoral enabled him to perform, during his period of office, two very remarkable journeys over territory hitherto completely unknown. The first (vide Geographical Journal, March 1929) was along the South-Eastern Borderlands of the Rub 'al Khali from near Ras al Had to Dhufar, the second (vide Geographical Journal, January 1931) from Dhufar for a distance of some two hundred miles inland. The two journeys, taken together, constitute the most important and most extensive piece of geographical exploration undertaken in any part of the world since the War. He has published in the Journal of the Royal Anthropological Society (June 1929), some preliminary studies of the tribes whom he encountered on his first journey. He has also published some important studies relating to the languages spoken by the Kumzara in the Musandam Peninsula (Journal, Royal Asiatic Society, October, 1930). Of more general interest is his article on the Musandam Promontory and its inhabitants (Journal, Central Asian Society, vol. XV, 1928). He is, at the moment of writing, engaged on a voyage of exploration of even greater interest and considerable peril.

A.T. Wilson

I commend these breezy narratives with confidence to the reader who desires, as we all should desire, to know something of the life that is lived to-day by a race not less intelligent) not less happy and not less interesting than our own. As we read these pages we may see the caravans and hear the tinkle of the bells on the roads beyond the towns, on precipitous mountain tracks and beside the desert edge. We may see the peasants working in the date-groves, the armed men levying tribute from the villages, with as little remorse as the fisherfolk from the sea, the Sultan holding his Court, and the tribes milking their camels. These are all human beings much like ourselves, and like us preoccupied by their own affairs. They have to get a living, and keep a wife, and, if God wills, bring up a family. If their daily lives do not appear to be so important to them as ours are to us, it is because they are on the whole more ready to sacrifice themselves for some cause which they believe to be of greater importance than life itself. They are conscious of being Arabs and are proud of their country; though unlettered, they are not unlearned, for they inherit, and keep alive, a common culture, as well as a common religion, and a common speech.

As Justus Lipsius remarks (In Epist. Ad Philip Lanoyum) —

"Humiles istae et plebeiac animae domi resident, et affixae sunt suae terrae, ilia divinior est quae coelum imitatur et gaudet motu";

or, in the words of Ecclesiasticus xxxviii —

They shall not be sought for in publick,

counsel, nor sit high in the congregation:

they shall not sit on the judges' seat,

nor understand the sentence of judgment;

they cannot declare justice and judgment;

and they shall not be found where parables are spoken.

but they will maintain the state of the world,

and all their desire is in the work of their craft.

A. T. WILSON - January 1, 1931

ADVENTURE 1

A PUNITIVE EXPEDITION AGAINST MARSH ARABS

INTRANSIGENCE

Mesopotamia! It was the spring of 1918, the last year of the Great War, British Arms had swept the Turks out of the Land of the Two Rivers into the mountains of Mosul, and British policy was engaged in reducing the Arab tribes in rear.

All was well in the Muntafiq marshes save for the non-submission of a single powerful Shaikh, one Badr bin Rumaiyidh, and he, troublesome fellow! was a constant source of unrest.

Improvement in the local tribal situation had followed on the success of the British arms. The fierce opposition encountered at the outset in this wild Muntafiq country [1] had grown feeble with the march of events — the withdrawal of the Turkish Army from the Hai River, the completion of our railway from Basrah to Nasiriyah, the issue, happy for us, of that long, stem feud with the Turk at Kut, the local "acid test", so to speak, that led victoriously on to a climax in our capture of Baghdad, and. during the past year, our consolidation of our gains. The tribes, "with their senses in their eyes", as their proverb had it, made up their minds that we had not made lavish sacrifices of blood and wealth for nothing, however altruistic our professions. They believed we had come to stay. They beheld our might, and naturally and cheerfully decided to cherish us whatever their own dark activities — raiding river-boats, cutting telegraph-wires, and looting the slain of battle-fields — had been when the issue hung in the balance. But that phase was over. They would behave in future, they swore: all of them, save only our Old Man of the Marshes.

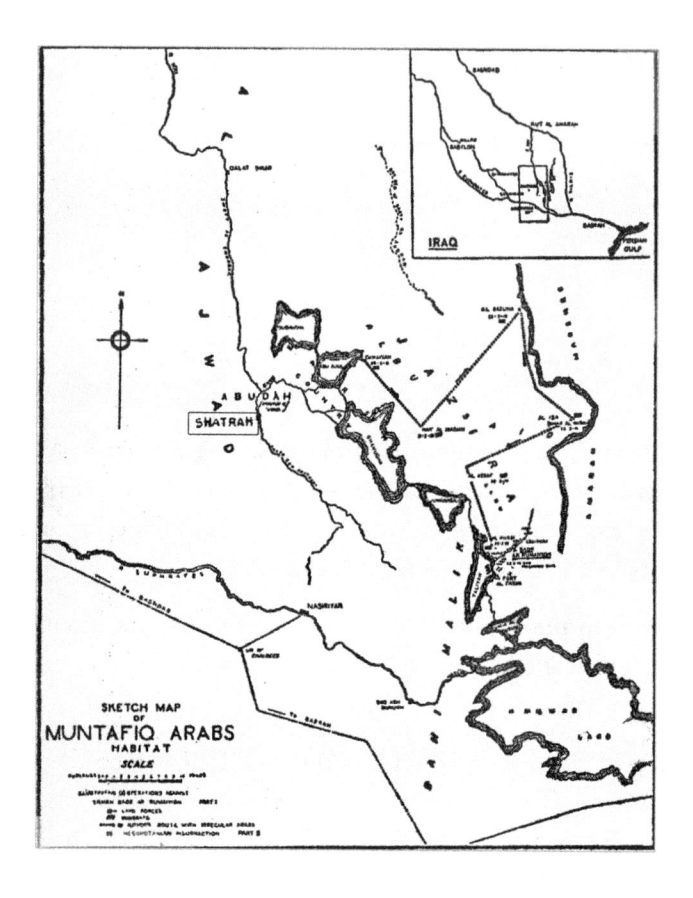

SKETCH MAP
OF
MUNTAFIQ ARABS
HABITAT
SCALE

"Submission?" queried Badr bin Rumaiyidh, Shaikh of the Albu Salih tribe, and paramount chief, at least nominally, of Bani Malik, a third of the great Muntafiq confederation. "Submission? Though it be for every other shaikh in this war-stricken land, yet for me: Never!" and he fingered the trigger of his 1912 pattern Mauser with an old desert warrior's fondness.

Anarchy and bloodshed had reigned throughout the marshes in late Turkish times, so that our own efforts to establish peace and order, however far short they fell of a standard to be desired, in comparison gave grounds for considerable satisfaction. The Turk, in spite of the prestige that attached to centuries of political domination, and of the heritage of a common religion, had, from the time of the tribally popular regime of Sultan Abdul Hamid, here been inept. He had succumbed before a more purposeful tribal spirit, for the tribal system is, ipso facto, antagonistic to the aims and methods of settled government: and National Arab, government in Iraq to-day may afford interesting speculation as to whether the tribal system will gradually wither under the influence of industrial development and methods of government based on ordered models and progressive ideas, or in time grow hostile to their agencies.

But at the time of which I write policy demanded, willy-nilly, our nursing the tribes as such. Our supreme need in a country predominantly tribal was tranquillity, in order that our military forces might devote themselves with a single mind to their main objective of destroying the Turk.

This condition we believed to be best achieved by a veiled rule through the natural chiefs whom the native soil had evolved, namely, the tribal shaikhs. The alternative of a premature experiment in bureaucratic government, staffed by the native inhabitants, was calculated to defeat our immediate ends, and had to be eschewed. At this time our prestige alone was sufficient to compel intertribal peace. And the tribes, secure from one another in an unprecedented degree, and able to sell their grain and dates and livestock to feed, at famine prices, our large army in the field, attained, in the few years that straddled the War-Armistice, to an undreamed-of wealth; they decked their women with fine gold, and rearmed themselves with modern rifles of which the gleanings of the battle-fields had provided bounteous harvest.

I am persuaded they had as yet not even thought of a day, soon to come, when they would turn these weapons upon the source of their prosperity, and so set in motion processes that would lead to its drying up. For arming is a point of honour throughout tribal Arabia; every tribe has its hereditary enemy, a past to revenge, a blot on its escutcheon to redeem, its individual standing to maintain, some *haqq* (right) or other to preserve or to pursue: and it were gratuitous to suppose that abnormal arming, springing from abnormal prosperity, had, at this juncture, any special ulterior motive. Indeed, under the slowly decaying Ottoman regime which formed his only experience, every shaikh had been a law unto himself; might was right; and a superiority in arms had become for the tribe the master aim, the key to accomplishment, the "Open Sesame".

But what of Shaikh Badr?

He, more of a recluse than most of his kind, had been out of his marshes for but one brief spell in his long life. That was to march down at the call of *Jihad* [2] to oppose the first wave of British invasion following the outbreak of hostilities. Then, at the battle of Shu'aibah in 1915, he had sworn never to pledge allegiance to us, and he had kept his word. And now, for three years, secure in his backwater, he had ignored our reiterated overtures for peace, had scorned our agents, and had harboured Turkish emissaries. As time went on and we became more and more firmly established, he must have foreseen the penalties of disobedience. Doubtless a time came when he thought his actions had gone beyond the limits of redemption. Partly to this, partly to his inability to conceive of any outside world — and the flat world in which he believed had for its centre his marshes, with a nebulous Ottoman Power revolving about their confines — and partly, perhaps, to a strain of megalomania in his character, must be ascribed his later recalcitrance. He seemed to regard us as part of Allah's inscrutable creation, infidels, who had come uninvited, he knew not whence, he cared not whither, whose star must surely soon set. Every other shaikh had made submission to Government. Badr alone clung to his old faith, a faith in the unalterability of his marsh regime, in the Turks' return, if only to their vague status as in the recent past. He alone of the shaikhly oligarchy refused to recognize the *Pax Britannica*: he alone would still set us at defiance.

Harold Dickson [3] was the Political Officer of the Muntafiq at the time, and Badr had been his one failure. Dickson had a psychological understanding of the tribal Arab, and a knowledge of the spoken language of the river which, so far as my experience went, were unrivalled throughout the country. He had a genuine, perhaps excessive, liking for the tribesmen, and I believe that he knew by name every man, woman, and child in some areas, where his inflexibility earned for him the nickname of *Abu Rassas*, [4] i.e. "the father of lead". This product of Exeter College, Oxford, and 29th Indian Cavalry, was a brilliant representative of the liberal school of Political Officer; he combined generous sympathy with unwearying patience, and he excelled the Arab at his own game of telling a story.

But these qualities, so successful elsewhere, were destined, alas! to prove ineffectual in dealings with the resolute Badr. They never got him beyond the stage of an interview with the Old Man, and it happened in this wise, as he afterwards told me.

He had been touring the Lake area to show the flag and to try to establish contact. In due course his emissaries brought a message from Badr which said: "To Nasiriyah. I will not come, but meet you here face to face, yes, by all means. Be, if you will, at a certain spot in the open plain to-morrow at daybreak. There you will find me, and neither of us shall come armed."

This, surely, was an advance, and Dickson looked round his own muster of loyal Arabs for encouragement.

None was forthcoming.

"Do not go" was their comment. "There is no good, but only evil, in that offer."

But the Political Officer felt that to heed their counsel were to close a half-open door. Go he must.

The rendezvous was a hut on a slight eminence in the open plain. At the crack of dawn he was there. But where was Badr?

Minutes passed, and never a sign of the Old Man. He would wait; but as the sun climbed the eastern sky so began to set the hopes he had cherished. Cursing himself for a fool for having been so easily duped, he was on the point of leaving when a speck on the skyline arrested his attention. The speck under his field-glasses became a moving cloud of dust, whence emerged a cavalcade of eighty horsemen which came galloping up to encircle the hut where he stood alone. They dismounted, and from their midst forth strode Badr. There could be no mistaking him. A tall, heavy, prepossessing figure of a man, but little bent for all his sixty-five years, a rugged face, deep, penetrating eyes, and a flaming square beard — that was the unforgettable impression he made.

"*Salaam alaikum*" (Peace be upon you), said he, coming straight up to Dickson in a disarming way, for it were darkest treachery to betray him on whom you have called down peace. For all that, it looked like a trap, and the Political Officer, feeling that Badr had behaved abominably in so outraging his own condition of a *tete-a-tete* was filled with rage and, turning, he plainly spoke his anger. The Arab Shaikh stood there eyeing him silently the while, then burst into laughter, and going up to him placed his wrinkled brown hands on Dickson's shoulders, kissed first one cheek then the other, and so fell to discussing the object of the meeting.

"Come with me," said the Englishman summing up. "Come with me under *hadh wa bakht* (safe conduct) to Nasiriyah. I will send a telegram to the Civil Commissioner [5] in Baghdad reporting that you have made your peace, and I promise you your life and an honourable settlement. Come as my honoured guest, and I give you a solemn undertaking that you shall return in safety to your village after a few days."

Eyeing the Political Officer quizzically at first. Old Badr seemed suddenly to unbend, and stretched forth his hand to shake the other's.

"Thy words are gracious, even as I expected they would be," he said. "Many thanks, O *Hakim!* (governor). To-morrow *insha'allah* (if God wills), we meet again. Let it be in this very place and at the same hour! Farewell, in God's keeping!" And he turned and was gone, as he had come, to the brave clatter of hoofs.

Dickson flattered himself he was on the right road at last, and mounting his horse to return to camp, set mentally to improvising the telegram that to-morrow should speed satisfaction to the highest quarters.

But it was a vain imagining. With the morrow's dawn came news of Badr's defection and flight.

What had ailed him after this promising audience? Surely no haunting fear? Why did he unaccountably disappear into his shell again, a shell which seemed predestined to yield to nothing less than cold steel?

And what would be the effect on friendly tribes whose submission had been achieved with very great labour? Badr's desire for self-aggrandizement might have far-reaching and evil consequences.

Dickson was discomfited. His hopes in an appeal to reason, his strong faith in pacific measures, were rudely shaken. Was he not the Agent of a Military Government? And surely Badr must realize our military strength?

Yet Badr seemed intent on setting his thumb to his nose and defying, with the "consecutive fifths" abhorred by doctors of music, the General Officer Commanding, Euphrates Defences.

A PRELIMINARY ENCOUNTER

28.5.1918

OPERATION ORDER

By O.C. River Column

(Ref. Map ½" to 1 Mile Survey Ghabashiyah, Khamisiyah, Nasiriyah)

1. *Situation.*

Shaikh Badr bin Rumaiyidh of the Albu Salih tribe has not up to date submitted to the British Government.

For a long time past his attitude has been passive and non-committal, but his obstinacy in not submitting delays the settlement of Albu Salih affairs.

2. *Intention.*

It is intended that the Defence Vessels *Firefly* and *Greenfly* and S9, with the detachment 99th Infantry, and dett. "d" Sec. Indian Machine Gun Company, accompanied by Political Officer Nasiriyah and Assistant Political Officer Suq, will visit the village of Badr bin Rumaiyidh on the

29.5.18, and direct him to make his submission to the British Government.

3. *Order and details of movement.*

On the morning 29th May, vessels in the order named will steam from Mazlik, the first named at 5a.m.

Defence Vessel *Firefly*.

"*Greenfly*.

S9

Greenfly will keep 400 yards behind *Firefly* and S9 400 yards behind *Greenfly*. Vessels will proceed via Hammar Lake, Fahud, Umm al Qutain Lake, Abu Ghalaiwin, and Taliyah Lake to a point opposite Badr's Village (sq. F.2.20.55).

4. *Protective precautions.*

Though no opposition is expected, yet as a precautionary measure on entry of vessels into Qutain Lake troops and personnel on all vessels will take full protective precautions against rifle-fire.

As a precautionary measure, should a landing be necessary, the detachments 99th Infantry, Mg.G.S., and Combined Field Ambulance will prepare to-morrow's food to-night.

5. *Action in event of vessels being fired on.*

In the event of vessels being fired on, machine-gun or rifle-fire will at once be opened on the hostile parties.

The vessels will move with caution as the navigation is at places uncertain owing to banks and shoal water.

6. Communication Det.

No. 3 Section Line of Communication Signal Co. will maintain communication between *Firefly, Greenfly,* and S.9.

7. *Reports.*

All reports to O.C. River Column on D.V. *Firefly*.

This was to be my first taste of Political work. I had only just left my regiment, the 1/4 Somersets, at Nasiriyah, to take up the appointment of Assistant Political Officer at Suq ash Shuyukh. Captain R. R. Haysom, a young captain with many languages and seconded from a Rajput regiment, was in charge, and with him I boarded S.9, according to orders, as she passed downstream at 7.45 a.m. on a scorching May 28th.

We were met on board by Lieutenant-Colonel C. de J. Luxmore, of the 99th Infantry, who was Officer Commanding the Column, and by Major Dickson, our local Political Chief, and were soon made privy to the plans against the Old Man of the Marshes.

Dense groves of date-palms line each bank of the mighty Euphrates, and in their clearings nestle mud villages, or, here and there, an occasional blue domed shrine to which Shi'ah pilgrims are wont to bring gifts. We steamed on until by noon we had come to a vast spread of water, the Hammar Lake, where the gunboats *Firefly* and *Greenfly* already rode at anchor. Never were visitors to a ward-room more popular, for we came with their ice ration, and the especial virtue of ice no man can appreciate more than he who has had to drink his beer hot in the Tropics under campaigning conditions with the shade temperature registering 120°. That night we transferred with O.C. Column to *Firefly*, and at the same time a consignment of 12-pounder ammunition we had brought along was also transhipped.

An early start had to be made on the morrow if we were to profit from the element of surprise, for we should have been deceiving ourselves by supposing that the object of our concentration was lost on the Arabs ashore, or that these would fail to send runners to our Old Man of the Marshes long before the black belching from our funnels rose above his horizon to warn him of the impending visit.

I woke to find our ship under way. Signallers and gunners were busy filling sand-bags with which to build a bullet-proof wall inside the thin iron bulwarks of the ship. Four and a half hours' steaming brought us to the far side of the lake, and by 9.30 we had come to an anchor in position 2,400 yards W.S.W. of Badr's fort.

A sporadic salvo of rifle-fire, apparently hostile in intent, had greeted us from the eastern bank, as leaving the lake we approached, up the narrow palm-fringed channel towards Badr's village; but we did not return it. "The dogs bark but the caravan passes by", was all it evoked from one of our Sowar escort, amused at this futile exhibition of defiance.

The early morning hours had been beguiled, as we came along, by Arab story-telling. The tribal Arab, perhaps on account of his illiteracy, is a practised raconteur, and his picturesque accounts of Badr's prowess and exploits kept us all entertained. Only a few months before, we were now to hear, the Old Man had captured a gunboat sent on a mission of a nature similar to this and had put to the sword every man jack aboard. Strange that never a whisper of the affair should have reached our ears, when the Arabs vouched for all its harrowing details! That ship, the romancer went on, had gone ashore upon a sandbank. The Arabs promptly proceeded upstream a mile or two, and feverishly set to work making grass ropes by the hundreds. These they weighted and threw into the river. Floating below water down-stream the grass ropes did what was required of them — they became entangled in the vainly revolving propeller, and, clogging the shafts, made further use of engines impossible. The rest was easy. When the British crew were seen to be deeply involved in salvage operations, Badr and his merry men in waiting launched forth, and the vessel was taken. So ended the figment.

Underlying the story was a moral, however. Badr was indubitably a man of parts. To take domestic courage alone. Had he not married sixty-five women, [6] an arithmetical arrangement of a young virgin for each year of life, so to speak, and when he went forth to war did not a troop of twenty of his sons ride at his elbow? Here was a Solomon and a Joshua in one.

No wonder the atmosphere of this land — for was it not the land of Shinar, of Babylon, of the Garden of Eden? — this atmosphere of patriarchs ancient and modern, coloured the ribald songs of the time. Typical was that in which the troops that morning were finding an impious joy.

· · ·

A PRELIMINARY ENCOUNTER

Adam was a gentleman who had no work to do.

Except to christen animals and keep off apples too.

When he got the push from Eden, Adam had to dig,

While Eve prepared pyjamas from the foliage of the fig.

Noah was the keeper of the Babylonian Zoo.

He used to take the animals awalking two by two.

He built an ark of gopher wood which on the waters swam.

And when the floods descended Noah didn't care a --.

There was a Mister Abraham, the father of the Jews,

He lent his wife to Pharaoh, 'cos he couldn't well refuse.

He led a life of bloated ease till nearly ninety-one.

When Sarah had the impudence to hand him out a son.

Esau was a farmer from the wild and woolly West,

His father left him half his land, and Jacob all the rest.

Esau saw the title-deeds were anything but clear,

So he sold the lot to Jacob for a sandwich and some beer.

Joseph was a genius with a head inclined to swell.

His brothers grabbed him by the pants and hurled him down a well.

He met a Mrs. Potiphar, whose ways were indiscreet,

When he had a deal with Pharaoh and cornered all the wheat.

. . .

Moses had a mother who was sorry he was born,
So she left him by the river in a basket all forlorn.
Pharaoh's daughter picked him up one morning on her walk,
And then the nasty cats in Cairo all began to talk.

There was a chap named Joshua, a captain of renown.
Who had the blessed cheek to stop the sun from going down.
Then he joined a German band and played the big bassoon.
And burst the walls of Jericho bassooning out of tune.

Samson was a boxer of the Darkie Johnson school,
And the Philistines he belted with the jawbone of a mule.
Then he met Delilah and she filled him up with gin,
And when she cut his curls off the coppers ran him in.

Solomon and David led the merriest of lives.
With millions of concubines and hundreds of wives.
When they both grew old they had such conscientious qualms,
That one of them wrote Proverbs and t'other sang the Psalms.

Uriah was a Hittite with a wife exceeding fair,
King David saw her bathing and he loved her then and there.
He called the captain of his host, and cautiously he said:

"Take out the ruddy Hittite and report to me he's dead."

There was a Mrs. Jezkbel, of rather bad repute,
Who went and married Ahab with a temper like a brute.
She leant out of the window, which he strictly did forbid.
Till someone shouted, "Chuck her down", and chuck her down they did.

Jonah was a sailorman, so runs the ancient tale.
He booked a steerage passage on the Trans-Atlantic whale.
When the fishy atmosphere grew heavy on his chest,
Jonah pressed the button and the whale did all the rest.

There was a troop of conjurers who gave a topping show,
Their names were Shadrach, Meshach, and Abed-n-e-go.
The best of all the tricks they did was at the King's desire.
When they hopped about with clothes on in the burning fiery fire.

We had reached the limit of navigation safe for ships of our tonnage; the last few dead-slow miles, indeed, had made perilous going. The lie of the low land alters from day to day with the rise or fall of the river, and there is really adequate scope to manoeuvre only when the floods are at their height in July and August. But the intense heat of those months militates against success of operations conducted by white troops, and if we could choose our time to throw down the gauntlet, the summer months would never be entertained.

The scene before us was characteristic. Both east and west banks were backed by dry stretches, which in turn gave place to temporary lake areas. Flocks were numerous, and spacious yellow fields in the middle distance a further sign, if this were needed, of a populous countryside. Badr's village lay to the west of a date grove, and between it and ourselves was a bare plain seamed with sunken roads which would favour an ambush of troops unacquainted with them. A glance sufficed to show that the landing of so small a force as ours was not warranted, even had this been contemplated.

Our mission, after all, was Peace; but it takes two to make peace. If Badr wanted peace he could have it simply by coming on board to parley. He would be assured safe conduct to go back if our proposals did not satisfy him, or if he required time to consider them; and in either case he would be no worse off than if he did not come at all. From where we were Badr's village looked deserted. No human being was to be seen, though a large Durbar tent and a smaller one standing over against the Fort, and a few tethered horses close by were signs of recent, if not of actual, occupation.

Suddenly from the larger tent emerged a figure, and straight-way made towards us. As it drew near the dignified carriage, well-nourished body, sophisticated mien, and sober habiliments bespoke the holy man. It was, in fact, Badr's religious adviser, Mulla Mishrif, chief priest and scribe — one of a class all powerful in their time, a time lasting well into the years of which I write.

The formalities over, he began.

"Why had we come? The tribe was excited by our visit. Shaikh Badr, if that was whom we were after, had unfortunately left for the interior that very morning, but his eldest son, Hasan, was present, and Hasan was our dutiful slave."

"Go back and fetch him," said Dickson; and Hasan in due course arrived.

"Where is thy father, o Hasan?"

"Shaikh Badr is an hour's ride distant."

"We have come to see him. No harm need befall him. No penalties need be imposed for his past misdeeds. All we desire is a formal visit to Nasiriyah, and an undertaking on his part to be in future no better and no worse than his neighbours."

"The blessings of Allah upon thee' returned Hasan.

"But we want him here. Is he willing to come aboard?"

"*Allahu A'lam*" (God is the more knowing), answered Hasan indicating his unbelief. "But we are thy servants. My two brothers are now in the village. Take them and me, at thy pleasure. Take us, if you will, as hostages."

This was exasperating. The shaikh was clearly playing at his old game. Dickson coaxed, promised, and argued in turn, but all to no avail. The go-betweens could scarcely be expected to speak their master's mind even if they knew it, and at the end of three hours' palaver the Political's patience was used up. He withdrew with the Officer Commanding the Column to consider the next step. It was soon decided. Mulla Mishrif was to be sent ashore with an official ultimatum to Badr to be on board within one hour, and Hasan, who was to remain aboard, dispatched a private message, at the same time— though it was not quite clear how far he might have been dissembling — requesting his two brothers to come aboard unconditionally.

This forced the nailing of the true colours to the roast. At 1.30 the Mulla handed in a written reply of polite refusal from Badr bearing his seal. Neither Badr nor his sons would come.

For the River Column to take this lying down, to depart leaving a reputation behind of having done nothing, was calculated not only to encourage Badr's further intransigence, but also to tempt the loyal shaikhs already in submission to leave us, in the belief that they could do so with impunity. Action of some kind was imperatively called for to show that the Government was in earnest. Such action on our part was anticipated ashore, too, for a sudden rush of activity around the tents, the cracking of bullets, the ululations of women and the war-dance constituted Badr's reply — the tribal *fiza'* or standard raising. This was a natural sequel to his verbal defiance; and soon some hundred and fifty tribesmen, rifles in hand, came scurrying out of the palm-grove to cross the plain and rally about the tribal standard now brought out before the tents. We were in honour bound to hold our hand till the expiry of the time mentioned in our ultimatum, other- wise we could have wrought much havoc.

At 1.40 this moment arrived, and *Firefly* first was ordered to open fire. One of her guns went out of action after a few rounds, and then *Greenfly* came neatly into action with a direct hit. The bombardment continued. First the big tent was blown to fragments, then the smaller one caught fire; some hits on the reed guest-house were registered, and, most telling of all, the west and north towers of the fort were breached.

Colonel Luxmore, commanding these operations, sat gallantly aloft on the highest point of the bridge, where he was best situated to watch and record movements ashore, to sketch and to spot for the guns. His exposed position drew a good deal of rifle-fire, all of it, fortunately, ineffective. There was no sign of life after our first salvo until a few men, presumably Badr and his bodyguard, rushed out, leapt into the saddle, and disappeared in a cloud of dust to the north.

"Cease fire" was signalled at 3.0 p.m., and following it the order to retire. S.9 had steamed ahead downstream at 2.40, and *Greenfly* and *Firefly* now followed on at cautious distances, expecting at every moment to be blazed away at from the date- groves fringing the river-bank, by tribesmen who, it was thought, would cut in behind our retreat. As we weighed anchor and forged ahead, hundreds of villagers became visible again in the plain, making for their desolate habitations. *Greenfly* went ashore on the mud more than once, and was only got off with difficulty. On these occasions *Firefly*, as rearguard, stood by while S.9, less able to give an account of herself, pushed on. These were exciting moments, for an Arab attack, if launched during salvage operations, would have had every chance of success, especially after nightfall.

The marsh Arab is, of course, as amphibious as a frog. A most powerful swimmer, even with one arm and in fresh water, he negotiates a stream with the other arm above his head holding his clothes high out of the water, thus enabling him to get into a dry shift 'on the other bank. In Turkish times and during the War, too, he had freely indulged in an unpleasant habit of applying this technique to more questionable uses. Waiting for the night he oiled his body, floated downstream alongside the craft he had marked down, sprang aboard, and silently dropped overboard again with his booty, which, legend had it, was brought ashore in comparatively dry condition.

Fortunately *Firefly* and *Greenfly* nowhere stuck hard and fast. It was during the tense moment of a grounding that an amusing incident occurred which illustrates the perfect sang-froid of the British "tar". A small fluffy pup of the nondescript origin, known generically to the Army of the period as a "Mosul Spaniel", fell overboard. Its owner, a hulking giant of a seaman, appeared on deck at that moment, and without stopping to consider hostile Arabs or to divest himself of a stitch of clothing, calmly walked over the side as he might step off a pavement. He disappeared under the water for a moment, then, coming to the surface, struck out for the pup, now receding in the fast-flowing current and struggling in vain to regain the ship. At length he overhauled it. Turning, he made the ship again, handed the pup up, and was hauled inboard himself, his dripping uniform clinging to his beefy frame. Uttering a blasphemous oath at the wretched little half-drowned pariah as he affectionately patted it, he joined in the hearty laughter of his messmates, quite unaware that he had done aught but the only thing there was to do. But the Fates were kind: no Arab lurked in those menacing palms but a stone's throw away.

Greenfly slid off into deep water, the River Column proceeded on its uneventful return journey, and by the morrow's sunset we had all got back to the scene of our normal avocations. Hasan, the shaikh's son, we had brought along as hostage, a prisoner under open arrest (incidentally, he broke his parole later); the Old Man of the Marshes was formally declared an outlaw, and it was bruited abroad that a rival had been appointed by Government his successor and Shaikh of the Bani Malik.

Haysom and I were dropped in a heatwave at Suq ash Shuyukh. There *tail bairdi* (the wireless of the reeds), or, more simply, Arab rumour, had forestalled us with a broadcasting of the expedition's itinerary, made vivid by the usual fanciful embroiderings; and I had learned by this time not to be shocked when my Arab bearer greeted me with a grin, and related, with evident satisfaction, a typical bazaar invention how, following the bombardment, the bloody head of one of Badr's innumerable progeny was recovered from the topmost branch of a distant palm-tree.

A LULL

A YEAR PASSED.

During the winter I had quitted Suq ash Shuyukh, on the Lower Euphrates, for independent charge of a Political District, Shatrah, in the Gharraf, the lower reaches of the Hai River. Though I was still in Muntafiq country, Badr lived beyond my borders, and "out of sight out of mind". I thought I had seen the last of him. I was wrong. The falling river had merely called a halt to operations.

To turn for a moment to picture the land. First and always, a vast, alluvial, sun-scorched plain, where Nature is in one of her sternest moods. The plain is the gift of the two rivers. These, threading their way tortuously and precariously across it, bring in spring and early summer a burden of red silt which is deposited as the floods subside. For five months, from May till September, the shade temperature by day is scarcely ever more merciful than 115degrees, making the nights with a fall of 30-40degrees blessedly cool and desirable.

Bertram Thomas and Muntafiq Shaikhs

A stone, even so small as a man's fist, is scarcely to be found anywhere on this immense plain; wherefore Babylon, its noblest city, unlike Nineveh and the cities of mountain-girt Assyria, was built almost entirely of mud and burnt brick.

The river, but a feeble trickle in winter, becomes swollen, swift, and sanguinary when the summer sun, melting the snows above Angora, sends an impetuous' flood through the land to mingle ultimately with the waters of the Persian Gulf. What now exercises men's minds is whether the bunded earthworks which the tribes have dyked against the event will hold, for the swollen river, flooding madly past, is at a level high above the plain. A single breach will inundate a whole countryside in the space of a night, and make short work of the crops of a winter's labour. To some exceptional flood of this nature, surely, was it that we owe the story of Noah. But the flood is also a blessing. It is the life-quickener of the country; its annual siltings are the foundation of luxuriant rice-fields; and who shall dismiss irreverently the snipe-shooting of the paddy?

The river is the sole water supply of the country, too, whether you live in a town which, as a relic of the British Army of Occupation, knows the doubtful amenity of chlorination, or in an out- district innocent of this experience, such as that in which I spent four post-War years.

But we must voyage downstream to get a fleeting glimpse of its life. The yellow stubble in the fields on both banks is what remains of the winter crops, wheat or barley or millet, or else of the rice crop of summer. The tribesmen live in small huts, consisting of a few bundles of unsplit reeds bound with green rushes and propped up against each other — wretched hovels at best, which cluster along the bank, and if the village be of any size a mud fort of the shaikh will there rear a battlemented tower out of its dingy midst. Never did distance lend enchantment with greater flattery. Nearby is the simple, unpretentious mosque, and over against the fort stands a giant yellow tunnel of plaited reeds, the *madhif*, or guest-house.

A pack of pariah dogs races along the bank level with your craft for a hundred yards or so, snarling displeasure at your intrusion. A solitary tribesman, dark of skin and naked but for a loin-cloth, stands thigh-deep in the water, a poised fish spear in his hand, gazing down intently for his elusive prey. Buffalo, massive lethargic brutes, laze neck-deep in these tepid waters, or swim leisurely from bank to bank. Clouds of flying insects swarm everywhere, and the air hums with mosquitoes.

A fleet of *mash-hufs*, the local canoe, lines the bank under the village, moored gondola-fashion to their punting poles stuck upright in the shallow mud, their high prows and sterns graceful as the coffee beaker's slender, curving line. With their dipping, shallow waists they make a pleasing picture. One of them darts past with feathery lightness to the strong, straight punting of some dusky son of the *ma'adan* (marshmen of non- Arab origin), its black bituminous body in strong contrast to its more ambitious rival, the white titivated *bellam*. The *bellam* responds to orthodox rowing with long-handled paddles, boasts, too, of canopied shade in the stern-sheets, where, reclining comfortably, the shaikh or green-turbaned saiyid rises smilingly to acknowledge your passing greetings.

On the banks play noisy naked children, whose bodies loving mothers have adorned with sacred amulets or tiny purses containing scraps of Holy Writ to keep off the Evil Eye. Washing their garments over a tiny stream are black-eyed matrons and young virgins, the latter disporting gay-coloured clothes to distinguish them, and, if they be *ma'adan* of the marsh, unveiled, the hussies! Their laughing moon faces, their hair plaited with coloured beads, their large flashing eyes and dazzling teeth, and their firm young bodies, straight as an arrow and full of grace, are things goodly to behold. Every limb is tattooed, and they otherwise beautify themselves with weighty silver ornaments, turquoise nose-rings, pendulous earrings, gold-coin fashioned necklaces, many finger- rings, and heavy silver bracelets and anklets. The nymph is conscious of her charms: and the marsh maiden is by no means unattractive.

Downstream there glides past a leviathan of a *mahaila* (river barge) under a single stretch of canvas, the green Shi'ah banner floating over her stem. Her motley freight of Persian and Arab pilgrims bound north for the Holy Places of Karbala and Najaf crowd her decks; below, her lockers are laden with corpses, *en route* for Paradise; [7] and for some solitary voyager, the journey is — who knows? — the valley of the shadow of death, for he comes to swear by the head of Abbas [8] to dear himself from some suspicion of guilt which is otherwise expiable only with his blood.

Here we leave the main stream to turn down one of many small channels that empty into the marsh proper. First a dense edging of bulrushes — fodder here for buffalo, or fuel potential for some distant town brick kiln. Then succeeds a mighty expanse of water, spreading away to a low, pink, distant shore which would scarcely be discernible were it not for a slender palm or willowy fringe that throws it into relief.

The marsh's surface is a sheet of glass with occasional splashes of yellow, pink, and green, where lotus ox-tongue and goose-flower mirror themselves in its pure face. A purple coot or pigmy cormorant floats listlessly by.

All is deathly still save the soughing of wind in the reeds. These, as we approach them, form a mighty army of green twenty- foot sentinels, thick and forbidding. Our frail craft is guided with unerring sureness into a narrow hidden channel that alone searches their otherwise impenetrable depths. At the edge a heavy crashing of reeds tells of buffalo disturbed by our passing; later an osprey takes to wing, followed by a crazy-looking flight of crane that flop clumsily away, skimming the drooping heads of the reeds. Here is the home of numerous otter and wild-pig, here the winter habitation of myriads of duck, teal, and snipe.

As we emerge on the distant side the sun is setting in a glorious paradise of colour — where else, except perhaps in Ceylon, do I recall such sunsets? — sinking gradually to the horizon, into which it seems suddenly to dip. Thera is an immediate and welcome change of temperature; the boatman ceases from his labours for the evening prayer; the wind freshens, to send black patches of cloud scudding across our bows; a V formation of loud- quacking geese goes flighting over well out of range, and darkness descends upon the frog-croaking waters.

But to return to Shaikh Badr. On the pretence that his own people had made things too hot for him, Badr paid a compliment to our River Column's visit by slipping back into the marshes, from where, however, he doubtless exercised a directing influence in Albu Salih affairs. To avail him of a ready means of coming in we had appointed a Native Political at Al Fathi, with a detachment of fifty levies under Captain F. W. Hall, an excellent officer who had served with the Muntafiq Horse since its inception and had now risen to command it. Our purpose was still to win Badr, if he was to be won, but it required excessive optimism to detect signs of such victory.

And now with unexpected suddenness he emerged from his obscurity in full war-paint. The month was April; he had been quiescent for nearly twelve months. A race-meeting at Nasiriyah had at this time brought in shaikhs from far and wide, and they arrived enthusiastic to enter their ponies and to back them — for with the horse-loving Muntafiq, while strong drink is strictly taboo, a small flutter on a horse is approved even by the most pious. Here was the old rebel's opportunity. And so, while the world made merry at the races he, with about two hundred men, suddenly appeared in broad daylight before the Government fort at Al Fathi, and when night fell made an attack on the levy post. He was driven off, losing four killed and three wounded, without inflicting any loss on our side.

But there was more in this manoeuvre than met the eye. Even Badr's boldness would scarcely have ventured to such lengths without external backing. In other words, there could be small doubt that he was acting with the connivance of the other shaikhs, avowedly loyal, and our guests at the races. Such an attitude on their part was more than intelligible. They felt that their power was being circumscribed by a peace-compelling Government, a Government that forbade the wiping off of old scores in the traditional and manly method of an appeal to arms, and, worse than all, they were now being called upon to pay revenue for the first time. Taxation! Monstrous inquisition! Little wonder, then, that they approved of Badr's activities for keeping Government on tenterhooks, and saw in him an instrument to serve their ends.

"Agitate", their self-interest was likely to encourage them to say to Badr behind the scenes. "We're with you. If peace is disturbed, Government can be persuaded to forgo revenue demands, for cannot we represent that to press our own followers in the present temper will have the effect of driving all into your camp and result in a wholesale defection from Government of the now openly and avowedly submissive Albu Salih?" Only such an hypothesis would explain, first, Badr's emergence, and then his maintaining himself, after an abortive attempt on Al Fathi, within six miles of our fort in the heart of Albu Salih territory.

At this stage Badr was clearly having the best of the argument. If matters were allowed to drift it would result in a further increase of his renown. Yet news of our fitting out a punitive expedition would be calculated to reach him, and all he need do would be to slip back into the marshes, wait for us to be driven home by a falling river, and then reappear with added prestige.

"Surely in vain the net is spread in the sight of any bird but the bird was no longer our only, if still our chief, consideration. For Ar Rumaiyidh villages had been flagrantly affording the rebel protection, had been aiding and abetting him, and they must now be taught a summary lesson if a dangerous situation was not to be allowed to grow.

COMING TO GRIPS

The heat of the Mesopotamian summer had begun to assert itself.

It was May 20, 1919, an oppressive day in Shatrah. I was dozing under a punkah when a mounted orderly from Nasiriyah was announced, the bearer of an urgent secret letter. Rubbing my eyes I stirred, and bewailing the importunity of some people's servants and the weakness of my own, fell to opening the letter. Its purport the reader may have already guessed — "the trail of the Old Man of the Marshes" again!

No one had been farther from my mind than Badr, whom I had long lost sight of in the busy preoccupations of a new district and normal administration. But it was ordained to be the war-path once more, though the role assigned to me was to be very different from the sheltered one aboard the river gunboat of last year's operations.

"You will raise a mounted force of two hundred friendly tribesmen at once", ran my orders, "and proceed to the Jazirah between the Muntafiq and Amarah marshes to the north and in rear of Shaikh Badr's village, there to co-operate with a main force which will attack it from the south."

G.O.C. Euphrates Defences with Political co-operation had been secretly organizing a spring offensive. The new River Column ordered to operate as before, from the Hammar Lake side, was to have a fairish stiffening of Regular Indian troops, a striking force, composed of 400 men of the 99th Infantry, 200 Sowars of the Muntafiq Horse, 100 men of the Suq ash Shuyukh Scouts, 2 gunboats and 3 aeroplanes, commanded by Lieutenant-Colonel F. D. Davidson, I. A.

Up to this moment I had been completely ignorant that operations were impending. Silence had been enjoined on those in the know, though there were definite limits to the surprise factor of secrecy imposed by a river and lake, the only safe lines of communication-waters — whose conditions of navigability, covering a brief season of the year only, were common knowledge. Veiled military preparations, however, had been going forward for some time. As unobtrusively as possible the levy garrison at Al Fathi had already been replaced by regular troops; gunboats and river steamers had recently been pushed out to use Hammar Lake at their normal base; and aeroplanes which had also been brought up from Basrah and centred on Nasiriyah, the nearest landing-ground to the coming scene of operations, were for some days kept screened and not permitted to fly over the town. On the political side, Badr's successor had fallen under a cloud, if, indeed, he was not a prisoner; friendly intercourse with Badr's ten-year-old son was being construed by the tribes as an indication of a reconciliatory attitude to the Rumaiyidh House; and, regarded together, these facts were calculated to lull the rebel into a sense of false security.

The plans showed Government to be acutely aware of the seriousness of Badr's activities and prepared for coping with it, and I buried my head in the newly arrived papers again to envisage my role in forthcoming operations.

Dickson's friendly D.O. was illuminating. "The main attack", it said, "is planned for dawn on 23rd. If Badr escape he will probably do so to the north. There you will be. He must be kept on the run and if possible your friendlies will close the bolt-hole."

As I turned things over in my mind it seemed to me that, unless the Old Man were killed or captured outright, he would, indeed, retire in my direction, and possibly with loyal and desperate retainers enough to give a good account of himself; if, on the other hand, he stole away and, made good the marshes, then my patrolling would be in vain. But eleventh-hour speculations, especially those that led to the horns of a dilemma, had to be discouraged, and were, in any case, soon swallowed up in the prospect of an adventure which was not wholly distasteful to me.

To-day was the 20th. The main attack was planned for the 23rd. Here was I, eighty miles from the position assigned for my co-operation, and as yet without a single recruit. Clearly I must raise my force as near to the scene of operations as possible if I was to be in position in time. To look to Albu Sa'id territory, then, was my only hope. Within half an hour I had tumbled a few stores and a saddle into my launch, which, after spluttering her usual chill objections, soon left Shatrah behind as we plugged up- stream to the Bada'a. Once we rounded the bend and found the current with us we moved at a fair speed, and crossing Lake Ajul made Dawaiyah four and a half hours later.

"*Salaam alaikum, Ya Sahib*" (Peace be upon you, O Sahib), said my old friend Shaikh Muhammed as he advanced to meet me, his son leaping to my horse's head with customary courtesy.

"*Wa alaikum as salaam*" (And upon you be Peace), I returned, dismounting at the same time as the crippled Mudir of Dawaiyah came up, a venerable old man, who had met me at the water's edge with ponies to bring my party thus far. After the usual round of handshaking we made our leisurely way across the open threshing floor, where heaps of yellow straw bore witness to a recent harvest, and thence to the *madhif* beyond.

We entered its comparatively dark interior. The softer light, after the brilliant sunshine outside, was restful indeed. Above was a vast arched ceiling of reed mats supported on robust arched reed pillars like the inverted ribs of a ship, a dozen or so of them set equidistant along its hundred feet of spacious length. A thin column of smoke (hence the mellowed stain colour of the *madhif* interior) ascended from a small square cement hearth just within the entrance. Here sat the inevitable coffee-maker beside his pestle and mortar, and his row of coffee-pots, black with age and service, ranging downwards in size like those in Southey's nursery story of the bears. His head lowered flat with the hearth, the old coffee man revived a reluctant flame with his own powerful lungs and soon had "Father *Dallal*" pinging on the fire, and before very long "Baby *Dallal*" was ministering coffee in prodigal fashion to at least a hundred half-seated, half-kneeling figures that lined the four sides of the *madhif*. As sitting on the ground is *de rigueur*, the velvet mattress had been hauled out for me, and with it the usual scarlet and green plush cushions. Accompanying the preferred coffee-cup, the shaikh, standing, as here becomes the host, advanced to offer the long tapering cigarette of the country, which he may or may not have lighted beforehand, holding it out perpendicularly at its extreme end between finger and thumb as with a conjurer's gesture of "Here, gentlemen, there is no deception!"

I took a few whiffs, and began.

It is discourteous in the East to come straight to your subject, and while I was inwardly bemoaning the waste of precious moments my lips were mouthing the Arabic words for crops and news that must needs be inquired about for the space that etiquette demanded. Whispering in public to your next-door neighbour, however, is no infraction of the local canons, and so at length I beheld, with feelings partly of amusement, partly of hope, my Arab assistant with his mouth close up to the Shaikh's inclined ear. This continued for two long unblushing minutes. It must surely, thought I, have for object the clearing of the *madhif*. And so it was. Soon only the Shaikh remained behind.

"Ya Shaikh Muhammad" said I, by way of broaching matters, "you know that Government is strong to punish wrong-doing, and generous to reward faithful service?"

"Government is a father," came the tortuous rejoinder. "First Allah, then the *Hukuma* (Government)."

"Well said, O Shaikh! But a father is angered with a slothful or unwilling son."

"God destroy the house of the father of sloth," said he, enigmatically.

"I have come to you in the *Hukuma's* name. Government has need of two hundred men and horses of the Bani Sa'id, and wants them to-day."

"I kiss thy hand, but... began the startled Shaikh. At the same time as making this tentative negative, he ran his deft fingers along the beads of his rosary, [9] divided them, counted sotto voce, and looked up with an "*Al Hamdu l'llah*" (God be praised). I took hope,

"Not to you, Muhammad, do I look to bear wholly the brunt of this demand. If the men must be drawn from the fields let them be drawn in just proportion from all sections according to their strength. These men are wanted but for a few days, and you shall none of you be the losers, *Insha'llah*."

"But wherefore so many, whence the purpose, O Sahib?" Shaikh Muhammad was more intelligent than most in his generation, and friendly withal, and I felt no compunction in unfolding my plans to him.

"Come," said I in conclusion, "there is no time to be lost. Send out horsemen to circulate these," and I handed him a sheaf of letters addressed to the sectional chiefs, which my Arab Assistant had written while coming along in the launch. The rendezvous was fixed for the morrow at the tents of the paramount chief. Shaikh Naif, some fifteen miles distant; zero hour was to be 8.0 p.m.

But the same night the shaikhs were to foregather with me here, and to be told as much as was good for them to know.

The afternoon was advancing, and, thoroughly tired, I turned my face to the latticed opening, the only ventilation in the *madhif*, to go to sleep. Overcoming the forces at work to cheat me I finally went off with a drowsy reflection that the *madhif* is a blessed enough institution provided you are insensible to flies, possess a philosophic temperament, and come armed with large quantities of Keating's powder.

When I awoke, most of the shaikhs to whom I had sent messengers had arrived. I could hear them at sunset prayers. My Arab Assistant came to apprise me of the general feeling. This was entirely favourable, and I was certain of getting my friendlies. No telegraph existed in these outlandish parts to enable me to report progress to headquarters: the nearest Englishman was stationed forty miles away to the north. I reflected how potent the prestige of successful armies can be. Here was territory which the Turks had practically abandoned for more than a decade because for them it was too remote and too lawless to administer profitably: territory that had not even known the tramp of British troops, for it lay well off the beaten tracks that followed the courses of the Euphrates and Tigris. Yet here, within a year of occupation, could come a British officer alone and raise the tribes to do Government's bidding.

The following day I rested preparatory to the start. It was to be a night march. I had ridden over in the morning from Dawaiyah — a scorching hot ride, as we skirted the flat shores of the lake — and I was congratulating myself that I had brought along my service saddle, for the discomfort of a saddle of the country is a thing not soon to be forgotten. It has a ridiculously small seat (Arab hips are unusually narrow), a high pommel, tryingly short stirrup leathers even at their longest, great square clogs of stirrup irons like a swashbuckling Mexican bandit's — in short, the *tout ensemble* extremely unpleasant for a six-foot European. The bit, too, although the pony doesn't seem to mind it, is unnecessarily severe.

Darkness descended. It was 8.0 p.m., the hour to start.

Not a tribal quota had failed me; even the light camel transport was there, and I moved off with my Arab cavalcade, two hundred strong, into the desert night, on the trail of the old rebel. Al Bazun, on the western fringe of the Amarah marshes, was my immediate objective. Thither we proceeded on a north-easterly bearing, trekking on across the plain through the small hours, to make it at dawn.

Resting for the day at Al Bazun, I split my force up into two, to enable one squadron to remain there under my Arab Assistant. With the other I planned to make another march that night to Al Isa, to the south, in the direction of the scene of operations.

We had been in the saddle six hours when dawn broke, and with it the full booming of the distant bombardment came faintly down the wind. Badr's village I calculated to be twenty miles W.S.W. of our position. I halted a little farther on, and my force was now, I thought, distributed to best advantage along these western marshes, the favourite haunt of Badr in his recent exile. The early morning air 'twixt marsh and desert was of sparkling clearness, and the first flush of morning lit up faintly, across a hundred miles of perfectly flat country in our rear, the low mountain-line of the Persian Pusht-i-Kuh.

Within an hour all our simple dispositions were made. The guns had now ceased their booming, and there followed an ominous silence.

One's first thought was: How fared the fight? Where was Badr? Dead? A Prisoner? In flight? Retiring in our direction as into a trap, and — unpleasant thought! — with a force that must swamp us?

I sent off in ones and twos a dozen of my party to neighbouring points to watch and wait and bring me information. More I could not safely spare. We were all thoroughly tired and hungry after two forced night marches. Killing and cooking a fat-tailed sheep of the country was the work of two hours, and soon we were applying ourselves ravenously to its carcass stuffed with rice and raisins.

Our position commanded a good view in every direction, and did not lend itself easily to surprise by an enemy. Two watches were arranged, and I confess I elected to be of the number for the first spell of "off duty". A heavy sleep fell on me and I was awakened only several hours later, when the day was well spent, by a considerable stirring and commotion in my camp.

But what of the main front, just under the mysterious skyline to the south?

The battle had been joined. According to plan, our force had got into position overnight without the enemy's knowledge. But something this morning had gone wrong with zero hour, and before the aeroplanes had arrived to drop bombs on Badr's village and the two neighbouring hamlets of Hafaz and Araithim, the villagers were astir for the dawn prayer, became alive to the danger that confronted them, and promptly made dispositions for flight — this, alas! before the first blow fell.

As a general rule tribesmen's rifle-firing is erratic and weak, but on this occasion it was heavy and accurate. Stout as was the defence they could put up, however, it could not stand against our superior force. Supported by Lewis guns from the 99th Infantry, the Muntafiq Horse were first across the Shuraish, drove the defenders out of Badr's village and out of Araithim, and then rallied for an attack on Hafaz, where Badr's green standard denoted the position of his main strength. Two miles beyond, a mounted body of his, a hundred and fifty strong, provided him with the means of escape if necessity arose, or the means of a flank attack on our infantry if a premature crossing of the Shuraish on their part placed this obstacle in their rear. This contingency did not arise.

Cavalry of the country were the obvious means of first closing with the enemy.[10] Our Muntafiq Horse, led by Hall, had already borne the brunt and acquitted themselves creditably, and now a troop of them were to sweep in and occupy Hafaz village. This they did, with 99th Infantry in support, but so impetuously that our aeroplanes, unaware of the ebb and flow of battle, unfortunately dropped bombs on the village after its investment, killing one and wounding four of our Sowars. But for this minor accident the attack had been an unqualified military success. Enemy losses in a few hours were 39 killed and 39 wounded, and by 8.30 a.m. Badr was in full flight to the north-west. Here the engagement was broken off, for no pursuit was ordered, though on the morrow Major Dickson, who knew the lie of the land better than anyone else, was given command of a fairish-sized reconnaissance party, which made a wide six-mile turning movement and burnt up the grain stocks in its path.

To turn back a day to relate how it fared with me "out in the blue" to the north. My awakening to loud and excited shouts in my camp had, alas! nothing to do with the fleeing Badr. It announced the arrival of Marrs and Rivett-Carnac, my two colleagues from the Amarah side, who had, it turned out, arrived on a mission similar to my own. In the circumstances no useful purpose would be served by overlapping. Shaikh Sikar al

Na'ama, a shaikh in the Amarah Division, was the local power in the land, and he was here present and ostensibly cooperating. His Arabs knew every reed in the marshes, and thus provided a far more efficacious means of patrolling them than could possibly be expected of my more distantly recruited Arabs. But Sikar's participation, I gathered, had been anything but plane sailing. When the first shot was fired. Government's Arab representative had presented his credentials at Sikar's tent.

"O Sikar," he said, "now must you raise your flag and call to it every horseman of your following. Think not of your former friendship with Badr and how you broke bread with him in his tents seeing that you were of the same tribe. There will be no pardon for you if you fail us. As for Saiyid Muhammad and 'myself, we have sworn the most sacred oath that we will be among the first at this enemy of Government. But if you will not call out your men, then we shall be forced to return to Amarah, and your name will be disgraced for ever."

Sikar had no recourse but to obey. The *fiza'* followed, and from every quarter horsemen galloped up at the sight of the banner, every man armed with modem rifle. The *hosa* (war-dance) followed, presenting a brave picture of wild and semi-naked marshmen, shouting their war-cries, swinging their rifles about their heads, and hopping around their banners now on this foot, now on that. Meanwhile Sikar's horsemen, of more exalted origin, took a sweeping circuit around the marsh Arabs. Here, normally, were the ingredients of a tribal row, but happily none materialized.

My party, clearly, could be withdrawn for employment elsewhere. Judging the day's developments favourable to my plan, and assuming that our main offensive to the south had, for better or worse, shot its bolt, I determined to advance to the scene of operations. This seemed a fairly safe move, though a blind one, as no portent of success or failure had come out of those large silent spaces of the Jazirah.

There followed a princely feast of grilled chicken, and so to saddle up. I waited for the first appearance of the moon, and then moved out again to cross the plain towards the northern boundary of Albu Salih territory.

Many of the animals were tucked up from over-marching, and I made frequent halts during the night, as much to rest them as 'to listen for sounds of any other body on the move. To enjoin silence upon my Arab Irregulars during a night march — and I remembered my own lessons as a North Somerset Yeomanry trooper in the Flanders of 1914 — was vain. The noise they made was hopeless. They had their own observances on the waging of war. One of the advance guard kept up a running string of battle-songs sung in a high-pitched but resonant voice to a rather thin tune. Many of these were, I dare say, reputable enough; many more were clearly impromptu efforts dashed with local colour; many, also, too extravagant and lewd to be set down here. One specimen of the doggerel, as I roughly translated it at the time, ran:

My warrior band heed my commands,

Be deaf to timid counsels;

Brave to drink of the waters of death,

For that which God hath ordained, that shall come to pass.

A warrior sleepeth not.

But is ever in readiness

To fall upon his victim

Like the cunning wolf in the chase.

We will butcher without order

This witless fellow Badr.

Forsaker of his female folk.

Who fleeth before his pursuers.

After a long, thirsty, noisy night we arrived at dawn within a few miles of Albu Salih country. Here we came upon a mighty Badawin encampment of Al Sulaim Arabs, with nearly a thousand camels, making north. Revived by copious draughts of milk we rested here for a few hours.

The Jazirah plain which we had crossed and re-crossed, though now a wilderness, bore evidence of a considerable former glory. I counted four sandy, age-old river-beds, as well as vestiges of an ancient dam, and saw many mounds, ruins of what must once have been flourishing townships. Here, indeed, was the ancient Tigris bed before that river changed to its present course, for the Jazirah was a smiling Persian province at the time the Arabs invaded and conquered the country in the seventh century of our era. Major Dickson, who throughout these operations was privileged as Contact Officer to fly over it, told me that the distinguishing feature from the air was an ancient dead river-bed which he thought must have been the famous Shatt al Akhdhar. Perhaps here will be found the sites of those dynastic cities of Babylonia so far unlocated: Larak, Awan, Hamazi, Maer, Bad-tibirq, Nisin, [11] and the rest.

The sun was getting high, and there was no time to linger over such speculations. We pushed on to make Al Assaf at 11.0 a.m., men and animals tired out after our series of night marches and disturbed, watchful days. As we came along, the heat had been excruciating; one's saddle, if exposed to the sun by a brief dismounting, became hot, and puffs of a fierce Simoom scorched one's face like blasts from a furnace. Badr, I was to discover some months later, was at one time in hiding within a few yards of my passing, and I must unwittingly have given him an uncomfortable hour or so.

I spent the whole of that day resting at Al Assaf, but dispatched a patrol at sunset to a point in the Jazirah where the rebel with thirty followers was said to be in hiding; this, however, proved to be a false scent. By 2.0 a.m. we were on the move again, and five hours later made Al Kurdi. The approach to it as the sun rose afforded some excitement, for the first thing the morning light showed us was a considerable body of horsemen moving along the skyline on our front. Who could it be? My mind was soon relieved of any apprehensions by their tidy, soldier-like formation

— this in contrast to the dog's hind-leg appearance my untutored fellows must have presented. It turned out to be Hall and his merry men. Neither of us was for taking chances, however, and each sent a horseman galloping ahead to make doubly sure of the other; then, reassured, we continued to approach the village, he to enter it on one side as I did so from the other.

Hall and I found a quiet, shady spot for post-mortem reflections, to the accompaniment of tinned sausages which were already promisingly sizzling on a camp-fire nearby. I was thirsty for news of the expedition and the story took little time to tell. Badr was a solitary fugitive somewhere in the depths of the marshes; and our main force retiring to Nasiriyah. This was the crucial point to determine my own plans for moving homeward.

Meanwhile it was interesting to compare notes, and we had the whole day before us. One of the lighter episodes of the main action was that at the outset, as the 99th Infantry advanced across the open by alternate platoons, an Arab youth appeared from cover on their right front. He stood about some little while and even hesitatingly advanced several times, though he appeared to be unarmed. Colonel Luxmore, in command of the 99th Infantry, could not follow this mystery, but thinking it a confidence trick, a lodestone to his men's eyes and attention while some dark scheme was being enacted elsewhere, told off a marksman to attend to the mysterious target. The shot missed, and the youth bolted and went to ground. Later in the day a mounted Arab away to the front of the 99th seemed a bit dogged too. The Colonel turned a Lewis gun on to him, when everybody was thrilled to see him fall heavily — quite dead, they decided. Away went the riderless horse, a grey, but a few minutes later the "dead" horseman appeared farther away to the north, running like a rabbit. The Colonel from whom later I was to hear the story first-hand added: "The laugh was now on me. The old dodger had purposely fallen off under some cover and had run along it until he was out of range. He wasn't touched, of course. Some Arabs on our side avowed that it was none other than the Old Man himself. But whoever it was, he was a sportsman."

Hall and I waited until sunset cool; then he marched out southwards, in the direction of Al Fathi Fort and I moved north with my friendlies along the shores of the Muntafiq Lake country, to disband them at Dawaiyah. There also I could find refreshment in a longed-for bath, and a welcome night's sleep, the first for a week.

At dawn on the following morning my launch was speeding to Shatrah. For me the pursuit was over.

CAPITULATION

THE RIVER COLUMN came sailing home with their tails up.

The situation in the Marshes looked unchanged, but appearance belied the fact. Badr was growing tired of an unequal contest, and Dickson felt that, when he went on the leave that was his due, the Old Man of the Marshes might consider he could come into Government without loss of face.

No logical finality could ever shape the affairs of the marshes. The shaikh protege of one regime was never sufficiently assured of the future; the *bete noire* might, by biding his time, come into his own, for human psychology being what it is no two men will view a situation in all its aspects alike.

And so it was that when Ditchburn [12] succeeded Dickson, Badr saw a glimmer of hope. This, Ditchburn with much adroitness, nursed into the flame of realization. It took five weary months. The flame sometimes flickered this way, sometimes that, and was always in danger of extinction.

To date, the rebel had been absolutely irreconcilable. He had the river and the marsh for allies, such allies as, under Allah's providential hand, were unseducible. But now at last our recent punishment of the tribes that had given him rein during his recent emergence had been effective; they would never risk incurring penalties again. Badr had become, therefore, an exile without hope from his own side. We reaffirmed his outlawry, though this in effect meant little. Perhaps any other Administration than a British one would, in time of war, have put a price on the rebel at the outset, and by the same token threatened any tribe with bombardment if they sheltered him. This formula, even with the air arm not so developed as it is to-day, would probably have brought instant success, and made an expensive River Column unnecessary; but we viewed it as being unsporting, even though precedent for such measures would not have been wanting. Kitchener, I believe, had employed them in the Sudan, and they were used against dacoits in India and on the North-West Frontier. But though Badr was a rebel against Government, the conditions were, perhaps, scarcely analogous. The isolated nature of his opposition, in a division otherwise loyal and quiet, drove us to no such lengths. But in these circumstances the Old Man's stand could occasion little wonder. He was batting on a home wicket, and was quick to discover how scrupulously we observed the rules of the game — how, indeed, we were to this end handicapping ourselves in placing the field. Naturally he would profit by this knowledge. But to give him his due he batted with a straight bat, and although forcing him to an occasional short run, we couldn't get him out, and up to now the honours were his.

Fathi Fort

But time was a factor favourable to us. And now Badr's chastened mood and a new regime brought about a change of front. One effect of active measures over the Albu Salih problem, unquestionably necessary at the time though they were, had been to keep Badr's name fresh on the lips of all men, whence he had bid fair to win the laurels of a hero, or at least a notoriety that was anything but displeasing to him. Indications were not wanting to show that the time had come to appoint his natural successor, Hasan, his eldest son, to the shaikhship, and to see what ignoring the

Old Man would bring about. There was no reason, too, why feelers started under no particular auspices should not find their way into the marshes.

So it was that one fine day an emissary, a Saiyid, revered man of God and still more revered son of His Prophet, brought from Badr a verbal acceptance of terms which Government would endorse. These provided for the rebel's abdication, subject to Hasan's proclaimed succession, coupled with permission for all members of the Rumaiyidh House to return to their native soil, save only Shaikh Badr himself, who would depart in voluntary exile to Mohammerah, there to reside as guest of our old ally. Shaikh Khaz'al. The future might be left to the healing balm of time.

Perhaps we grasped at this olive branch too avidly; for a few days later Badr recanted in the hope of getting better terms. Two hot, dreary months of inevitable summer inaction followed, and then Badr, able to stand his eclipse no longer, decided at last to test the quality of British mercy.

It was October. Ditchburn was touring the Hammar Lake.

He and Captain A. Platts his energetic assistant at Suq ash Shuyukh, were seated in *mejlis* (public assembly), surrounded by a hundred tribesmen. Of a sudden three horsemen were sighted and reported galloping across the plain in the direction of their tent. As they approached, the shrill ululations of women outside announced some event of more than passing interest. It was, indeed, the swan-song of the Old Man of the Marshes.

The horsemen dismounted. One of them was the rebel himself: he had come to make no less than unconditional surrender.

It was a memorable moment. With bowed heads the tribesmen filed silently out of the tent. Badr came forward to where the two British officers now stood to do honour to a subdued foe. The sands were about to run out, the old tenacity of purpose to crumble.

Bending down he removed his head-dress, and in the manner of the country tied it slowly to the leg of the chair of those to whom he was making submission.

'I am of no more count than a *shabana* (common soldier) of your Militia," he said.

Then, rising to his knees: "You have put down the mighty from their seat" — this in the spirit of the old megalomaniacal Badr. But he had said enough.

The Politicals returned jubilant to Nasiriyah. The fateful news was telegraphed to the Civil Commissioner in Baghdad.

Back came the reply: "Congratulations. Joy shall be in heaven...."

ADVENTURE 2

AS DISTRICT OFFICER IN THE MESOPOTAMIAN INSURRECTION OF 1920

PROLOGUE

THE READER MAY POSSIBLY BE unfamiliar with Arabian War Politics, and it is not intended here to lead him into that controversial maze in which many able men have intricated themselves. But it is due to him, perhaps, to be given, as a background to this story, a brief sketch of the salient Arabian events, stated without embellishment, from which he may catch a glimpse of that difficult political complex out of which the Mesopotamia troubles of 1920 chiefly sprang. He may, on the other hand, choose to pass straight to the story.

For twenty-six generations the Arab countries of Syria, Mesopotamia, and the Hijaz had been in the hands of Turkey. In the decade before the War there were signs of an Arab revival. It was less a cultural renaissance than a political separatist movement, which drew its inspiration from Western liberalism. In Mesopotamia it took root in Baghdad and the towns chiefly to the north of it, where it was confined to the intelligentsia; the tribes to the south, steeped in obscurantism, were not affected by it. There were, it is true, elements which in pre-War days had approached British Consuls with the embarrassing suggestion that the Great and Benign Government should forcibly relieve the Turks of their administrative burdens; but they were not typical, for the tribesman, a consummate individualist, is in feeling and fact a constituent of a form of patriarchal society, sufficient unto itself, which in sentiment runs Counter to organized Governments whatsoever, whether Turkish, British, or Arab. He did approve distantly of his old-fashioned Sultan Abdul Hamid and his Pan-Islamism, but he regarded the Committee of Union and Progress, composed of the free-thinking, anti-traditional, and Europe-aping Young Turk, under the inspiration of his religious leaders, as evil incarnate.

The tribesman, with his rifle at his side and living in remote and inaccessible places, is governable only so long as he is convinced of his ruler's power and will to govern, as well as of that ruler's genuine desire for his welfare. That is a cardinal condition, and must be remembered in connection with all events that took place in tribal Mesopotamia.

In the year before the Great War administrative problems had not yet arisen; it was the Arab Nationalist movement, insignificant as it may then have appeared, that was interesting certain high quarters. Lord Kitchener, who as Commander in Chief in India had come into contact with Caliphate influence amongst Indian Muslims, was now in Egypt. In the Arab Nationalist movement he saw the possibility of an Arab Caliphate, and in an Arab Caliphate allied to Great Britain the means at once of countering *Jihad* in India and of parrying German ambitions in the Middle East — should ever Turco-German relations, which had grown apace in the recent Balkan Wars, culminate in a World War.

The World War came, and with it Turkey's intervention. The choice of a candidate to lead the Arab movement fell upon Sharif Husain of Mecca, the Keeper of the Holy Places. Of the immediate objects of the Arab Revolt, one was to hoist a signal to Islam that the Holy Places no longer obeyed, but actually repudiated Constantinople: another to attract Syrian and Mesopotamian elements to its side, and so undermine the enemy position in those countries. The Arab Revolt was sustained during the war years and immediately afterwards by considerable sums of money from the British Exchequer, and by political engagements entered into by the British Government to free from the Turkish yoke the Arab provinces involved.

It was these engagements, or rather the difficulties attending conflicting interpretations of them, which afterwards gave rise to misunderstandings and were the source of many of the troubles that later agitated the Middle East.

The term "Arab Revolt" is perhaps a little misleading. In Arabia proper it was confined to a narrow strip of western littoral, the Hijaz Province — for Arabia is a geographical and not a political entity. Most of the other Arabian Principalities were not concerned; Najd, Shammar, Muscat, Bahrain, and Kuwait, each with its own independent and hereditary ruler, would in any case have repudiated the elevation of the Sharif at their expense, and the Arab revolt was not for them. Its martial activities were limited to the Hijaz and the Mediterranean theatre of war. These areas and Mesopotamia alone provided the political occasion for it.

Representation of British interests throughout Arabia proper —except for the Red Sea littoral — was vested in the Government of India. The Red Sea littoral and, more particular, the engagements with the Hijaz concerning the Arab Revolt were a Foreign Office responsibility. So it came about that the two Arab theatres of activity were managed by two separate Offices of State. The Mediterranean theatre came, by way of the Arab Bureau and Egypt, under the Foreign Office. For Mesopotamia the India Office was responsible.

As the War approached its end there emerged two divergent views regarding Arabian policy: (1) that of the Arab Bureau, deriving its inspiration from the Nationalist intelligentsia elements of the Arab Revolt, and (2) that of the Indian School, administering Mesopotamia itself, and involved in the interplay of the Turkish, Persian, and Najd questions.

In the Arab Bureau view, Sharifianism and Nationalist bureaucracy was equated with the independence of the Arabs, and it looked to the proper fulfilment of British war-pledges in the handing over of Syria and Mesopotamia (if possible, the two States federated) to the kingship of respective members of Sharif Husain's family, with administrative control vesting in the hands of a Nationalist bureaucracy.

The Indian School was for a more gradual Arabicization of executive control in Mesopotamia, in the light of the backwardness and insularity of its tribesmen, the lack of peace with Turkey, British military commitments at the time in Persia, the Russian menace, and the susceptibilities of Bin Sa'ud, the now all-powerful Najdi ruler and a determined enemy of the Sharif.

The one was idealistic; the other traditional. The issue was not simplified by the French view, which was anti-Sharifian. The Sharifians, as the Nationalists of the Arab Revolt came to be known, were also unwilling to recognize the French, and insisted upon the fulfilment of war-pledges by Britain alone, who had initiated them. Their sympathies were naturally pro- Arab Bureau and anti-French and anti- Indian School. In the two years following the War, their patriotism took the form of engineering two insurrections — one against the French in Syria, in which they failed to secure their objectives, and the other against the British in Mesopotamia, in which they succeeded.

Broadly and briefly the War commitments that led up to this state of affairs were as follows;

(I) At the outset of the Revolt in 1915-16 the British Government communicated an offer to the Sharif which stated, *inter alia.*

Subject to... [certain Mediterranean littoral districts] Great Britain is prepared to recognize and support the independence of the Arabs within the territories [including Eastern Syria and Lower Mesopotamia].... When the situation admits Great Britain will give to the Arabs her advice, and will assist them to establish what may appear to be the most suitable form of government in these territories.

On the other hand it is understood that the Arabs have decided to seek the advice and guidance of Great Britain only....

With regard to the vilayets of Baghdad and Basrah, the Arabs will recognize that the established position and interests of Great Britain necessitate special measures of administrative control in order to secure these territories from foreign aggression, to promote the welfare of the local populations, and to safeguard our mutual economic interests.

(II) In March 1916 the Sykes-Picot Agreement was secretly signed between France and England. This settled the boundaries of their spheres of influence in the Arab countries freed from the Turks. Syria was to be a French zone: Lower Mesopotamia would go to Great Britain.

(III) In November 1917 the Balfour Declaration was made which established Palestine as a separate enclave.

(IV) On November 7, 1918, after conclusion of the war with Turkey, an Anglo-French Declaration was issued. It stated, *inter alia*.

The end aimed at by France and Great Britain is the complete and final enfranchisement of the people so long oppressed by the Turks, and the establishment of national (Governments and Administrations, drawing their authority from the initiative and free choice of the native populations.... Far from wishing to impose upon the populations any particular institutions the allies have no other desire than to assure by their support and active assistance the normal functioning of the Governments and Administrations which the populations have freely given themselves.

During the early Armistice period the French zone of Syria was in British occupation, the occupation of General Allenby's victorious army. The Sharifian force, an adjunct to that army, with its nucleus of British officers logically assumed the administrative executive of government. In its ranks were the *Ahd al Iraqi*, a Nationalist organization of Mesopotamians, and these now applied themselves from their *pied a terre* to the problem of the "liberation" of Mesopotamia; in other words, to secure the executive control of the administration there as they appeared to have achieved it in Syria, preliminary to loosing the fetters of foreign influence. Syria was henceforth the chief source of Arab propaganda, and a stream of gold, directed at undermining the British position in Mesopotamia, issued thence.

To revert to the Anglo-French Declaration, which appeared to endow Nationalist activities with a moral cause and a stimulus. The results of this Declaration were unfortunate. It seemed, for all its democratic appeal and high idealism, to those called upon to give effect to it on the spot, more suited to societies with developed institutions and a corporate sense than to a tribal country wholly lacking these conditions.

How to give a "complete and final enfranchisement" to a politically inarticulate people? The population south of Baghdad were an almost solid Shi'ah *bloc*, nearly wholly illiterate, living in a rude but self-contained tribal society, which in many places had for decades been unused to any government at all. Their real desire was probably for freedom from any sort of Government bigger than their tribal unit.

How to set up a "National Government and Administration drawing its initiative and free choice from" a country, largely peopled by such untaught men? The setting up of a native Government at all clearly postulated a personnel drawn wholly from one cultural class — the Sunni intelligentsia, chiefly of Baghdad and the northern towns - a class to which the tribesmen, in their dealings with British officers, had declared, when no issue pended, their rooted objection. To have embarked prematurely upon the supersession of British personnel by the local effendi, who, moreover, were either without experience or had acquired it in the Turkish School, would not, in the opinion of the Mesopotamian authorities (quite apart from the questions involved concerning Turkey, Russia, Persia, and Najd), have satisfied the condition of "the initiative and free choice of the people, which they would freely give themselves".

In short, the Shi'ah and tribal factor which existed in Mesopotamia, alone of the Arab countries, made it extremely difficult to frame an acceptable constitution there that could square the terms of the Anglo-French Declaration.

Up to the time of its issue the great bulk of the people of Mesopotamia had been resigned to and content with British Administration. With Oriental fatalism they had accepted the decision of arms, and were prepared, as the Arab proverb has it, to "kiss the hand you cannot strike off". The bombshell came with President Wilson's Fourteen Points at the Peace Conference, and within a month of it the sequel — the Anglo-French Declaration. Amongst the Baghdadis the appointment of an Arab Amir was immediately canvassed, and a cry of hope went up from the coffee-shops. In the tribes nothing happened for some time and then a dim idea got abroad that the future held an Arabian Nirvana: no more taxation, no more land rent, no more interference, but only tribal "liberty", emancipated from any coercive authority. This idea gained ground. As for the Holy Places, the torch-bearers of an exclusive faith were enraptured at the declared self-effacement of an infidel Government.

A solid community of anti-Government interests was invited to be up and doing, and a solidarity was created which had no previous existence.

At the outset the Civil Commissioner, under instructions from home, took necessary steps to ascertain local opinion. There was no formed opinion at this stage, 'and therefore no means of ascertaining it. Public meetings were called by "Politicals", who loyally took every measure in their power to encourage the people to say whether they would like an Amir, and, if so, whom, what type of administration they desired, and so on. But the mental horizons of the people coincided with their physical horizons. The tribes had never been invited to help frame a constitution before, and they usually replied — this to ingratiate themselves with their present masters — that the British were a most desirable connection. Gradually, of course, the man "with his senses in his eyes" got a feeling of promotion in his blood. Up to this time he had thought that only Allah could shift the British, and he would behave accordingly; now he had it put into his head that he had only to flout authority and the British would remove themselves. He thus became a ready tool for agitators, religious and Nationalist, and these in turn found nourishment in abundance in the British press, a section of which was loud with propaganda against the Mesopotamia "adventure" and with a demand to cut the painter.

Thus was the seed of trouble being sown, and soon we were to reap the tragic harvest whirlwind.

As if an ill fate were making doubly sure, extraneous events were contributing to an uprising. Syria was astir, so was Egypt. Self-determination was a principle that held the political field. Article 22 of the Covenant of the League of Nations stated that "the wishes of the communities must be the principal consideration in the selection of the Mandatory".

Whatever Mesopotamia had not said, there had been a unanimous feeling that the British connection was desirable. But the Sharifians in Syria regarded Article 22 as *prima facie* quashing the Sykes-Picot Agreement, under which Syria was willy-nilly to be a French Mandate. They therefore indulged in anti-French intrigues. President Wilson had suggested at the Peace Conference a plebiscite for Syria. For this purpose four representatives of the Allied Powers were to proceed thither; but the terms of reference could not be agreed upon, and the American representative was the only one of the four to go to Syria. In an invidious position he became a focus for the forces of unrest. Damascus rioted.

The arrest of a pro-French Syrian notable, by British troops in occupation, had already brought matters to a head. The French attributed their troubles in Syria to the machination of British officers serving with the Sharifians. However unmerited such a charge, there was an acrimonious outburst in the French Press — a most unfortunate moment for the Anglo-French relations to be strained, for it was at this time that Egypt was seething with agitation for the abolition of the British Protectorate. It was decided to withdraw all British troops out of the Syrian zone. The French thereupon took over the country and Sharifian administration.

Within six months the Amir Faisal and his army of the Arab Revolt were at war with the Mandatory Power, and in July 1920 the French army in Syria now drove them from that country at the point of the sword.

Great Britain recognized the Arabs' considerable claims on her for their war services. But Palestine and Syria presented closed shutters. Thus Mesopotamia remained the focal point for Arab Nationalist aspirations.

COMING EVENTS

THE EARLY MONTHS of 1920 passed pleasantly enough in Baghdad. For instance, there were the Pleasant Sunday Afternoons of Miss Gertrude Bell, after the usual Sunday morning ride, often taken with that eager, distinguished woman herself. These "P.S.A.s", as they were called, were held in Miss Bell's garden, and the political intelligentsia of Baghdad were invited — a. gathering of those whose brothers for the most part were in the Sharifian camp with the Amir Faisal in Syria. The P.S.A. afforded a free platform, and the young Arabs expressed their convictions about the politics of the day — the Sykes-Picot Agreement, Zionism and the Balfour Declaration, the Anglo-French Declaration, Mosul and the Turkish question, and their own hopes and aspirations.

Again, I had the privilege of living in No. 1 Political Mess, the senior political mess in the country, whose numbers included our brilliant chief. Sir Arnold Wilson, Miss Bell, and others. This mess never knew a dull moment. It had acquired a magnificent piano from the old German Residency in Baghdad, and I vividly remember the guest nights, on which might be heard J. M. Wilson's lusty *Prologue to I Pagliacci*, and my own memorized parlour tricks, Chopin's *A Major Polonaise*, and Schumann's *Fasschintgschwank aus Wien*. Visitors, the good and the great, who came out to the country at this time made No. 1 Mess their domicile. They ranged from 'peers of the realm and prospective governors of Indian Presidencies, making a preliminary survey of the land, to world-renowned archaeologists on pilgrimage to this Babylonian paradise of theirs, now safe at last. There was, moreover, a stream of officials on leave or returning to their Divisions — personalities such as Leachman and Soane, men with an unrivalled knowledge of the land and the people they had made their life study, who regarded the P.S.A. askance, if not as a positively dangerous institution.

Madhif reed house with Cattle

But the bondage of an office stool — for I had been posted as Second Assistant in the Revenue Secretariat since returning from home leave — was less to my liking than the comparatively free life — most of it spent in the saddle — of a District Political Officer. For this I longed again.

It was May, and the insurrection was upon us. There had been rumblings already, and the Civil Commissioner considered the number of troops in the country inadequate to ward off the storm. G.H.Q. took a more rosy, if a rasher, view. The question of increasing the garrison before the necessity had actually arisen was one that, committed by the exigencies of finance and the process of demobilization at home to a policy of reducing the Army of Occupation at the end of the year, it could not cheerfully face. Moreover, it had irons in the fire in Persia, where the North- Persian Force — "Norperforce", as it was called —

constituted a check to the Bolsheviks' striking down through the Caspian Sea: a move that was always thought possible in those days. But the cause of economy was scarcely served by the establishment of a Military Hill Station in Persia in addition to the Army Camp at Karind. To Sarimil, however, had come out the previous winter the wives and families of the Army of Occupation, and G.H.Q. now announced that it intended itself to move up to Persia for the summer. Civil apprehensions on the political situation were thus treated somewhat lightly; whence came this amusing topical parody [13]

> Half a lakh, half a lakh,
> Half a lakh squandered!
> Up to the Persian Hills
> G.H.Q. wandered,
> laired on by Hambro's brains,
> lagged by Julian's pains.
> Pushed on by Lubbock's trains,
> G.H.Q. wandered. [14]

> "Charge for the camp," he said.
> Was there a bill delayed?
> No, though contractors knew
> Someone had blundered.
> Ours not to calculate.
> Ours but to render straight
> Forms, cost, accounting, eight,
> Monthly in triplicate.
> Ours not to query what
> G.H.Q. squandered.

> Wars to the west of them.
> Wars to the south of them.

> Battles all round them,
> Volleyed and thundered.
> Careless of tribes that kill,
> Firmly they sat and still,
> Dug in at Sarimil.
> Then they came back, but with
> Half a lakh squandered.

> Honour the brave and fair
> Wives who remained up there.
> Breathing the common air,
> No longer sundered;
> Mixing with me and you,
> Just as though G.H.Q.
> Might have been human, too.
> Why one camp would not do.
> All Karind wondered.

> Honour the brave and bold
> Taxpayer, young and old.
> Who, although never told,
> Paid by the hundred.
> 'Think of the camp they made',
> Think of the water laid
> On, and the golf-links made.
> Think of the bill we paid.
> Oh, the wild charge they made!
> Half a lakh squandered!

I heard a ring on the phone.

"Captain Thomas, please."

"Speaking."

"Secretary to C.C. speaking -Sir Arnold would like you to come round and see him." I was shown into the Civil Commissioner's office, a large room, well carpeted, but otherwise innocent of furniture except for a writing-table, a few chairs, a bench on which our political chief was wont to take his night's slumbers, and pillars of files standing about that engaged him for fourteen hours of the day.

"Take a chair! Read this, Thomas."

It was from the Political Officer of the Muntafiq Division and read: I have received an urgent report from the Assistant Political Officer, Shatrah, that the tribal situation there is looking black, the tribes are buying rifles and refusing measurement of their crops for revenue purposes. If the Khafajah and Abudah tribes combine a most difficult situation will arise. The inaccessibility of the district, lack of means of communication, and its own notorious turbulent spirit will make it impossible to subdue. The Assistant Political Officer there has tendered his resignation.

I looked up.

"Well, what do you make of it?" said the C.C. "You have served there longer than anyone else, I think."

"I'd very much like to be posted there, sir," I replied.

The following day I was sent around to G.H.Q. to see the Chief of Staff. I took a letter for him from the C.C.

It read:

I have asked for a gunboat to be sent to Kut, and I request that it may be placed at the disposal of Captain B. S. Thomas, whom I am sending down as A.P.O. Shatrah. It should move from Kut to Hai with a British machine-gun detachment on board under instructions from A.P.O., Shatrah, subsequent to his arrival at that place and thence to Shatt al Gharraf and to Shatt al Bada' (which is as far as it can get with safety).

Captain Thomas knows the district well. It may become necessary to send a couple of planes to Shatrah, where there is a good landing-ground. They should be sent to Nasiriyah with instructions to proceed to Shatrah if and when asked for by the A.P.O.

Twenty-four hours later I reported to the Political Officer, Nasiriyah, the headquarters of the Muntafiq Division in the Lower Euphrates, two hundred and fifty miles down the line, having proceeded there by railway — a German pre-War dream, that railway, and a war contribution by the British to the Land of Two Rivers.

From Nasiriyah I went by horse to Shatrah.

SHATRAH

SHATRAH AGAIN! for a second term of service. It was a pleasing prospect. I already knew many of the people individually, certainly the influential amongst them, and I liked them, as an Englishman does like the tribesmen when he gets to know them. The market town for the surrounding tribes, Shatrah lay remote from the main highways of Mesopotamia in its spacious heart, the fertile plain of the Jazirah beside a tailing channel of the Hai River.

My house occupied a central position on the river front. It was the Arab type of house, built round a courtyard, and inadequately windowed on the outside on account of the Muslima's veil and prying eyes. The ground-floor rooms, which were my offices, opened on to the courtyard — a joyous courtyard, paved with inscribed bricks four thousand years old of the Priest King Gudea of Lagash, the ancient Sumerian city, the ruins of which lay a little way up-stream; outside the first-floor rooms, which were my living quarters, a verandah ran round the interior square of the house, and from it the usual flight of steps led to the roof. Thither I retired in the cool of the afternoon for a pipe of peace, and looked out across the city walls beyond the tiny river, over vast yellow cornlands that stretched away like a calm sea to die encircling edge of the sky. Overlooking my roof was the tall turquoise slated minaret of the Friday mosque, where on hot evenings the Faithful chose the roof beside its domes for their prostrations. Beyond and behind it were the flat houses of the town, and amongst them a Boys' Primary School and a Dispensary — both innovations which Shatrah owed to British administration. These progressive institutions were appreciated, though I had encountered a little opposition to start with when I introduced a globe into the school and called it the earth, for some of the parents, scenting a heresy, objected to it. On the side opposite to the mosque were my stables; the days of motor-cars in such districts as Shatrah were only just dawning. I preferred in any case to do my touring on horseback, for that always seemed to me the right way of studying the Arab and his language and of letting him get to know you, besides being so much more fun; and the surrounding country bred prolifically the usual undersized but beautiful Arab hack.

A bazaar which flourished in those fat days of the land ran the length of the town, a street or two removed from, and parallel with, the river. It seethed with country folk, bright of garb and loud in their guttural tongue. Many of them were young tribal bucks armed to the teeth and flashing in their war-like array. The bazaar catered for a catholicity of Arab tastes now that Shatrah had come in touch with the outside world. There were tiny shops gay with the gimcracks of India and Japan. An interior galaxy of mirrors, with a life-size flesh-coloured picture of a bust of buxom womanhood at the entrance, was the sign of the shop of the barber, who in these parts is masseur, and physician too; at least he is the practitioner of blood-letting — a popular cure for fever and the malady obscure. Most shops trafficked in the country's stock-in-trade — its winter crops of wheat and barley, and rice in summer; there were fruit stalls of melons, pomegranates, oranges, dates, gourds, and the like; the inevitable grocer's stall that was hung about with sugar cones and displayed a chess-board effect of coffee-beans, tea, tobacco, and spices resembling every kind of sand. But it was the shop glad with a riot of silk and knick-knacks, and lit up with shafts of sunshine coming through the holes in the bazaar roof which I could never bring myself to repair, that held the tribal girl spellbound; there you would see her gazing in wrapt devotion and waiting for some one to buy the load of firewood that she carried on her pretty head, thus to endow her with the means of acquiring her fancy, if there should be cash left over after buying tobacco for her husband.

The Shatrah District was an area about the size of an average English county. It was the geographical centre of the Muntafiq confederation of Arabs, whose habitat was the lower middle Euphrates, extending northwards here, astride the Hai (or Gharraf) River past Qalat Sikar to the confines of the Kut Division. It had never known the tramp of the British soldier as the Euphrates and Tigris had done; it was, in fact, a notoriously turbulent part of the country, where for years past the Turks had had but a shadowy hold, if, indeed, they had held it at all. So the Muntafiq habitat remained an Arab enclave when the rest of Mesopotamia had for centuries passed under the Ottoman yoke.

Here the Sa'dun, an Arab family of noble origin, had for the past three centuries been the titular lords of the land, and might have continued so had they remained satisfied with tribal homage and a nominal tribute. But their exactions and a changing tribal temper gave the Turks their opportunity of putting an end to what they considered an anomaly, a situation similar to that of an isolated Indian Native State surrounded by a solid British India. In 1881 the Turkish force, said to have been 18.000 strong, inarched southwards from Kut. Coquetting with the tribes in whose ranks disaffection had become rife was scarcely necessary to induce them to turn upon their alleged task-masters, the Sa'duns. These fled, many of them to Muhammarah, to find asylum with the father of the present unfortunate Shaikh, and only after six years did they begin to trickle back, a forlorn band of exiles, to dwell on the borders of their lost domains. The Turks followed up their military success by appointing a governor at Shatrah, and ten years of strong and peaceful administration ensued — an inevitable lull after the tribes had beheld the might and the will of their masters. But now this peaceful interim seemed to be coming to an end through the fading effects of time and the return of their former overlords, an encroachment which the tribes viewed with concern. The movement, they were ready to believe, was no part of the official policy, but was facilitated by local officials who were willing tools where the bribe offered sufficient inducement. At the root of the tribal objection was a new land law which upset their own prescriptive rights. For what had happened was that, in compensation for the Sa'duns' surrender of their sovereignty, the Turks '.conferred upon them rights of ownership over large tracts of tribal territory: a title approximating in practice to freehold in English law. Now "proprietary rights" and "rent" were institutions foreign to the tribal mind. That the attempted system of leasehold which followed should have set the tribes by the ears is not to be wondered at, and for the following twenty years the district was in perpetual state of unrest or convulsion. Agrarian discontent, a fertile source of trouble in all agricultural countries, thus became aggravated among the Muntafiq, and woe to the adjudicator of land disputes! Indeed, across the stream from my house (ominously situated) was a small graveyard containing the remains of three Turkish *Qaim Maqams*, i.e. governors, and predecessors of mine, who had not given local satisfaction, and who, therefore, had died at their posts from other than natural causes.

Then came the Great War. The Shatrah tribes rose under the fanatical preaching of their religious leaders to march under the banner of *Jihad* against our invading army, assured that in fighting the infidel they were carrying out the Divine Will, and that, if they fell, their bodies would most surely be transported to the Celestial Theatre of Delights. Whether or not it is an illusion to suppose that the fighting capacity of the Arab is increased when the issue is a religious one, there is ample evidence to show that the Muntafiq had little stomach for the battle of Shu'aibah. But there was profit in it: for following upon our ' out of the opposing forces and the suicide of the Turkish commander, the Shatrah tribes fell upon the retreating Turks, their erstwhile comrades, so that in place of the crude Arab muskets they set forth with they returned to their villages armed with modem rifles and plentiful ammunition.

General Townshend's spectacular advance to Ctesiphon set them scurrying into Nasiriyah to acknowledge the British Government. But as soon as the tide of fortune turned, and our retreat to Kut and its investment followed, these tribes broke off relations with us and promptly resumed them with the Turks. Shatrah once more became the headquarters of Turkish agents, and these, by means of bribes and gifts of arms and ammunition, induced a rising of the Gharraf tribes against our Euphrates force resting on Nasiriyah. Seventeen thousand tribesmen marched down under their redoubtable leader, Shaikh Khaiyyun al 'Ubaid, and engaged a glorified brigade of ours at Butaniyah. Hand-to-hand fighting took place, and the Arabs retired only after inflicting casualties of 148 killed and 35 missing. Butaniyah was a battle which ended not too well for us and showed the fighting mettle of the Shatrah tribes. Offensive operations we had been preparing against them were allowed to lapse, and for three years they thus maintained themselves unmolested. Our blockade measures, necessary to prevent supplies getting through them to the enemy, while hitting the people, brought handsome war profits to successful smugglers and provided ulterior motives for the continuance of the conflict, apart from the arms and ammunition by which the tribes profited at the hands of their allies.

But with the fall of Baghdad in 1918 they once more came in, protesting loudly their joy at the triumph of just government! — all the leaders, that is to say, but one, for Shaikh Khaiyyun al 'Ubaid still remained obdurate. Shatrah was soon afterwards (June 1918) visited for the first time by a small party of British officers, and six months later I was transferred from Suq ash Shuyukh as its "Political".

The tribal leader in all these events was this same Shaikh Khaiyyun of the Abudah, a man of fabulous wealth, of unquestioned authority, of strong and resolute character, and mighty in battle. He had dominated the whole river for fifteen years, and had been a thorn in the flesh alike of the Turks and of ourselves.

THE LEGACY OF THE TURKS

Pending a peace treaty with Turkey, War and post-War Mesopotamia was, in the eyes of international law, still Occupied Enemy Territory'. British administration of it was thus conditioned; it was inevitably of a military and provisional character. International usage required that the criminal law lately operating must, as far as compatible with the safety of the occupying army, be carried on. That law had been the Ottoman Penal Code, a system based on the Napoleonic Code, which experienced British officers entitled to a judicial opinion considered admirable for Turkey Proper but singularly ill-adapted for Lower Mesopotamia. Military law enjoined upon us the obligation of collecting revenues ordinarily taxable on the population, to which end the departing Ottoman officials' contribution had been the removal with them of most of the tiles and records.

The Turkish administration of Mesopotamia of late years had been discredited by most European standards, and deservedly so. It was corrupt; it was effete; and the land withered under its blighting influences. The recognized object of officials seems to have been to make a good thing for themselves out of it. The biggest posts are said to have been auctioned in Constantinople, and the highest bidder, portfolio under his arm, came, as everybody knew, unblushingly to recover his investment, plus a reasonable capital appreciation during his term of office. But in order to stay the distance and insure against his recall, he had to see that other appetites at Imperial headquarters were appeased from the Mesopotamian pie. Local Regie (tobacco), Auqaf (religious endowments), Sanniyah (Crown Estates), Ottoman Public Debt and Customs Departments must all remit their quota of annual income to the Sublime Porte. The example of official integrity set at the top was said to have permeated down through the grades of Government employees, who, whether Arab, Jew, or Turk, were, from their associations, considered to be corrupt or corruptible.

In such circumstances international administrative interests could scarcely be expected to thrive. As a matter of fact, public security, law, and order had practically no existence outside town areas, and the degree of administration imposed varied with the character of the localities, and their respective capacities of being turned into commercially paying propositions.

Mash-huf Reed Boat in the Iraqi Marshes

In this wild Muntafiq country something like anarchy had normally prevailed, except in one or two towns. Its people were not of the kind to yield easily, for, though now tillers of the soil, they had sprung from the wayward sons of the desert. They originated in one of those human eruptions which from Babylonian time onwards have periodically come surging out of Arabia's vitals. Whatever the causes — drought, the pressure of over-population, or the proselytizing zeal of a new religion — the tribes have pre- served fundamentally the mentality, the customs, and the sanctions of their ancient deserts. Hence, in the Lower Mesopotamia that I knew, blood-feuds were normal and respectable, womankind was regarded as an inferior order of creation, right was to him who could assert his strength, rebellion was endemic. The Muntafiq tribes were too strong, too militant, to allow' the Ottoman administration more than a precarious footing, and were left to enjoy an almost taxless and uninterrupted existence. The remote tribal shaikh of the Gharraf was a law unto himself and a menace to his poorer neighbours. Now and again some bold official would apply the favourite Turkish precept, *divide et impera*, but it was productive of no lasting result, if, indeed, of any immediate effect. Of security for the merchant, the landlord, or the official, there was none, and the weaker brethren could only look for it by enlisting under the banner of some robber baron of a shaikh or by plying him with presents and palliatives. His lair was a fort on the river-banks or in the marshes, and there he posted his "braves", and there kept a fleet of *bellums* with which to launch out and to despoil.

There was no railway as yet to lend itself to the peaceful purposes of trade. The trader had, therefore, to pay the tribal exaction as he passed or be plundered and incur the risk of death. The Turks, engaged in their Balkan wars, had neither the power to bend the local chieftains nor the will to yoke them to the cause of law and order. Turkish action, as translated on the spot, was based on the concept of the right of the conqueror. This, of course, was also the guiding principle of the robber shaikh, so that there was a common ethical standard. Hence the arbitrary sale of title-deeds over tribal tracts to absentee landlords; and these *ashab tapu* (title-deeds) in the fullness of time were to come to a "just Government" to exact their statutory rights — a fertile source of injustice to one party or the other or both. Hence also the law courts had been conducted in Turkish and in accordance with the Sunni canon, despite the fact that the population to the south of Baghdad was almost 100 per cent. Arab and 90 per cent. Shi'ah.

The town Arab of Baghdad and to the north saw things in a different light. He was a Sunni, if not a Turk, at any rate a co-religionist of the Turks, and thus profited relatively by the privileges of a Sunni domination. He had received a Turkish education, and most probably had to look to the Ottoman service for a career.

To form any just appreciation of the interior situation in the days of British administration, it is essential to be clear on this singular feature of the Mesopotamian population. Between the native townsman and the tribesman there was a cleavage, geographical, social, and religious.

The townsman of the official class was predominantly recruited from Baghdad and the towns to the north; he regarded the rebellious and non-taxpaying tribesman as an enemy of the State, and shared the traditional view of merchant and landlord fellow-townsmen that the tribes were dissenting barbarians at whose hands they all suffered acute depredations.

The tribes of Iraq south of Baghdad, on the other hand, were almost exclusively Shi'ah in religion, and regarded the official and the landlord as natural enemies of their liberties and the passing merchant as the fat lamb which Allah had sent them to be fleeced for his heresies.

Now Shi'ah and Sunni in those days did not stand for academic differences. Intolerance in this land of obscurantism and hot passion was not free from animus. The relationship between the two sectaries, aggravated, perhaps, by different cultural levels, by supposed conflicting economic interests, and by the Ottoman legacy of a Sunni domination, was similar to the relationship of English Dissenters and Anglicans at the time of the Stuart Restoration.

Shi'ism is the great dissenting body of Islam. [15] Its devotee, the Mesopotamian tribesman, in the nature of his mystical creed and by reason of his illiteracy, had come to take his politics from its hierarchy. This was so when Constantinople traditionally turned the cold shoulder on the Shi'ah divines of the Holy Places, and how much more so now that the hand of that unsympathetic Power lay stricken! This hierarchy consisted of a chief *Mujtahid*, the Pontiff, so to speak, the *Mujtahidin* — bishops, and the ulema — clergy. And though in point of fact priestcraft is anathema to Islam, the paradox existed of the riverain tribes being the most priest-ridden of men. The power of the *Mujtahidin* lay in the theological concept that they are the interpreters of the Divine law, and that interpretation might vary with inspiration from time to time. The interpretations accepted by that other great division of Islam, the orthodox Sunnis, on the other hand, are one of four orthodox systems — Shaf'i, Hanbali, Maliki, and Hanafi. These systems are of great antiquity and are held to be immutable. The Shi'ah holy places of Najaf and Karbala, the Vatican of Iraq, thus held for the tribesmen the keys of heaven and hell, Here lived Persian divines, steeped in the lore of the Holy Books which they alone may interpret, books written in the sacred Arabic script, the mother-tongue of Paradise, and the language through which God had made his revelation to man!

When the tribal pilgrim went, as he did almost annually, to Karbala and to Najaf, and to a lesser extent to Kadhimain and to Samarra, to make his devotions at the shrines of the saints, he placed himself under the guidance of one of these divines, became lavishly generous under a religious stimulus, and assumed for the time being the somewhat ironical role of a creature of submissive obedience.

To the tenet common to both Sunni and Shi'ah — "There is no god but God and Muhammad is the Prophet of God" — the Shi'ah them. adds, "and Ali is the Saint of God". But the chief theological point of difference between the two sects, apart from the interpretation of Holy Law already referred to, is the question of succession to the Prophet. With the Sunni, succession is a living issue; with the Shi'ah it is a dead one, or at most is in abeyance. The Sunni holds the Caliphate by an elected succession. The occupier of this office was customarily the head of the strongest temporal Muslim Power of the day; the role fell for centuries, therefore, to the Ottoman Sultans. This attitude is heretical to the Shia. He holds by an hereditary succession, a succession limited to twelve holders of the office called Imams. Ali was the first and greatest of these — the corner-stone of the edifice. His bones, with those of other early Imams, lie in the Holy Places of Iraq. The twelfth and last Imam Mahdi disappeared as a boy into a cave, where he still lives, though hidden from men's eyes, and will come again to wage war against the infidels; whence the periodic upheavals in Shi'ah countries caused by the appearance of a claimant upon the scene. The Sunnis repudiate the word "Imam" in this sense, and are therefore regarded by Shi'ahs as heretics.

The Imamate conception stands for a theocracy and excludes the sanctity of other temporal power. This principle is sometimes advanced in support of a view that the tribes south of Baghdad, whose Shi'ism was a very real faith to them, rose in insurrection for purposes other than the desire of a Sunni Ruler and a bureaucratic Arab State.

BRITISH METHODS

THE BUSINESS of a District Political was to govern, and the objectives of Government were the pacification of the tribes and the introduction of law and order in place of the habitual chaos that had previously obtained. A District Political had to administer justice, collect revenue, purchase supplies for the Military, set up a Municipality, and co-operate with other Departments — Education, Irrigation, Agriculture, and Public Works, if and where these were operating.

Apart from ethical considerations the necessity for introducing law and order amongst lawless tribes was clearly in military interests as a means of securing our lines of communication and for the maintenance of local supplies. Shipping and world conditions subsequent to the Armistice, which had made costs of overseas supplies prohibitive, made it very desirable to feed the army in the field as much as possible from local resources. Oddly enough, the most lawless areas happened often to be the most fertile ones.

As I have observed, Shatrah had never seen as much as a squad of British soldiers; my authority came, therefore, from the reflected prestige of our resounding victories that had swept the Turk from the land, and from our good name for honest dealing.

I was the only Englishman in a district of, perhaps, 130,000 souls. My nearest colleagues were stationed at Nasiriyah, 24 miles to the south (my senior officer), and Qalat Sikar, 36 miles to the north. These I contrived to meet at intervals of a month or so. Speaking Arabic and learning to think, also, in the local dialect were, naturally, obligatory.

For force one depended upon native *askaris*, of which I had thirty. The *Shabana*, as we called him, was one of God's own. A tribesman whom we ourselves recruited locally, who brought his own rifle and horse with him, and was put into uniform and cloaked with authority. His duties were, in turn and out of turn, those of escort, 'messenger, gaoler, policeman, and soldier, and well he performed them. Brave and bold, he was altogether a great fellow, though one learned to avoid using him where possible in his own district. There, in the nature of things, he had old scores to settle, and it was inadvisable to expose him to the temptation of exploiting his position to get even with personal enemies. But twenty miles from his village he was a pillar of strength. Springing from riverain tribesmen — a. race almost non- politically minded — he was capable of tremendous personal loyalty, and the *Shabana* came, with time, to develop first into militiaman and then into Arab levy, in which capacity he did magnificently during the troubles of the insurrection.

Besides the small force of local scallywags, administration was entitled to support by air action in case of any serious disorder. But I never found it necessary amongst Muntafiq tribes to ask for an aeroplane for punitive purposes. Punishment from time to time was necessary, of course, and I fancy I made a record score once, when by means of *Shabanas* twelve offending towers of the Bani Sa'id were demolished on a single occasion — an act that seems to have been not undeserved, since their owners stood by me to a man when the troubles came.

My experience taught me that the tribesman was amenable if he knew the why and wherefore of things, and if he were patiently listened to while, at almost unendurable length, he unfolded his grievances. My practice was to spend more than half my month touring the tribes, whom I thus got to know personally. I usually took with me some four shaikhs (on whom I rang the changes) drawn from another part of the district; these were thus a sympathetic medium with mouth and ears.

The Gharraf Arab, wild and woolly as he was, did respond to the personal touch.

Shatrah had been given a wide berth by the Turks for many years, but even when they were at the wheel their relationship with the tribes was such that officially a Sunni Qadhi administered the *Shar'a* law —an act of non-recognition of Shi' ah dissent. As the tribes were almost wholly Shi' ah, it was not surprising that the Government court had been boycotted. As in all tribal Arabia an unwritten code was found operating among the common folk, and here the magistrate was the tribal Shaikh or a respected Saiyid. The results on the whole were satisfactory, for they were consonant with the local conception of justice, or had, at any rate, the sanction of immemorial custom. This system we recognized and made our own in the Tribal Disputes Regulations, though the fellow who came off second best usually brought tales to one's office that there was no justice except at the hands of *Hadhrat al Hakim* — i.e. oneself. Such petitions were often frivolous, though not invariably so, for *dhulm*, petty tyranny and self-interest, were factors not absent in the psychology of the river chieftain, who must not only have a giant's strength but also use it, in his circles, if he would prevail. With almost all tribal cases the procedure was to hand them over to a tribal court I convened and over which I presided, or absented myself, as the case might be; I then passed judgment according to its decisions.

That was the approved method of administering tribal justice and of giving satisfaction, though an occasional case came along where considerations of humanity, or, rather, a more enlightened sense of justice, compelled one to interfere. Such a case, I remember, had occurred at Suq ash Shuyukh. There a lad of seventeen was brought before us charged with the murder of his mother. He did not deny the crime, and explained that it had come about in this wise. She had confessed herself to be with child, though his father had died many years before. The disgrace that a bastard brother would bring upon him was intolerable, unless he could expiate it. Now he loved his mother and was minded to spare her. So he brought in some sage old tribal women who attempted to bring about a miscarriage. Had they succeeded he would have spared his mother's life, but as things were there remained only one thing to do to insure his own good name being untarnished and to enable him to sit down with honour to the coffee-cup in the tribal *madhif*. From this step he did not shrink. The blood-stained dagger was produced with which he had stabbed his mother between the breasts as she slept. The tribal court to which the case was referred dispatched it in an hour or so. They found that the murderer had acted honourably, and they recommended his acquittal. It was only with difficulty that the tribal conscience could be persuaded of the justice of Government punishment, which was forthwith meted out to him. In the six months before he gained his liberty he was found to be an excellent gardener, and turned his skill to good account at Political House, Suq ash Shuyukh, where I resided, and where the garden to this day blossoms as a memorial to him.

Criminal law, as applied to non-tribesmen living in the town, I administered myself in the old Turkish Court Room of Shatrah's rather splendid Sarai. The Ottoman Penal Code of the late regime had been superseded. We used as a temporary measure more simple regulations, which had been evolved in Baluchistan in circumstances similar to our own. During my previous sojourn in Shatrah my court was that of a Second Class Magistrate, with powers to imprison up to six months, but with experience I had come to be invested with First Class magisterial powers and a two years' maximum. We of course conducted our cases in Arabic— a reform that gave satisfaction, for cases in the courts in Turkish days were generally heard through interpreters in Turkish.

A reform which gave considerably less satisfaction was the institution of revenue collection. Taxation was necessary for many reasons; it was lawful; it would represent a palpable act of tribal submission; it would help feed our army of occupation and thus reduce the burden of bringing supplies from overseas; and later, it would provide the ways and means for financing schemes of amelioration. Our fiscal system naturally took the form of the Turkish one to which, theoretically, the people were accustomed. In effect ours was more uniform in incidence, more efficient in method, and, as far as we could make it, was bereft of its old-time corruption. Turkish practice had come to be a patchwork arrangement where the assessment varied in every area in proportion with the local tendencies to yield or resist; it was, in short, opportunist and commercial in its aims and ends, and thus it overtaxed certain districts, undertaxed others, and abandoned some to no taxation at all. Shatrah had of late years belonged to the last category, and our revenue policy seemed to it, therefore, revolutionary indeed.

But with the operation of constructive schemes it was easier for us to point to the disinterestedness of our aims than it could have been for the Turks. The revenues, such as they were in pre- War days, were, as already shown, in part earmarked for the Imperial coffers of Constantinople, and in any case there were never any funds left over for local improvements. Thus the country was bled. Our objects were different. We would take with one hand but give back with the other, on scientific and productive lines, calculated for the country's good. A public telegraph and telephone service, a road, a school, and a dispensary marked the fruits of our labour in Shatrah to date, and an important public works cum irrigation project was in hand.

Nature seemed ill-disposed to Shatrah, which, without the intervention of man, was doomed to decay from the silting up of its river. The town was situated downstream of the bifurcation of the Gharraf. It lay, alas! on the wrong fork of the **Y**, for its twin, the Bada' channel, year by year took an increasing volume of water at Shatt ash Shatrah's expense. The project of bunding the Bada' must absorb, as was clear to the locals, most of Shatrah's revenues; yet we had applied ourselves to it unstintingly and with very little local pressure— indeed the idea was our inspiration. If the Arab's "senses are in his eyes" as he kept on saying, the financial aspect of the scheme could not but have impressed him as an earnest of our good intentions. Yet the mind of the average tribesman in that land of chronic individualism was incapable of rising beyond the interests of himself and of his immediate present. To him it was a nuisance that we must call upon him for labour, even though we paid him wages. It was not the work that irked him, but the absence it entailed from his village, the separation, if only for three days at a time, from some little black-eyed "bint" he had taken to wife.

Compulsory labour necessary for such ameliorative schemes as this, plus the pruning measures for getting rid of the bad features of Turkish administration — inefficiency, corruption, ineptitude, and, worst of all, the injustice that these led to — involved the tightening up of authority. And authority of any kind sat uncomfortably upon the Mesopotamian tribesmen.

It was not enough that he had become abnormally rich as a result of his associations with us, for that condition was tempered by our "despotism" in requiring him to surrender as revenue a percentage, even though a legal percentage, of his unprecedented and undreamt-of war wealth, so that he threatened to perform the trick of the dog in the fable, that, having acquired the substance of a bone, coveted the shadow in the river.

This tightening of authority was vexatious in another way. It had brought the boredom of perpetual inter-tribal peace in place of the customary incessant tumult of the land: and compulsory peace was uncongenial to a war mind. Had not our predecessors followed an opposite policy, set shaikh against shaikh, and encouraged them to fight it out? Where was our respect for tradition? Yet another misfortune to be charged to the account of an exercise of outside authority was that it inevitably changed the scale of interior feudal values. It clipped the wings of all those powerful shaikhs who recently enjoyed unfettered liberty; it banished the days of murder, of plunder, and of insecurity. The chieftain, then, was what he was in virtue of his own strong right arm and his personal prowess. It could not be expected that he should welcome a "reduced" position in the eyes of his universe. For he was not, as may be supposed, the popular representative of his clan. On the contrary, he was sometimes the best hated and most maligned man in the district. [16]

And so it came to be that during my first term of service in Shatrah, the one man I found myself crossing swords with was Shaikh Khaiyyun al 'Ubaid. Silent and sullen of manner, only very occasionally visible, he gave the impression of supreme arrogance. The indictment of the Turk, and of the Sa'dun, must, it seemed, be true — he was not to be trusted.

THE RUMBLINGS OF REBELLION

I RE-READ the telegrams that were in my hand.

To Aviation Baghdad.

Aeroplanes will stand by at Samawah for two days after Political Officer Diwaniyah reports that he considers bombing of Sufran should cease. It may be necessary to send them to Nasiriyah, thence to Shatrah if and when asked for by A.P.O. Shatrah.

From Communications Basrah.

To P.O.

G.H.Q. reports gunboat *Greenfly* en route to Kut. For information of yourself and Thomas.... *Greenfly* arrived 1140 hours. Personnel for manning guns live B.O.Rs. Nine B.O.Rs. reported to-day to man machine guns.

From Civil Commissioner.

. . .

I had conceived the plan of arresting Shaikh Khaiyyun and of sending him to Nasiriyah or Kut for deportation out of the country. But the proverbial catching of the bird by putting salt on its tail here assumed all its old formidable logic. Open daylight arrest was out of the question. There were too many belted retainers for that.

Shatrah Walled Town Iraq

Days passed, opportunity lacked. I received and returned calls of old friends, and every day rode out to all my favourite haunts and around the neighbouring countryside to see the crops. The tribal Arab is easy to renew acquaintance with, and his welcoming felicitations flowed with accustomed facility. Here in Shatrah all was well. So at least it seemed. But the situation in the neighbouring Division to the west was very different; in fact, it daily grew more menacing, and I wondered how long it would be before the danger overflowed into Shatrah. Now, too, came news of agitation in Baghdad. But the local effect was small. The Shatrah- Baghdad affinities were negligible — it was the Shatrah-Diwaniyah affinities which counted.

I determined on a tour to ascertain the feeling in the district and to cultivate some of my old friendships with those who were a power in the land. The floods enabled my motor launch to come up to my front door, so to speak. At this season it was possible to travel by launch only in the eastern areas of my district, for the Bada' River, which at other times of the year is a network of narrow channels under an easy self-control, at this time spills into a chain of ever-growing lakes that temporarily submerge the surrounding countryside. Later on, when the floods subsided, the new alluvium floor would become rich paddy-fields of rice. But I was bound across and beyond these lakes — which incidentally mark the line of the Tigris as it was when the invading Arabs of the seventh century' wrested the land from the Persians — to the fragrant plains of Albu Sa'id. This was the most remote part of my district, and here the local feeling would give me some indication of the way the wind was blowing. I resolved to seek out an old acquaintance, one Shaikh Naif.

It was July 12th when I landed at Dawaiyah, and, changing launch for horses, set off in the cooling afternoon of a tropical day for the tents of the Shaikh. He had instigated a murder late in my predecessor's time — a legacy which it now fell to me to settle. It was a normal tribe case in which a nephew of his had killed another nephew in order to seize the latter's lands. I arranged the usual blood-money of Rs. 500, a course acceptable to the tribe, and invited Naif to accompany me back to Shatrah to discuss the land question. He took fright at this idea, but on my assuring him that I had no intention of imprisoning him he agreed. We set off; but as we were ambling leisurely across the plain towards Duwaiyah I espied a party of twenty-one mounted men, an uninvited escort of Naif's tribesmen, on a flank about a mile away and proceeding suspiciously in a parallel direction. Unhappy in the knowledge, I promptly wheeled my party round in their direction, and so rode just across their rear to some tents at hand, where I announced I would stay the night. There had been no attempt by the Shaikh to break away, and no attempt to rescue him — not a murmur of anything untoward, in fact, but to-day was not the day for taking chances. Provocative courses had to be avoided.

Shaikh Naif came round to see me in my candle-lighted *madhif* late that night. He was penitent, and disclaimed all responsibility for the acts of his tribesmen — irresponsible followers, he said, of the murdered man. I used discretion rather than courage, and told him I would not take him to Shatrah on the morrow if the local situation embarrassed him, but I could not have the Arms Law defied before my eyes, and ordered the confiscation of the twenty-one offending rifles. Eleven of these were promptly forthcoming, and a week later the Shaikh came in to Shatrah bringing the other ten with him. The bluff was successful. Eighty miles to the west of me the insurrection had already begun, and the tribes had risen in Samawah, where the "Political" dare not go outside his own limits; the railway line near by had been uprooted, and a station-master killed. News of these events had not yet reached the tribesmen on whom I had successfully imposed the rifle fine, but trouble was in the air, and in any case it would have been folly, in the absence of troops to support me, to show weakness or to let the locals think that Government had its tail between its legs.

I was back in Shatrah. The news of the insurrection in the neighbouring division and of troubles in Baghdad now rang in the bazaar. But the tribal shaikhs, friendly as before, came to see me, and work proceeded harmoniously enough. "Why don't you arrest the agitators?" they asked. "They are few, but if you do not they will grow to be many. You cannot be afraid, you who have vanquished the Turks."

Whatever the causes of events elsewhere two things were clear in the local situation: (i) that the spirit of Nationalism did not exist; and (ii) that there was no alliance between the local and neighbouring tribes of the middle Euphrates for the purpose of overthrowing Government.

The situation demanded a dispatch, and what I wrote in those fateful days of Ramadhan 1920 was this:

Submitted in place of a monthly diary.

Having completed six weeks' residence in the District and carried out an extensive tour of the tribes, I feel now able to give a slight appreciation of the local situation. At the outset it is my conviction that the disquiet is, broadly speaking, agrarian and not primarily political. Nationalist activities there have been, and no one would underrate their seriousness, but one is on perfectly safe ground in estimating them. The politically minded, made up of a small coterie of town intelligentsia, is not more than 5 per cent, of the population. In the tribes Nationalism is unknown. Constitutions conceived on howsoever liberal lines will not affect the local situation one iota, at least not for the better. The root cause of unrest is objection to taxation. There can be no doubt that the bigger shaikhs would welcome a return to the status quo ante, a condition of their own unfettered control, no taxation, and no land rent. Small shaikhs have been taught to whistle to the same tune, though they know their interests lie with us, and make no attempt to conceal the fact when out of earshot of their big brothers. The bulk of the townspeople, in particular the comfortable shopkeeping class, enjoying a security of life and property hitherto unknown are for a large part pro-British, but in view of our declared policy of one day withdrawing they are naturally timid of showing any definite leanings.

Discontent in the tribes springs from taxation, disquiet in the town, the fear of relying on a broken reed. Our friends are threatened with Britain's withdrawal and know what that means; their attitude is the perfectly reasonable one of ingratiating themselves with their oppressors past and prospective. To the tribesman the prospect is not nearly so forbidding. True, it augurs a regime of blood and of right to the strong, but under the Khaiyyun aegis he knows that rent and revenues are alike repudiated.

Khaiyyun dominates the situation. He is too wily to be trapped. The only alternative course is the less satisfactory but inevitable one of our continuing, without scruples, to coquette with him. I have impressed upon him the fact that in the long run he will best serve his own interests by being a good servant of Government's. It should never be forgotten that the one man capable of engineering a rising on the Gharraf is Khaiyyun al 'Ubaid. No trouble could be sustained a week which had not his connivance or support. He took a leading part in the recent unrest just before my arrival, and I incline to the opinion that he believes himself now to be Government's marked man; he is therefore anxious to make good, and on the numerous occasions he has come to see me lately he has declared his future intention to be that of loyally serving Government....

News of events daily trickles through, and refugees in small numbers, chiefly women and children, have already found their way into the district. "The Arab's senses are in his eyes", and in the long run it will be found that the temper of the Lower Gharraf will be determined by the strength of our right arm in suppressing the ebullition across the border. The situation here is quiet, but not normal.

Accurate judgment on the situation was devoutly to be desired, for a mistake in the light of events taking place throughout the country and likely to develop here might cost the reporter his life.

The days wore on. There had been no deterioration in my position, so far as I could see, nor cause for alarm, Shaikh Khaiyyun and I had become fast friends. We owed this to adversity. He was wanting to go on the Pilgrimage and was being frustrated: I had wanted other things equally in vain. But "all things work together for good". If our official relationship had in the old days been strained, perhaps because each thought the other was occupying too much the centre of the stage, there had never been a suspicion of animosity in our personal dealings. Indeed, I had fed his hawks at various times, had given him a sporting gun, had enjoyed his hospitality; all this in the intervals between my official admonitions. I had, in fact, always had a sneaking admiration for Khaiyyun as a man, for one thing, because of his frankness, but most of all, perhaps, because he was a supreme example of his kind.

During this second term of mine at Shatrah he had shown unusual signs of being well disposed, and, like all the other shaikhs of the Division, seemed not to be adversely affected in his relations with Government as a result of external events taking place hostile to the central authority. He had been in the habit of calling on me at dusk. To-night he asked whether he might come round for a longer session after dinner: there was an important matter he would like to discuss.

Round he came, an imposing figure of a man. Of middle age, nearly six feet tall, swarthy of skin and inscrutable of expression, Khaiyyun had somewhat Mongolian eyes, which, with his long, drooping moustachios, gave him the appearance of a Tartar.

"I propose going on the Pilgrimage to Mecca," he said, after the usual formalities were over. "Will you please give me a pass both ways?"

I cogitated the matter. His plan involved his proceeding via Nasiriyah or Basrah. At either place his arrest would be easy. But my giving him a pass was tantamount to "safe conduct from Government". To arrest him then would be to play him false — unthinkable treachery even by the meanest standards. But supposing we did not arrest him? His absence on Pilgrimage would then be in effect the same as his deportation. And here was a difficulty. Khaiyyun's behaviour since my arrival had been exemplary. The general situation throughout Lower Mesopotamia, on the other hand, had changed and was still changing. Shatrah was actually proving tractable though we had feared in Baghdad, and though it had been reported by P.O. Nasiriyah, that it would be the first place to rise in rebellion. It now occupied a different position in relation to the general situation. As a result of this the plan of yesterday was obsolete to-day. Khaiyyun I found to be a stabilizing factor on the Lower Gharraf, at any rate for the moment; and I tried to visualize the situation with him absent and with the temper of the Gharraf changed for the worse. I was led to a single conclusion. If Khaiyyun was the one man who could raise the tribes, he was also the one man who could prevent their rising.

He looked at me across the table while these thoughts flashed through my mind.

"I propose starting on Monday," he said.

I took a bold and ingenuous course.

"Shaikh Khaiyyun," I said, "I will tell you something. You are aware of the gunboat at the Bada'. That gunboat I summoned for the express purpose of arresting you and taking you away."

His face became serious. There was an awkward pause.

"And why do you tell me this?"

"Because," I said, "if you proceed on the Pilgrimage you will be arrested and deported out of the country as a political prisoner. It is the course I previously recommended, and Government approved of it."

"But why are you telling me so?"

"Because I desire your welfare, and I ask in return for your friendship. We are living in troubled times. The Gharraf must remain loyal to Government."

Khaiyyun saw that I could have caught him, that he himself was proposing to walk into the trap, and that I was delivering him.

There was gratitude in his voice when he spoke and the hand-shake of a pledged word.

"Sahib," he said, "we have often been at cross purposes. From to-night we are friends. Have no fears for the Gharraf."

He was a reticent man at all times, and I felt confidence in our new-found friendship.

The next day I joined *Greenfly*. I was going upstream as far as Qalat Sikar to compare notes with my colleague there. She was proceeding then to Kut, anxious to return to the deeper waters of the Tigris, for the floods were abating, the Hai River was falling, and at its bar she would have only a foot or so of clearance. Her withdrawal in any case could not be delayed for many more days.

HOLDING THE FORT

COULD we stave off a general tribal rising? It would depend upon our ability to nip the early trouble in the bud, and this turned on the adequacy of our forces in the field.

The first omen had been far from propitious. In the late winter, Dair az Zor, a district in the Upper Euphrates on the border-line of Mesopotamia and Syria, had been the scene of a Nationalist inspired challenge to our occupation. The withdrawal of the British authorities there, and supine acquiescence in a state of affairs for which the Syrian authorities later repudiated responsibility, had a pernicious effect.

The trouble spread hence to Rumaitha — the first challenge in the Lower Euphrates. This was the acid test, so to speak, and, alas! local authority could not be supported here and Government had to evacuate. This in the light of our military weakness was the burnt-offering to the principles of war. Henceforward and inevitably insurgence became a rolling snowball (if the phrase as applied to a mid-summer rebellion in the tropic plains of Mesopotamia may pass). Nothing could be more clear, it seemed to the rebellious Arab, than that we lacked the powder or the will to maintain ourselves.

But Shatrah must keep the flag flying: that was my *raison d'etre*.

It was the first week of the troubles. I was on cordial terms with my own shaikhs, and felt a certain confidence in the local position. I knew them all from close contact — had known them, indeed, for nearly two years — and I was banking on their loyalty. Yet it would have been folly for a Christian to close his eyes to a certain psychological fact, namely, that they were men of inflammable temper, and deeply imbued with the obligations of their Shi'ah faith. *Jihad* — the virtue, nay the necessity, of fighting the infidel — was one of these, and they would not for long oppose the *fatwah* that proclaimed it, or defy the dictates of their religious leaders in the Holy Places. My chief fear, then, as a solitary British officer and the representative of Government in my district, lay in a sudden sweeping wave of religious fervour. Khaiyyun had already come to me in late June protesting against the arrest of a Najaf divine, a son of the ruling Chief Mujtahid. This arrest, he said— and I knew he spoke by proxy — was regarded by the tribes with sorrow and dissatisfaction. And although our personal relations were now so very much closer than previously, I still had to remember that Khaiyyun was a deeply religious man in the tribal sense of the word, and that his undertakings to me, made in good faith though they might have been, would always be contingent upon an edict from the Chief Mujtahid, the Najaf Pontiff.

My duty was to remain as long as I could at my post and use what influence I possessed to prevent my tribes joining in the rebellion.

The Gharraf was the storm-centre of the Muntafiq confederation, and if it rose it was the signal for a general rising of the Muntafiq tribes. Now these straddled the railway from Basrah, which was still intact as far as Nasiriyah, and provided the best means for the advance of an army to re-occupy the area in revolt, when the necessary reinforcements should arrive from India. Nasiriyah garrison was pitifully inadequate at the time and would be so for two months: it consisted only of three platoons of Indian Infantry and two hundred local levies and police, against which the Muntafiq tribes represented a potential hostile strength of twenty thousand rifles.

The Gharraf, moreover, formed the link between the Euphrates and Tigris; and in the event of its defection, the troubles would most probably spread to the Tigris tribes, where the river was the one remaining means of communication and supplies between Basrah and Baghdad. Shatrah assumed, therefore, a position of considerable tactical importance, and my hanging on as a missionary of peace to keep the tribes in check was imperative.

The insurrection had, indeed, broken out in the adjoining district. Samawah, sixty miles to the west, was beleaguered, the railway was torn up, and Rumaitha was being evacuated. The British and the Arabs were at war, refugees, mostly women and children, came drifting in, and the news of British casualties of one hundred and fifty killed and wounded spread like fire.

The second week of the troubles brought reports of a glorious Arab victory and a crowning defeat for the British a hundred miles or so north of the scene of neighbouring operations. A mobile column, consisting of a battalion of infantry, two squadrons of cavalry, and a field battery — the Manchester column, as it came to be called — had been treacherously attacked at night near Hillah by overwhelming numbers of tribesmen and had suffered severely. There were 20 killed, 60 wounded, and 318 missing, of whom about half were to be accounted for afterwards as prisoners. The Arabs were thus deeply committed at both ends of the Middle Euphrates, and from Hillah and Samawah the flames of rebellion now spread inwards like a prairie fire. Our evacuation of Diwaniyah had grimly to be faced, and the column fought its way out northwards. This left my western boundary completely in the air, but the Shatrah tribes stood steadfast. Only my Arab assistant, my second in command, decided that the place was a little unhealthy, and left. He appeared to have taken alarm at a sudden recrudescence of arms traffic, for good rifles and plentiful ammunition, relics of the Great War, were, not unnaturally at such a time as this, obviously marketable commodities.

The third week.

While in the palm-groves by the waters of Babylon a battle was fought, murmuring asides arose from the neighbouring district of Qalat Sikar, to the north. My colleague there and I used every morning to talk to each other over the telephone, but now something had happened to the line. It was impossible to get through. He had just previously reported the probability of a rising in his area, judging that the tribal plans would materialize in the course of a few days, and had asked for aeroplane demonstrations.

But now that telegraph wires were cut, I had to report for the information of the aeroplanes that they should not expect their customary landing **T** laid out at Qalat Sikar. Only one machine could be spared, an old R.E.8, a war type with odd upper wing extensions, and nowadays regarded as not having in its nature been too friendly to man. She landed at Shatrah first and flew me up river the next day, but we saw nothing hostile below us, and Qalat Sikar was found to be O.K. And so back to Shatrah.

For me the days passed excitedly. News, sad news, alarming news, tainted news, came filtering in every day, much of it distorted by its carriers, some of it, perhaps, locally invented. The town was ever agog. From time to time Shatrah became panicky, but I was able to carry on, fortified by the knowledge that the tribal chiefs, headed by Khaiyyun, were a solid bloc of support to me and able to overcome hostile counsels. At intervals of a few days an aeroplane would pass over on a reconnaissance, usually at a "safe" height, that is to say, by the standards of the period, 2,000 feet, though I have seen bullet holes through the wing canvas sustained at that altitude from Arab ground fire. Once a week a machine flying rather lower than usual would circle over my house, an indication that it had a message to drop. Then a policeman would rush over to the landing-ground and collect the bag, with its brightly coloured streamers, which came hissing down from the skies.

It would be a welcome letter from C.C. — a circular letter generally to those of us in the Muntafiq out-districts who still kept the flag flying.

My daily telegrams to you on the situation (this one said) are, I hope, sufficiently full to keep you adequately posted. The latest events are... The policy which I consider it necessary to ask you to adopt as regards Shatrah and Qalat Sikar is for the A.P.O. to remain at his post as long as he can keep the local shaikhs or sufficient of them together on the side of

Government and good order. If and when he finds the situation untenable I will do my best to ensure that an aeroplane is sent to take him away. As a precautionary measure it would be well for you not to keep more cash than you need about and destroy all surplus currency notes, keeping a record of the numbers of each note burnt. It is only a matter of time before the tide again turns in our favour, and I hope that the ten minutes of tenacity which Napoleon referred to as being the deciding factor in a campaign will enable us to maintain our positions in areas as yet unaffected by disturbances.

The final paragraph was a typical heartener; there was not an officer in the country who would not respond to a really great chief who inspired his respect, his loyalty, and his admiration.

I was not affected by the financial reference, for I had but a few hundred rupees by me, and this in coin which I required for messengers and incidental expenses. I had no occasion to "buy" the shaikhs. Khaiyyun himself was notoriously rich, and never profited a penny-piece either during or after the troubles; the loyalty of the other shaikhs likewise was spontaneous — they received neither payment nor promise of payment.

The fourth week.

I had already wired Nasiriyah on July 28th:

With reference to your secret telegram of yesterday and in confirmation of my subsequent telephone conversation I consider that evacuation of the Gharraf now to be premature. We must hang on at all costs. Am strongly of opinion that if an aeroplane were put at my disposal for peaceful demonstration, the question of evacuating Shatrah need never arise.

Aeroplanes, however, were wanted too badly elsewhere. But living in exciting scenes that became all absorbing, one naturally regarded one's own district as the centre of the political firmament, around which the nebulous districts of others dimly swam.

Meanwhile, Nasiriyah, with other sources of information, was wiring to the C.C.:

Danger spot Shatrah. Khaiyyun outwardly loyal, but rumours that he is holding secret meetings and feeling his way in regard to the attitude of the Gharraf tribes. Hostilities broke out a month ago: our well-wishers, also (air enemies, are beginning to realize how weak we are militarily. Arms and ammunition are being bought and sold freely; carrying arms is now more noticeable in the districts where land-grabbers are beginning to man their war towers and old enemies are watching one another and waiting. News of the evacuation of Diwaniyah has reached Shatrah where there is no effect as yet. I am sanguine that we shall tide over the anxious period until the arrival of the Brigade.

The reference to Shatrah was one to which I could scarcely subscribe. True, there was the usual band of malcontents, the inevitable young "blood" itching for a hand in the making of local history, and wild rumours of secret meetings. But I relied on my personal relations with the leading shaikhs to avert the evil day.

Now came disturbing news indeed from neighbouring Qalat Sikar. My opposite number there had been ambushed when returning after dark from a friendly visit to a tribe just outside the town. A party of six Arabs holding a *nullah* had opened fire on him at short range. Happily no one was hit, but there were two horse casualties.

A demonstration by aeroplanes was asked for, and a visit of two Bristol fighters from Baghdad was arranged. These were to refuel at Kut and fly over Qalat Sikar, making Shatrah their first stop. Overcome by curiosity they came down at Qalat Sikar to 1,000 feet, to see whether there were any signs of hostility. There was none, but a party of *Shabanas* on the aerodrome attracted the attention of one of the machines, which thereupon landed to inquire after the "Political" while the other remained in the air and circled round.

Unfortunately the landed machine in taking off had its engine cut out at a hundred feet, so could not turn to make the landing- ground again. Hence it force-landed in the "rough" and crashed. The pilot of the other machine — D'Arcy Grieg, who was later to acquire fame as a Schneider Cup candidate — came on to me afterwards at Shatrah bringing me a

Popham panel and the depressing news about the crashed Bristol, a complete "write off", alas! — though luckily the pilot was unhurt.

Here was the hand of God again. Qalat Sikar was already suffering from the preachings of a *mu' min*, one of the lesser clergy who had recently arrived with the mischievous gospel of rebellion. Thus did the hand of fate salute him. A most unfortunate local impression was created.

The fifth week

Almost simultaneously with these deplorable events at Qalat Sikar, the Samawah tribes flared up. Crossing the river on rafts, spurred on by an agitator who was said to have mysterious funds and paid a golden sovereign for every sleeper torn up, they attacked the railway downstream of the town. Now it was Nasiriyah's own turn. Small parties of Arabs took to sniping the town each night. On one occasion they attempted to break in, presumably to raid the bazaar or create an atmosphere of fear and insecurity, and a party did manage to effect an entry into the date gardens on the left bank, but these were sporadic adventures of no serious import and were a problem that did not c.xiirci.se the small local garrison overmuch. I heard of these incidents on the phone the day after they took place — 6.0 p.m. was a general routine for exchanging Nasiriyah-Shatrah news and I began to think Shatrah was the one peaceful spot. With the gradual deterioration in the situation, Nasiriyah was now asking Baghdad for aeroplanes and more aeroplanes. "If," said one telegram "we fail to send aeroplanes to Qalat Sikar I feel we shall have to evacuate it, and if Qalat Sikar falls, Shatrah will have to be given up."

"We cannot send even one aeroplane daily to Qalat Sikar," came the reply, "we have only five available altogether in Baghdad, and they have to be used elsewhere."

One aeroplane did arrive. It came to Qalat Sikar to evacuate the A.P.O. The C.C.'s letter to him brought by hand of the pilot ran:

I have received and discussed with G.O.C.-in-C. letter X telegram Y. Shortage of aircraft makes it impossible for us to send planes regularly in sufficient numbers to the Gharraf. Any such planes as we have can probably be most effectively used elsewhere. It will, moreover, be difficult to extricate you even by air should the situation at Qalat Sikar get worse, whilst the impending arrival of regiments at Nasiriyah will probably sufficiently stabilize the situation at Kut and Nasiriyah. I am therefore directed by the G.O.C.-in-C. to instruct you to proceed forthwith in this plane to Nasiriyah and await further orders there.

The A.P.O. was loath to leave, but the order was peremptory. And so I now found myself marooned in Shatrah, more or less in the air, for the encircling districts of Rumaitha, Diwaniyah, and Qalat Sikar had all been evacuated, and Samawah was in the throes of a siege. Nothing stood between Shatrah and Hillah on the Euphrates and between it and Kut on the Tigris but a phalanx of hostile tribes.

The sixth week.

My shaikhs still came to see me, but some had lost their optimism. They had a feeling, one sensed, that they were backing the wrong horse. Were we leaving the country? they asked. If not, why had no troops arrived? There was reason for their questionings. Troubles did not come singly. The evacuation of Qalat Sikar coincided with the grounding of the gunboat *Greenfly* in the Euphrates between Nasiriyah and Samawah. There, with all aboard, she was abandoned. For a military retreat to Ur had been decided upon, and the risk involved in relieving her was too serious for our already slender military resources. Alas! her gallant captain and entire crew were never to be seen again. A mystery veiled their end, but the absence of any' trace was regarded as meaning that they could have been shown no mercy. Two nights later, some eight miles below Shatrah, the telegraph wire was cut and several poles were removed. This put me out of touch with Nasiriyah except by runner. The journey, twenty-four miles each way, took a minimum of two days to accomplish, and one felt, in consequence, rather cut off from the outside world. My shaikhs cheerfully undertook the job of providing runners, though I was careful to duplicate all important messages. In this I had the assistance of my old friend, Haji Almas, a staunch person whom I had recently elevated to an eminent position in the Municipality.

How well I remember my first meeting with the admirable Haji! Never could I then have dreamt of our present relations. It was on the occasion of my original appointment to Shatrah. My servant announced at breakfast that a notable had come to call on me. I indicated that he should be shown into the office downstairs to await my arrival, but my "farrash" came back rather agitated and nervously suggested that there would be nothing unusual if I received so honoured a man in my private quarters. So Haji was shown upstairs. He was a townsman, large and fat, pale and soft, an enormous figure of a man in brown *abba* and weighty woollen *agal*, as he stood filling up the doorway. Nature's normal lines seemed somehow awry, and I soon realized that a foreign body of sorts lay concealed beneath his bulging *abba*. I rose to greet him, whereupon he made a speech of welcome, and said that he felt the occasion was one upon which he must voice the sentiments of the people of Shatrah. Those sentiments were warm ones. Happy were the people, nay, blessed in my arrival! And as for himself, my humble servant, he had brought a token of esteem and respect — and thereupon produced from beneath the ample folds of his mantle an enormous and ornate marble clock of the presentation kind which occupies a central position on the mantel-shelf.

"How kind of your honour," I said, motioning him to a seat, "but you will appreciate that I am not permitted by the Government I serve to accept such a valuable present."

I was really nonplussed at having excited "esteem and regard" within twenty-four hours of arrival, particularly as I had never set eyes on Haji Almas before — though may be there was a precedent in Turkish times for the procedure. My first impulse was one of irritation that he should have supposed me amenable to this sort of thing, and I'm afraid I showed it.

"As a British officer, Haji, I must tell you that we buy any clocks that we may be in need of. I cannot accept your present," said I, in answer to his fresh importunities.

It was Haji's turn to be annoyed.

"Not accept it, Sahib?" said he incredulously, "then it is a great shame for me. I can never take it back. If you will not let me leave it here, I must throw it over the verandah into the courtyard below and smash it to pieces.'

"Ya, Haji," I remonstrated, "I am a man of peace, and I want us to be friends, but you must take your marble away."

"Impossible!" said he with an air of finality, "if you cannot accept it I must destroy it."

"Haji Almas," I retorted, getting up, "you shall not make a mess in my courtyard. If you throw it over, I shall be reluctantly compelled to throw you over after it."

Haji now registered a change of mind, and said he cherished an ardent desire above all things for peace and concord. He there- upon returned the marble clock to the shadows beneath his *abba*, and, retiring backwards to the; doorway, smiled an undiscomfited smile, and departed.

It was a week later that I appreciated the significance of the gesture. One of my duties was to auction certain municipal taxes. These were farmed generally to local merchants amongst whom there were competition and regular bidding. It was my duty "to knock down" the various farms, and amongst the stubbornest bidders was Haji Almas. He already held one Government farm. He desired another, and this, under my hammer, so to speak, he got. And the reason he got it was, that he was the highest bidder. I was offered no more marble clocks during my service in Shatrah.

Two years later, in the time of trouble, Haji Almas was loyal to the core. He brought me the news of the bazaar: of gatherings, and of what was said and thought at them, of the activities of certain ill-disposed men in touch with the headquarters of agitation, men who were ripe for rebellion as soon as opportunity presented itself, and of the general consensus of opinion which remained steadily friendly. But the situation in Shatrah was none too happy. Much of the information had to be discounted on the theory that it was intended to please. This drove me back on the logic of probabilities. The fall of Qalat Sikar had depreciated our shares. There was one chance of their rehabilitation, and that was if I could move up the Gharraf with representative friendlies and re-occupy the place. For this purpose I had asked that Captain Hall, who normally commanded the Muntafiq Levy Corps, be sent out to me. With Hall left at Shatrah to keep the flag flying, I thought I might make the move forward with a hundred friendlies — on the principle that offence is the best defence — and by this means arrest our waning fortunes. Meanwhile, the Qalat Sikar shaikhs and some hundred or two followers came flocking into Shatrah, a gesture that seemed to give promise of success to my design. In reality, however, as I was to discover some days later, their arrival had no friendly intent; they had come at the bidding of an influential local Saiyid for a very different purpose — namely, to engineer united action with the Shatrah tribes in a bold march on Nasiriyah. Had such unity been achieved, our tiny garrison could not have withstood the tribal onslaught for a single hour. Khaiyyun damned this plot with faint praise. He pledged his support only when Nasiriyah should fall. So the Shatrah tribes took up a non-committal attitude, and the conspiracy fell through.

The seventh week.

Hall had arrived. It was a great comfort to have another Englishman in the place. Living alone during the last few weeks had been rather a strain, with the country for two hundred miles to the north-west aflame with insurrection, the uneasy expectation of sudden developments at any moment in Shatrah itself, and being for nearly a week out of telephone touch with Nasiriyah and the outside world and having to depend on "runners" who might at any time prove unreliable.

Our first job was to open the boxes of bombs which Hall had himself sent me disguised as beer boxes at the outset of the troubles. They were for last and desperate courses. In preparation for emergencies, we got the bombs ready, and thereafter kept them under our camp-beds on the roof — scarcely romantic bed- mates!

A day or two later Hall, who had motored to Nasiriyah with my dispatch reporting a changed Gharraf situation and to bring out stores, was ambushed on his way back. The van was brought up suddenly as the road came to a dead end where the bridge over a *nullah* had been removed. Thirty men. who had just completed the destruction, leapt out of the under- growth and covered him and the driver with their rifles. Providentially, the Khafajah Shaikh, their own tribal chief, whom I had sent as escort, was in the back of the van, and he promptly emerged to save an ugly situation. A bridge was hastily improvised, and Hall's party came on, the Shaikh bringing the ring- leader of the offenders along to me at Shatrah.

One of the petty Shatrah merchants, a notorious agitator, was at the bottom of this affair. The night before he had sent out messages to certain Khafajah elements notorious for their lawlessness, with news that Shatrah had been seized by Khaiyyun, and that Hall and I were prisoners in the hands of the Arabs; whereupon these gallants removed five miles of telegraph poles, and were now annexing the bridges along the Shatrah canal for firewood. In the course of the next few days wire and road communication with Shatrah was cut off, and our means of escape — if it were to come to that — were reduced to flight in disguise by night or by aeroplane. But things had not yet come to that pass.

Sporadic destruction of this kind was not nearly so alarming as a new factor which now appeared in the situation. The son of a former Chief Mujtahid was reported to be about twenty miles north of and advancing upon Shatrah, preaching *Jihad*. That gospel had had, alas! too much success along the Euphrates already, and its propagation here was a most disquieting prospect. When an obscure *mu'min* from Qalat Sikar had arrived in Shatrah a fortnight earlier on a similar mission he had been silenced. This thwarting I owed to the influence of Shaikh Khaiyyun. But the threatened visitation was under auspices of quite another kind: a curate then, this was a bishop. To make confusion worse confounded, a new Supreme Pontiff had just recently been installed at Najaf. He represented an incalculable, albeit a decisive factor locally, and Baghdad, whither I addressed inquiries upon his attitude, could only say that he would probably incline to the side of the extremists. The shaikhs who had stood by me, my strength and support, of late showed symptoms of wavering. It would be no treachery, I felt now, if these men were swept by considerations of self-preservation into the other camp, for our fortunes were reaching their lowest ebb, and there were no signs of an army to restore our position, though actually its arrival was imminent. Yet those shaikhs who were standing their ground were sufficiently influential to justify my still hanging on. Better the storm should spend itself around Shatrah than be free to hurl itself against Nasiriyah, with its miserable garrison, and as yet unprotected railway.

The eighth week.

In the Middle Euphrates, Government had been entirely withdrawn, and the Arab tribes there were delirious with success. The news of it all could scarcely fail to embolden the local elements of disorder. And now the fall of the British post at Khidhr, on the very doorstep of Nasiriyah, was the last straw. Shatrah's time surely drew near.

Disaffection appeared in my force. Sowars and Police were reported to me to be mortgaging their rifles at £30 a piece (an indication of the Arab's prosperity in those times) against the fall of Government. This was borne out one night when, the temptation being so strong, and the penalties no longer apparent, ten men deserted, bag and baggage. Hall and I walked down to the Sarai the following morning, had a parade, and disarmed the remaining twenty, bringing the rifles back to my house. I then placed the force under Khaiyyun's orders and made him responsible for law and order in the town — a regrettable step, but one demanded by a perilous situation. Two hundred youths were to assemble daily in front of my house and demonstrate, the tribes were carrying arms again to a man, *mu'mins* were moving in and out amongst them preaching *Jihad*, and rifle-firing throughout the night, both inside and outside the town walls, became a normal practice.

I had ceased to have authority. Khaiyyun, still my counsellor and friend, assured me that, so long as I remained in Shatrah, everyone would respect my flag and my person; but it was clear to me that my presence was a source of growing embarrassment to all my old friends; the storm cloud of opposing forces grew hourly more menacing, and if and when it burst, my allies might be unable to stand against it. In any case the notion of my staying on under recent developments, that is to say, in a situation I could not control, was intolerable to me.

Matters hastened to a climax. Two days later, on August 25th, arrived the apostle of *Jihad* — the great *alim* already referred to — a saint-like, bearded figure in white, with a turban of the same colour and of episcopal proportions. He had been preaching rebellion as he moved down the Gharraf, and on his arrival the whole town rose to meet him. A big demonstration with banners took place outside my house, rifle-firing from the roofs of the houses saluted his entry into the town, and certain of the shaikhs were said to be writing orders at his dictation to bring in the tribes.

The place was obviously too hot to hold us any longer. I decided upon evacuation if that were possible. SOS messages were secretly sent by runner to Nasiriyah to ask Baghdad for planes; but this one remaining means of rescue presented difficulties.

First, the landing-ground lay some half a mile away on the other side of the river beyond the town walls, and our walk thither would be through a crowd among which the fanatic might lie in waiting; secondly, if a machine were shot down by such an individual, air reprisals would not be very good for Hall's health or for my own.

I sent for Khaiyyun, and told him confidentially of my plans, thanked him for his unswerving loyalty to Government, and assured him that the people would in time be grateful to him for his foresight in delivering Shatrah from the wrath of an avenging army which must soon sweep across Iraq, restore law and order, and punish evil-doers. I entrusted him with the office that I was laying down.

It was the morning of the 27th. The drone of distant aeroplanes broke upon our ears. It was a welcome sound for two Englishmen. The immediate job was to remove the bolts from all rifles in the house and detonators from the bombs. No sooner had we buried them than Khaiyyun arrived, bringing along with him a party of all my faithful Shatrah shaikhs. The two machines circled round and round my house at a considerable height, thus observing their instructions that they were not to land if there were signs of hostility, but were to go on to

Nasiriyah. There was, therefore, no time to be lost in showing ourselves.

Hall and I emerged, followed by the shaikhs and a vast throng; so we passed in solemn procession along the river-front across its now drying bed and on to the landing-ground beyond. There was no demonstration of any kind. Not a sign of disrespect, but rather a hushed dignity about it all. This was a relief. One of the machines had landed, the pilot prudently remaining in the cockpit, its "prop" "ticking over" preparedly.

"There is no danger," I said. "You must come down and be introduced to the shaikhs." This was an encouragement for the other machine, which, according to programme, was circling round in case of treachery, to land and follow suit.

I was resolved there should be no precipitate farewell; and so for five minutes we all chatted merrily. I was wondering whether I was not acting badly in leaving my post, seeing that I could do so peaceably, but I read again the letter which the pilot had brought from my Chief in Baghdad. It ran;

Two aeroplanes herewith to evacuate you both to Nasiriyah. You are hereby directed to leave Shatrah by plane. No change in conditions subsequent to the dispatch of your request by P.O. for your evacuation will be considered by me to justify your remaining and this must be regarded by you as a definite and final order to leave Shatrah.

I made a small speech to the assembled Arabs, and said that I should return to them as their Hakim as soon as law and order, which could not be long delayed, were restored. Meanwhile, I was handing over the reins of office to Shaikh Khaiyyun.

I was to keep my word with them, as they had kept theirs with me.

There was a screech of accelerating engines, and a solid blast of wind against our faces as the machine raced madly forward and climbed into the air.

At length we were gliding down into the aerodrome at Nasiriyah, and as I alighted amidst the old familiar uniform of British troops a load of care vanished from my mind. An hour later I found myself standing before a map and explaining the situation to the General — for the long-awaited Brigade had at last arrived. I became Intelligence Officer first to the 74th Brigade, and then, as more and more troops came, to the 6th Division.

Our tide was on the turn. The erring tribes capitulated. The fury of the Mesopotamian insurrection had spent itself and the Muntafiq tribes had lived through it all to redeem an unholy reputation for revolt. They did not rise against us. Possibly their comparative remoteness from the fanatical influences of the Holy Cities was partly responsible; certainly they had profited least from the stream of gold which flowed fitfully from the British Treasury into the hands of the malcontents via Syria.

Six months had passed, and I was back in Shatrah as "Political" of the Gharraf — for the additional district of Qalat Sikar had been added to my duties, 'there I remained for six of the happiest months of my life, and there divided my leisure, the leisure of a solitary British officer, between hunting a pack of long dogs and indulging an amateur's enthusiasm for archaeology. Tribal swords had been abandoned again for ploughshares, and my shaikhs saw to it that I was never without a squad of clandestine spades to dig in the ruined city of ancient Umma.

Then came a day when I must leave my beloved Shatrah. I was being transferred. On the eve of my departure I was invited to a garden-party. I found the place thronged with shaikhs and local notables. It was a farewell gathering.

"There is something we want to present to you," they said as I was going. "It is a sword. It is the sword that led us into the Battle of Butaniyah."

A very precious possession is that sword to me, recalling old and unforgettable loyalties.

ADVENTURE 3

CAMEL JOURNEYS IN AND ABOUT THE SULTANATE OF OMAN

ON TREK WITH THE SULTAN IN THE WESTERN BATINAH

We pushed off from the tide-swept steps of the Palace at Muscat one early dawn. In the stern-sheets with me sat Saiyid Sa'id, the youthful Heir Apparent, who, home on school holidays from the Chief's College at Ajmer, was not less enthusiastic than I over the adventurous prospect of a three-hundred-mile camel journey.

Muscat - Jalali Fort and Palace

This preliminary trip to the camel rendezvous four miles up-coast sped midst the merry chatter of two of Saiyid Sa'id's kinsman companions. Our gay white boat, the State gig, leapt forward to the long steady strokes of six lusty Baluchis, as though anxious to escape the gloom of the rock-girdled harbour. As we rounded the bold western arm of the harbour, we saw the name Diana, in fresh white six-foot letters, beside a beautifully painted tricolour, recording the recent visit to the Sultan of a French sloop of war. Thus must every ship leave her card in Muscat, hence the first thing to strike the visitor on entering the cove is that all about him the cliffs are emblazoned with ships' names.

Once in the open sea we turned towards the hog-backed island of Fahl, now pink in the morning light. There was a sparkle in the March morning air. A sheet of unruffled sea spread away, relieved only on its far rim by little splodges of white triangular sails of frail fishing craft which listed crazily to the light breezes. In the deep bay to our left shone the white houses of Matrah, nestling beneath a wall of jagged mountains, here and there crowned by a bold tower — memorial of some adventurous Portuguese invader of the sixteenth century'.

This scene was shut out as we passed under low serpentine cliffs that here dive steeply into the sea, and form further submarine precipices, so giving to the Gulf of Oman, in contrast to the shallow Persian Gulf, its great ocean depths. Sih' al Malih, our immediate destination, came in sight after an hour, and, turning into the little bay, with its clear green water, we ran up on the sand.

My faithful Khuwara, besides a dozen other camels, was there — Khuwara whose hump had already known me for a thousand miles. But alas! I must shed her of her new glory, for the gay trappings with which she was caparisoned were scarcely suitable for the workaday world. Meanwhile, Saiyid Sa'id, as he waited for me, fingered his newly acquired sporting rifle, hoping to blood it on a gazelle or a hare that the desolation before us seemed to promise.

Bertram Thomas on his camel 'Khuwara'

Across sandy undulations we moved, between red transverse hills that ran back to the scowling face of the ridge above Wataiyah. Scanty pasture, the short-lived grazing that follows rain or heavy dew, existed in patches but there was never a well to gladden the sight. "Water is the fount of life, we have made of water everything living," says the Quran, and with the pastoral inhabitants of thirsty Arabia, it is the supreme consideration. Ask a man what manner of country such and such is, and he will surely reply in terms of its water. Hence the Badu stranger of our escort had his fierce black eye riveted to the troughs of these sandy billows, watching for a moisture patch or some other indication.

"That is the place to dig for water," said Saif bin Ya'rab suddenly, by way of a general challenge, as he pointed to a depression a short distance off. His companions looked at the old man incredulously. "But what if water is found there," said one, "is this not the earth of Wataiyah, and is not the water of Wataiyah brackish?" Saif was adamant. "Dig there on a Wednesday," he returned dogmatically, "let the hour be four o'clock" (i.e. in our forenoon), and he pointed his stick over his left shoulder to indicate the sun's position. "And you question the sweetness of the water? Hallah! Hallah!" (By God! By God!) How many of Saif's Badu companions subscribed to his beliefs in a propitious day and hour for striking sweet water I cannot say, but the Badawin are a superstitious race, and Saif, as astrologer and a master of the science of sands, was held by them to possess occult powers.

At length we topped the rise, here sprinkled with acacia. Below us lay the spacious green groves of Wataiyah. A small white house, the squalid survival of a former Sultan's country residence, peeped from between its palmy depths. Here the Sultan of Muscat had arrived overnight and was now awaiting us. An extended line of fifty bearded Arabs, brown-skinned men in white robes, and glinting with the steel of rifle, belt, and dagger, emerged from a distant thicket and approached us chanting to slow accustomed step. In their centre and to the front was a man of middle stature and mature age, a dignified figure — no other in fact than the Sultan himself. At thirty yards we couched our camels to dismount and approach on foot the country's Ruler, who also advanced to receive us. Such is the ceremonious yet simple welcome of the Arab.

The Sultan, full of his usual bonhomie, fell to questioning me about the morning's trip. He asked me whether the arrangements he had made were to my liking, then, pointing with a sweep of his stick to a dozen bivouacs, told me of the tribal composition of the host with which we were to sweep through the land. The grove was alive with their gaunt camels, great, slow-moving beasts that lazed blinkingly in the open, scorning the shade of the acacias favoured by their idle Badawin masters, or standing, knee-hobbled, nibbling away at the prickliest thorns within reach of their long, upstretched necks. Under a spreading *ghaf* (acacia) a large carpet had been laid for the *burza* (assembly), and thither the Sultan and I proceeded, the Badawin following, to range themselves in a large circle along the edge of its spacious shade. Here the *fuwala* (dates, or some simple kind of food), the coffee-cup, and the incense-burner must go round before the party disperses if the newcomer has any title at all to a meed of honour.

The *burza* is a morning, afternoon, and evening affair. It is the manner by which a shaikhly personage shows his bounty: indeed, a hungry Badu is apt to judge his lord and master by this very criterion — the frequency of the coffee-cup. For me I confess it was ten minutes of extreme discomfort, because long and intractable European legs were never meant for the sitting position — not to mention the rising and resuming with every new arrival. My legs sometimes rebelled with "pins and needles", or temporary lifelessness, against this tyranny of the half-sitting, half-kneeling posture in which the Badu spends a large part of his day. His left haunch rests on the ground, the right leg is bent perpendicularly at the knee, making a kind of firing position approved of by Musketry Regulations, and the right arm more or less outstretched hangs limply over it. His rifle, butt resting on the ground, he holds perpendicularly by the other hand, or retires it slantwise over his left shoulder. His equally inevitable cane occupies the same position, or is pressed back against his cheek, its slightly crooked end masked by his brown hand. There these Badus sit for ten weary silent minutes, none ever speaking, except to return a "Yes" or "No" to an occasional laconic remark addressed to him by the host. The slaves stand without waiting for the magic word *Gahwa* (coffee), with a stress on the middle syllabic that has no literal right to be there, a word that sends them scurrying to their ministrations.

The *burza* over, all slowly dispersed in their tribal groups, and the Sultan, taking me by the hand, led me to the white house wherein we were to await the morrow's move.

These Arab country houses are very much alike, being entirely without amenities or decoration from a European point of view: they resemble much more a combination of shooting-box and frontier outpost — the functions of which, indeed, they nearly fulfil. Glass windows are unknown, as is reasonable in so hot a climate, and interior decoration, where plain, sun-made brick does not wholly forbid it, takes the form of a simple plaster stucco — again, not to be wondered at in a land where the ornate comes in for Puritanical criticism. Representation of the human figure, the human face, or of things created, partakes of the nature of "the graven image", and is against divine ordinance. So said the Prophet Muhammad, like the Prophet Moses, dealing with a similar state of society and a kindred race. I myself have known unpleasant experiences when choosing the wrong place and moment to produce a camera.

Camels Wataiyah

The upper chamber in which I found myself was typical. Low, square-shuttered, iron-barred windows level with the floor surround the four sides, and each is carried up to a blind, pointed arch, a shelf flush with the upper window-sashing making a sort of alcove wherein gay coffee-cups, water-ewer, and incense-burner are the usual furnishings. The exposed rafters are black with smoke stain, for the chimney is unknown in tropic Oman, but to-day the whole floor is covered with gay coloured carpets, requisitioned, no doubt, from the neighbourhood for an auspicious occasion. Ornate wooden pegs punctuate the walls at man's height, and from them depends an armoury of rifles slung barrel downwards, common double-edged swords, cartridge-belts, powder-flasks, and daggers of us visitors. Nothing else in the room is permanent. Our camel rugs were brought in and strewn about, and to-day in the comer was a heap of fresh fruit — Quetta apples, Baqubah oranges, and Indian limes, which we owed to the weekly British India Mail boat— luxuries to be added to by a friendly shaikh, whose letter just to hand announced the dispatch of a sack of pomegranates and another of walnuts, the produce of the interior Jabal Akhdhar.

The Sultan and ourselves, an entourage of seven, were all huddled in this one room, and the others, having shed their accoutrements, at once relapsed into playful conversation.

"Why aren't you married, O Wazir?" was fired off at me by an uncomprehending Arab, as our enforced intimacy broke down barriers. I say "uncomprehending", because almost all Arabs of this class marry, or, rather, are married by their parents, on reaching the age of puberty. They can divorce at will without incurring penalties for bigamy — all this without affecting their reputation or the current of their lives.

I expatiated on the difficulties under which a Christian laboured, especially one serving in the East, and pointed to the comforting doctrine that for a man it was never too late.

"Ah!" said the Sultan, knowing of my secretly cherished desire, "Quite right. *Insha'allah*, I will help to marry you one of these days to that which is near to your heart — *Rub 'al Khali* (The Great Southern Desert). *Insha'allah!*"

"A virgin indeed," quoth Khan Bahadur, his private secretary.

"Amin!" I muttered to myself. (So may it be.)

The hour for the midday siesta was announced by a flagging in the conversation and a stretching out of limbs, and soon we were all sleeping heavily.

Europeans in the East almost invariably take what day sleep they have in the afternoon after lunch, but the tribal Arab of these parts is a believer in the noonday sleep — a time perhaps advanced by his rising at dawn for prayer.

I was already astir when a slave came up to announce the midday meal. After ablutions and prayers my companions buckled on their dagger-belts — an observance I noticed to be rigid for meals or any even semi-public appearance — and we trooped downstairs. There we found that a few of the more important shaikhs had been invited. Three enormous dishes of *haris*, a paste compounded of flour, shredded meat, and fat, crowned with a cup mould of melted butter, were laid out in line on the ground; for the rest, there were similar smaller dishes of fried fish steaks — (i.e. *kanad* (rock cod), beloved of the Sultan, who held that every fish delicacy of his European tour paled before its succulence) — dishes of meat, so prepared in small fids as to suggest a *rechauffe*, and clods of dates. Bowls of delicious curds were there also, but only a few, for the produce of the poor pastures of Oman, as of Palestine, cannot compare with the marsh and river areas of Iraq. Hence we assembled about these dishes to apply ourselves *abu khamsa* (the father of five), i.e. with the fingers — the right hand is *de rigueur* here as throughout the Orient of course; and with a *"B'ismillah"* (In the name of God) — the grace — we fell to.

Suddenly the absence of an invited guest of consequence is remarked. "Send for Shaikh Fulan" (So and So), the Sultan orders, and in due course, the meal proceeding the while, the laggard arrives. But over food the otherwise invariable salutation of *"Salaam alaikum"* (Peace be upon you) is not observed, nor is handshaking permissible.

"Ka' innahum" (As they are), says the latecomer.

"*Wa anta minhum*" (And you are of them) is the response by way of welcome.

As the meal goes on, the European legs are getting cramped. A white left hand which might be strapped to my side for all the good it is, suddenly lunges forward, only to be drawn back, abashed. On such an occasion the meaty tit-bit that clings tenaciously to the bone, and is the cause of the lapse, is about to be abandoned, when a merciful neighbour — I always had the good fortune to sit next the host — stretches forth his right hand to hold the bone while the morsel is removed.

But at a meal one can never keep pace with the Badu, armed with his perfect finger technique, and with a monumental digestive organization; he consumes more food in one unmasticated mouthful than a European can deal with in five minutes. With him eating is a stem and rapid business.

"*Al huwa min wayn?*" (Which way does the wind blow?) inquires the Sultan, as the end approaches — an allusion to the gaping holes in the side of the great common mountain of rice, indicating the position of the best trencherman. "A westerly wind," someone shouts back, having a butt at his neighbour, and the possessors of repleted appetites burst into loud guffaws. Belching, polite in any case, now becomes excessively so, and with the Badu there is no surer way of conveying to his host a lively sense of the quality of his hospitality.

With an "*Al hamdu L'illah*" (God be praised, i.e. returning thanks for food) all rise and silently trail out. At the entrance, the Sultan and I are met by a slave carrying a ewer of water, soap, and towel. The *hoi polloi* gravitate sheep-fashion to an enormous tub of water in the middle of the compound, and there perform their ablutions. The remnant of the food is now gathered up by the slaves and taken away to their particular apartments, "below the salt"; but no woman is at any time in evidence, for what manner of man would demean himself by eating with her!

"*Allahu Akbar*" (God is great), rang out from fifty Believers' voices. "*Allahu Akbar*" thundered back a hundred others on the same high-pitched note. This *takbir*, or magnificat, of the Badawin was the signal of our mounting and departing. Few spectacles are more moving than a large body of mounted men in the silent parts of the earth, and as I, the only European of their number, stood upright in my stirrups and looked back over the column filing past the little mosque on the edge of the palm-grove, I decided that we made a brave picture

Emerging into the Wadi Adai we were joined by more Badus from both flanks; drawing rein, they halted in their tribal groups on our immediate front, awaiting the coming up of the Sultan, to give him the salutation, "Peace upon you. Our Lord," and so, falling in, to follow in rear. But verbal obsequiousness finds no counterpart in action, for the poorest free-born Badu is so obsessed by the absolute Omnipotence of God that he considers no man his superior, and will speak with the easy freedom that springs from that consciousness.

Our road lay through a bleak, arid, and almost treeless valley, its pebble bed here and there relieved by a volcanic outcrop, which widened out to where some high sand-dunes skirted our right. In the distance to the left, a patch of green under precipitous hills that faced seawards, marked the environs of Boshar. On towards it we pressed, past three old forts to which distance lent a semblance of nobility. The first of these that edged the grove brought its old muzzle-loading gun out to do the honours. A perfect ring of blue smoke rolled up to a great height, and, dissipating itself, hung in a cloud down the valley.

The Wali of Boshar, Shaikh Ali, had come out to welcome us. A perfect aristocrat is this local representative of the Sultan. Oddly enough he is the brother of the Sultan's enemy and usurper in Interior Oman, the present Ibadhi Imam. Shaikh Ali's hospitality was always complete, and I was now to indulge in the luxury of a room to myself. Though I dislike herding arrangements, I must confess that where discomfort is unavoidable, the finicky European has much to learn from the cheerfulness and complaisance of his darker and fatalistic brethren in Arabia.

After an enormous breakfast and lunch the hour for sleep came, but, though the sun had risen high and waxed hot, I could not put away from me the temptation to go off for a bath in the hot springs that make Boshar and Ghalla famous. This water is full of minerals, particularly of sulphur, and its reputation for health-giving properties in the days of old brought more than one Sultan of Zanzibar two thousand miles across the sea to enjoy it. So I repaired to my favourite spot, a small walled enclosure under a tree beside the little mosque at Boshar. I had bathed here many times before, without ceasing to wonder how its tiny fish life could survive the temperature. But this year the water seemed to have much cooled off, and I was not driven to the usual resort of putting a toe in gingerly, following it timorously up with a leg, then cautiously sitting down and so by slow degrees taking the final plunge.

A spot where the stream comes oozing hot out of the side of the mountain is held to be possessed of a devil, and, in sickness or adversity, evidence of a devil that must be propitiated. I came upon a curious commentary on this one day when, as I followed the stream up to its source, I saw on a rock a little freewill offering of a tiny basket of dates and some raw eggs.

Two hours before sunset we were in the saddle again. Leaving Boshar we moved back a short way down the wadi, to cross the sandy ridge along an alignment of a proposed new motor-road, which will be the first of its kind in this fair camel country.

Climbing to the top of a lofty sand-ridge ahead, whence the far side slopes down to the sea, we were rewarded with a panorama of much interest. Behind and to the right is the great dark serpentine mass that raises its jagged cliffs about Muscat and for seven miles beyond to Yiti. To the northward stretches away the noble but paler limestone range of the Hajar in a gentle curving sweep. Starting here at the coast, the Hajar range swings gradually in to a maximum distance of forty miles at a point about seventy-five miles north, and thence bends symmetrically back to strike the coast again at Khutma Malaha. Thus enclosed between it and the waters of the gulf of Oman is a crescent plain, the Batinah, the chief province of the Sultanate of Muscat to-day.

A uniform threefold nature characterizes the Batinah throughout its great length. First, a stretch of shining sandy beach, very gently shelving and almost everywhere innocent of rocks; secondly, a mighty palm-grove, one of the three largest in the world, which marches with the beach continuously for a hundred and fifty miles, in places two or three miles deep; and thirdly, a great wilderness of shingle plain that stretches back from the palm-grove to the mountains, a plain often skirted with acacia jungle where it meets the palm, and elsewhere largely covered with camel scrub. This plain is the sun-scorched haunt of gazelle.

My journey with the Sultan was to take us through this populous province: now along golden beaches, past little Arab ports ever associated with Sindbad the Sailor, and little fishing villages whose men go forth to grope under the sea for precious pearls; now through the shady date-grove; and now along the hot dazzling plain beyond.

From the crest of the 'hill we descended into the acacia plain below, on reaching which we broke into a merry trot, and so turned towards the shallow Wadi Ubaidha. The air was fragrant with the scent of new budding verdure as we made our way for an hour through acacia jungle. We fetched up at a most delightful camp at the back of the little patch of palms called Ubaidha.

Stretching ourselves on the soft sand in the balmy afternoon air was a pleasant relaxation. And now as the hour of prayer approached arose the question of the correct time, for the Faithful most be punctilious in prayer observances. It seemed that their watches varied, and though I was not taking much interest in proceedings, the Sultan suddenly referred the matter for my arbitrament.

"What is the hour, O Wazir?"

I glanced at the watch I kept Arab time by.

"Exactly twelve o'clock," I returned vaguely, a remark that was greeted with a shout of laughter; for the sun still shone brightly well above the skyline: and Arabic twelve o'clock is, of course, the moment when the sun's upper limb disappears below the horizon. In effect, therefore, my decision was unanimously brushed aside, and it was not till twelve minutes later that the Faithful prostrated themselves, and we all set our watches accordingly.

The Arab system of taking sunset as twelve o'clock as opposed to ours of deciding that hour by its crossing the meridian, is a most error-promoting and laborious arrangement: it involves regulating one's watch every evening. One might well be on the high seas for the uncertainty of it. Their observance of lunar months has much more to be said for it.

The evening wore on, but not to fulfil its early promise. Gone was yesterday's brilliant sky, when the mid-moon of Shawwal made it possible to read. To-night she was enveloped in a pale opaqueness and dank, hazy clouds. Our horses — we had brought seven with us, and these were preferred to camels by Saiyid Sa'id and his kinsmen — were still very fresh, and the Wali of Boshar, who had now joined us, had introduced a mare, scarcely conducing thereby to the peace of mind of the rest of the stable, which in consequence had to be split up and tethered singly. There was much whinnying and answering whinnying as night fell, till one of the stallions — in Arabia an entire remains an entire — refusing to be comforted, broke loose and was secured again only after savaging his syce.

Up betimes in the morning, we were in the saddle by 5.30, and, setting off through a plain of scrub and acacia, kept close to the sea, here screened from view by a slight ridge. A treeless plain succeeded. This, Umm as Sabkha, true to its salt, flat nature, brought one of our horses slithering down, but its rider promptly vaulted back on to his saddleless mount to the playful taunts of his fellow-riders, and we proceeded into hummocky sand country, to halt just short of the old ruined fort of Hayil.

Allahu Akbar! came echoing and re-echoing from the four corners of our camp, our Badawin having spread themselves over an area of a mile and more beneath the widely scattered acacia, here vividly fresh with young leaf. Our slaves were promptly despatched to the palm-grove for food for man and beast, and soon came small brown donkeys struggling along under loads of firewood and lucerne, and shepherds, springing up from nowhere, dragging sheep for the slaughter, or with bowls of milk and cream, for our more privileged circle.

Fulfilment of last night's weather portents came with sudden *shamal*, a north wind that sprang up with an onslaught of sand. This was torture to our eyes, noses, and ears; it buried our saddles and completely blotted out the great range of mountains that but a moment before had looked down upon us from a glorious distant prospect nearly ten thousand feet above.

Respite came when, two hours before sunset, we saddled up and dived into the date-grove that broke the fury of the sandstorm. Here were leafy lanes beneath natural bowers of bordering palms. Women, clad in reds and yellows, harmonized with their bright beds of saffron. Fields of melons and lucerne under the thick palms succeeded. The scene was one of rank luxuriance.

In a clearing beside a great almond-tree, the generous vivid green and red leaves of which give ample shade to man and beast, is the well that is the means of all this life. The bulky creaking rig construction above it is one of the features of the date-grove; it recurs at intervals of every two or three hundred palms. Two split palm trunks incline at an angle of 60 degrees to carry a spindle of mimosa wood and a picturesque, if crude, wooden wheel, both of local handicraft. The lofty wheel suspends above the gaping mouth of the well, and over its rim is passed a rope which carries the water-bucket, the other end of the rope being yoked to a bull. From the base of the rig a pit slopes gently away. the length of which corresponds to the depth of the well. Thus the water-bucket is raised by the action of the bull — usually of the humped Brahminee kind — walking down the pit, and on reaching ground-level, the bucket automatically empties itself into a surface tank from which the garden is irrigated. The bull's return journey up the slope sends the bucket down into the well again, and so the process continues. "Oil the wretched thing", says a European impatient of its creaking and whining, but the owner has another view, for every well has a different note and he, from the far end of his garden, may thus know whether all goes well with his own. The cacophony from many wells operating at one time is really not unmusical. The effect is that of a weird assortment of stringed instruments, the 'cellos seeming always to delight in drowning the violas and fiddles, and the ensemble is a sort of tuning up of an orchestra.

Emerging from the grove after forty minutes we came across a wide pebbly wadi bed opening to the sea, one of seven similar *bathas* between Ghubra and Manuma, the deltaic outlets of the important Wadi Sama'il.

A still larger one was crossed diagonally as we approached the village of Sib. Behind the grove, and standing in its own grounds, was the elaborate country residence of the late Wall of Matrah, my lamented Council colleague. A row of chanting, white-robed Arabs stood in the open plain before it, rifles held to their hips, to send up a cloud of white puffs, followed by the muffled crackle of a *feu de joie*, while a distant gun boomed forth a welcome.

Mosquitoes, thick swarming and of menacing note, here make the lofty house-roof the only possible place for sleep, and thither we retired after dinner.

The Sultan was in no sleeping mood, however, and he and his entourage whiled an hour away at a game which seems to me to involve more memory and more poetry than most Europeans possess. "A" recites a first line of any poem he knows. "B" must follow suit, but is limited to a line the initial consonant of which is the final consonant of "A's" line. "C" does the same thing, taking his cue from "B," and so the round continues until some- one falls out.

Sib is a sort of Brighton of Muscat, into which the population of the capital pours, almost *en masse*, in the summer months. There is at this time a migration of the town population of South-East Arabia to the date-groves, and the poorest tinker will wander off for three months, without any visible means of supporting himself. Here is the simple life indeed. He comes along with a straw mat as his only possession, and enters a date garden, the owner of which has never seen him before, but recognizes his immemorial right to shade, before private ownership in dates had been devised. No one would think of turning him away. His wants are few, a handful of dates and water from the copious well. He may not, however, take from the trees: that would be theft. It is to the dates that have fallen to the ground that he applies, without question, his prescriptive right, and he will get more only if his professional services, which the garden owner may or may not want, warrant it — a species of ethics, which, as a boy, I applied clandestinely to many a rosy Somerset orchard. "Picksuring," we called it.

It seems always to have been the custom for the Muscat merchant of standing to invest in a Sib garden — whether for the state of the soul that goes with ownership of landed property, or whether as a summer residence for his family matters little. The result has been good — for at least the gardens have not been devoted purely to commercial ends, and their owners, men who have crossed the seas to Iraq, India, or Zanzibar, have introduced plants and flowers they have met on their journeyings. These gardens are a tangle of tropical growth. Nature is given water and then allowed her own way. The air is heavy with scent of jasmine, henna, and roses; fruit- trees are borne down with such leaf and fruit as lo suggest that they have never known the pruner's knife.

Hopes of ripe papaya which had drawn Saiyid Sa'id and myself to a part of the garden where these tall and slender trees appeared, must, alas! be postponed, we learned, to a later season; mangoes too — the crop of which this year promised to be prolific. We then espied a coconut palm, and soon had the black gardener swarming up its smooth trunk, a feat he accomplished unaided by the usual rope of the date-picker. The bare shining blade from his belt soon sent six enormous brown pods thudding down to earth. To extract the nut was now the problem, for the fibrous pod is so thick and tenacious (which may be very well if copra is wanted) that it yields only slowly and reluctantly to the dagger. This is a source of much provocation in a thirsty land. Once it is set free, however, a few jabbing horizontal strokes of one's dagger remove its brown beard, when a small white ring shows where milk will ooze at a gentle piercing, for the young coconut is full to the brim with delicious milk; and its flesh, too, when fresh, is soft and yielding as a melon's, so that it may be eaten with a spoon.

But where are the great groves of Dhufar? Here in Sib there are not half a dozen coconut palms, and, shades of Palgrave! the whole Batinah cannot boast a hundred.

A snake had been killed in a bed of lucerne hereabouts over- night, but local snakes cannot be very poisonous, as one finds that the usual penalties of snake-bite sometimes yield to readings of Holy Writ. Still, they are unpleasant creatures to have about, and in the absence of a path one timorously uses the bare ridges that mark the water ducts. The Sib gardens stand alone in not being primarily date gardens. All other kinds of fruit-trees flourish, especially the lime and citron families with their green pungent foliage, and the mango, a finer tree to look at, and densely leafy too; but guava, quinces and plantains also abound, and beneath their shade grow sweet potatoes, eggplant, cowpeas, onions and vegetable-marrows and such-like humble fruits of the earth. If one came here two months hence, one's host would supply grapes and apricots, nectarines and pomegranates. These, however, would have been brought from the milder climed slopes of Jabal Akhdhar and nearly eighty miles inland.

Saiyid Sa'id and I emerged from the garden in time for the morning *burza*. Here, as throughout the Sultanate where Government forts and seats of Government are to be found, a raised plinth running along the edge of the wall at the door entrance, with another parallel one a few feet off, marks the scene of the *burza*; only here, and at this ceremonial, does one encounter in the social life of the Badu, the European counterpart of sitting aloft, so to speak, though these mud benches are well carpeted and pillowed. An old shaikh drew my attention to a lad sitting at the far end. "That boy's grandfather," said he, "had a beard which stretched down to his knees, and such is custom, would not have it cut. On occasions he would divide it into two and take it up over his head, scarf- like to tie in a knot on top. Shameful indeed would it have been to cut his beard, and" — this with a twinkle in his eye — "when he was minded to flirt he is said to have tucked it into his shirt front." This unwillingness among tribal Arabs to cut the beard is curious. Whether or not it is to facilitate matters on the Day of Resurrection, as some say, I do not know; certainly the nails are pared without misgivings. Among their women, too, they never burn their shed hair, and if they do not bury it, one may come upon bunched tufts protruding from the clefts of ancient garden walls.

A Banian petitioner now came to complain of the local Government, but the *burza* had already been protracted, and the hour for breakfast was near, so the Sultan directed him to come and state his case to me afterwards. The administration of these tiny townships is very primitive -patriarchal, in fact. The Wali, or Governor, who dispenses a summary justice, assisted by a Qadhi, or judge of Holy Law, and some dozen soldiers, are its framework; and the petition of the Banian, the only one of this sect in the place, shed a curious light on the rude but time-honoured police system. By night the safety of property is vested in night watch-men, here a body of three scallywags, tribesmen of the Bani Ruwaiha; if theft occurs, it is by this system of *Hararis* — a system known only in the remoter corners of the Middle East — the *Hararis* themselves are liable for compensation.

I once found myself as Political Officer in Southern Mesopotamia, obliged by public opinion, after exhausting every other means, to appoint as chief of these night-police, the arch-thief of the place himself, a man who had spent many years of his life in Turkish dungeons designed for expiating his more dangerous and less successful coups. And here in Sib it seemed that four months earlier, Sudairi, the chief of the *Hararis*, had presented himself at the house of the Banian one morning with the distressing news that the Iranian's shop in the bazaar had been burgled during the night. The panic-stricken Banian betook himself to the Wali, and tried to make it clear to him that the world had come to an end or would shortly do so. The Wali, the Banian, and the chief scallywag then formed a trio of investigators, and went to the scene of the burglary. They found the shop rifled; it had been entered by way of another shop less fruitful of spoil. The Wali, who would draw his pay at the end of the month anyhow, and had had a satisfactory breakfast that morning, was inclined to take the long view of Allah's everlasting mercy, but otherwise was not conspicuously helpful at that early hour, while the suppliant saw at a glance that the crashing in of a door, breaking down of a brick wall, and rifling of two shops must have involved men, time, and noise, to such an extent that the *Hararis* could not be so wholly unknowing as they declared. Now if the Finger Print Expert does not flourish in the sands of Arabia, the Sand Tracker does. Indeed the *Qaffar*, as he is called, becomes, where he enjoys a good local reputation, a pillar of society, and the drawer at my hands of a monthly stipend. Here is a genius who can identify every living creature on his beat by merely gazing at the ground, for man goes unshod. And so it happened that the *Qaffar* of Sib declared that the thieves were none other than the Night-Watchmen themselves, who all three were thereupon sent to Jalali Fort at Muscat, and there, in the absence of a local habeas corpus, still linger.

I owed the visit of the Banian to me this blessed morning to a twofold object. First, to argue his claim for 500 rupees compensation for the stolen and damaged property. Judging by experience, I thought 125 rupees represented a fairer evaluation, and before the interview ended it was conceded that this latter figure represented an eminently desirable sum of money. Secondly, he complained of a travesty of justice for which the *Qaffar* was negatively responsible, for while there were five foot- marks, there were only three prisoners, and while he, the Banian, did not pretend to be a tracker, he knew by intuition who the other two were. The accused turned out to be two of his old and hardened debtors!

It was the usual hour of ten o'clock Arabic time when we broke camp. Stepping across the threshold of the. house the Sultan had halted, and murmured in a low voice what might have been a couplet from a poem. Curiosity getting the better of me, I was constrained to ask for its meaning. "What is the good," was the smiling reply, "you are an Unbeliever; but," he added, "I will write it down for you some other time. It is a verse from the Holy Quran:

Verily, He who has made the Quran binding on you;

He will bring you back to the destination

and our belief is that whoever repeats this, as he departs from a place, God will spare him to return."

"*Allahu Akbar!*" came the manly shouts of our freshly mounted Badawin, and as we moved out each tribal element rode square across our front, drew rein, and, with a characteristic sweep of the cane in the Sultan's direction, gave the customary salutation. But the Badu with a high freak inflexion of voice on the second syllabic pronounces *Salaam, Silaum*, which to one who has lived in Palestine recalls the Hebrew *Shalaum*, heard daily in the streets of Jerusalem.

"*Makran al Awwal*" (Trot in front), motioned the Sultan. The order was taken up and shouted by relays ahead, so that the leading files soon broke into a trot, and all behind conformed in turn. This pace of from five to six miles an hour is most economical for beast, and if one has a comfortable saddle and a good mount, most pleasant for the rider. The Badawin, pleased with the order, burst into a chant which suited the pace, in their high-pitched but rugged voices.

In contrast to yesterday's ride through the heart of the date-grove, to-day we moved through the pleasant acacia jungle where the date-palms fringe the plain. Overhead thorny branches, which here and there make one bend in the saddle to avoid them, are to the Badawin perfect camel fodder, and to the Banian and Luwati merchant a source of wealth when cut and exported as firewood to Bahrain, Dubai, and Southern Persia. Whether the jungle shall be cut or not is often the subject of dispute between conflicting interests.

On our way we passed various palm frond villages, and an occasional deserted old mud fort with its attendant mosque. The Ibadhi mosque is unique in having no minaret to speak of, and where it has fallen into disuse it would be sacrilegious to remove such of its interior fittings, doors, and furnishings as have survived the hand of time, even though they might be wanted for a new mosque. The Sultan lamented, therefore, that the builders were so shortsighted as to have built enduringly on temporary sites. There is, in theory, no priestcraft in Islam, and yet, paradoxically, the Faithful are among the most priest-ridden of peoples. The power of the literate *Mutawwa* (religious leader) in this illiterate and backward area perhaps naturally looms large. Despite the Puritanism of Ibadhism, and its many at least superficial resemblances to Wahhabism, it has its own reservations about the sanctity of the mosque. True, the building is unambitious to a degree, boasts not even a minaret, and to attempt to beautify its interior would be a mortal sin; yet, say the *Mutawwa*, are its bricks and stones of a truth holy. A companion riding at my elbow remarked: "You see that mosque squat and lowly: but we are taught that screened from our eyes there continues up from its foundations a mighty pillar of holiness through the seven heavens."

Here at last was Wadi Manuma, marked by its giant ghaf tree. A slight trough of clean sparkling wadi bed just out of sight of the sea and edged with plumed palms made a glorious camping-ground.

"What do you say to a *mushuwa* dinner?" said the Sultan to me, when the sunset prayer had ended. I returned the Arabic equivalent for "an excellent scheme", though in fact I was to enjoy nothing more than a brimming bowl of camel's milk that evening, for I was very tired. The morning inspection of Sib, followed by the afternoon ride, had deprived me of my midday sleep, and now the sheep for the slaughter must needs be brought from a mile's distance, and its death and preparation, followed by the elaborate processes of *mushuwa*, would mean waiting a length of time which I could not cheerfully endure. The following morning, however, I heard all about the excellences of the repast.

Mushuwa is our grill. But into the remoter parts of Arabia, grilling irons have not yet penetrated, and the method of a heated pile of rubble, known, I suppose, to our Stone Age fore- bears, is still rapturously employed; and that it is good I can bear witness. But even stones were here wanting, and so our Badawin had recourse to their other device. A shallow oblong pit, eighteen inches to two feet wide, was dug, a wood fire was made in it, heavy logs were brought to turn into hot ash, and the pit soon came to exhale the breath of the furnace. The Badus with their knives now took to stripping palm fronds of such length as to rest transversely over the pit, and on the sharpened ends the meat, cut into fids, was spiked, and rows of these were suspended in position above the red-hot embers to make that succulent delicacy, kabab.

The acacia and scrub grew thinner as we proceeded on the morrow, though early signs of new budding spring foliage gladdened the heart. The sandier nature of the soil here concealed treacherous blind holes, which brought two of our Badus tossing over their trotting camels' heads, a none too pleasant experience when the rifle is habitually slung loosely under the shoulder and is thus likely to slip across the back during the fall.

But a worse occurrence was to follow. The frantic shouting of a dismounted old Badu standing away to the right now attracted my attention, and, on looking closer, I saw that his camel — an angry bull camel had the old man's hand and wrist clenched in its teeth as in a vice. Seconds must thus have passed, for the whole column now engrossed by the scene, had come to a standstill. The camel had lifted the old man bodily off his feet and held him suspended in the air while neighbouring Badus slithered down from their own camels and struck with their canes at the brute's head. The latter relaxing his hold, the Badu fell in a crumpled heap to the ground, his hand bleeding profusely and arm hanging limp. The Badawin continued to beat the savage beast, which frothed characteristically at the mouth, bellowing and bunching out its red tongue, but the importunities of the old man, its owner, made them desist, and in due course he mounted it again, and, giving us a wide berth, enabled us to proceed.

What had caused this outburst was uncertain. The regal camel ration of lucerne and dates may well have increased the brute's spirits, for no Badu could normally afford his mount such daily luxury. Over or unusual feeding is sometimes fatal to camels, and the partially habituated brute, when thus tempted, does not know when to stop, and suffers. The raw and unhabituated, on the other hand, turns up its supercilious nose at anything new fangled which it has not been used to foraging for itself in the desert scrub. The sex of the present offender provided another theory. Bull camels are always more ferocious than cows, though at this season both are generally exemplarily behaved, and when riding *en masse*, as we were then, with constant collisions and much jolting, a normal spirit of forbearance was desirable. With the Badu any notion of "dressing" is unthinkable, and the equivalent of "observing a half horse's length between files" would fill him with derisive mirth.

In Oman, the bull camel is usually used for transporting goods, the Badu choosing to ride the cow for her gentler movements. Quite the reverse ideas I found to prevail in Southern Baluchistan, when on a shooting expedition after ibex there, and the bull was generally ridden because of the belief that riding the female interfered with her breeding qualities. No such heresy rules here in Oman, where, perhaps, some of the finest camels of Arabia are reared. Indeed, of our two hundred camels there were scarcely at any time more than a half-dozen bulls. And while the cow camel after her fourth year is covered every second year, only one in fifty bulls seems permitted to indulge its progenitive instincts, for in a countryside there is always one bull with more outstanding qualities than the rest, and the Badu cow-owner comes from far and wide at the critical time to engage his services. The camel's antagonism to man at such a time is very usual, and only a year or two ago in Dhufar, I remember, a Badu was so savagely attacked that crushed bones in his forearm led to the whole limb withering.

Anxious for the poor old victim of the morning episode, we sent for him as soon as we made camp. Along he came holding up his stricken arm. There were two deep tooth-mark contusions in the back of the hand and wrist, through which the red raw flesh protruded, and the old unwashed brown hand was still streaked with the blackness of its own dried blood. [17] The old man worked his fingers, and with confidence born of hope, perhaps, declared that no bones were broken. *"Min Allah"* (God's will), he said fatalistically, and went off uncomplaining to his village the next day for domestic treatment, and that was the last I saw of him.

Barkah Fort, an imposing pile — imposing, that is, from a distance, for like the old rusty cannons that lie strewn about it, it is ramshackle with age and beyond repair — has a great historical background. The natural centre of the Batinah Province, it was Barkah that excited the covetous eyes of Sa'ud, the Najdian invader, who sent thither his Wahhabi hordes at the beginning of the last century, and here to this very fortress Sa'id, the greatest Sultan the country ever knew, came as a boy. Hither he lured and slew his uncle, the Regent and Pretender and thus succeeded to the throne. And now for a century the place had the tradition of being administered by some exalted member of the ruling family [18].

Here we had arrived on the previous evening, having struck across the palm-grove to make the beach a mile to the eastward. Thence our course lay along the yellow strand. It was a memorable scene, with our camels' feet laved by the surf, and with our Badawin, the headdress streaming in the breeze, shouting their wild war-cries. Two dhows rode peacefully at anchor off the shore, their high decorated poops, and strangely forward raking masts giving them a fairy-like look, or suggesting that they had come straight out of an Elizabethan or medieval port.

We had dismounted to occupy large *sablas*, camel-frond huts of considerable proportions pitched open to the sea and richly carpeted for our reception. My reflections on the superiority of the *sabla* to the tent in virtue both of its ventilation and of its protection against the sun, were disturbed by the cry of a party of lepers who had come down to the beach to beg from us. Leprosy is not uncommon along this coast. Smallpox too — there had been a few cases recently segregated in the gardens close by— is endemic.

The Wali of Barkah, a venerable old man, had brought along the recently arrived Walis of Musana'a and Suwaiq, two seats of government that lay immediately before us, and also some of the local nobility, to make their *salaams* to the Sultan; and the Sultan was entertaining them with the story of his trip to England and its wonders, though I trembled to think with what effect, as all the old country people of the Ibadhi persuasion are conservatively religious, and likely, therefore, to be suspicious of the land of the Unbeliever.

My thoughts were suddenly interrupted by a chuckle from the Sultan.

"Hilal," said His Highness by way of attracting my attention, "Hilal has just eaten sticky halwa (Turkish delight), but declines to wash his hands from the ewer, nor will he partake of our coffee."

"Why?" I asked, mystified.

"Because both the ewer and the coffee-pot are silver vessels" — they were, indeed, of a rather fine filigree work — "and with the ultra-religious among us the use of silver and gold vessels is forbidden."

This to most of those present may have appeared a little display of self-righteousness for such an occasion, but I professed, while having no such scruples myself, to appreciate devotion to an ideal. The Ibadhi male adult is denied on religious grounds the personal use of gold or silver, or of silk for dress, but many among the Faithful compromise with their convictions in a gold-crowned tooth, and all delight to adorn their rifles, swords, and daggers with the precious metals. Hilal, the Puritan, himself, I observed, sported a silver ring and a silver-hafted dagger apparently without a twinge of conscience. But curious are the workings of the mind, as the drift of conversation was about to show. It was now the old Wali's turn for a hearty laugh. "Hullo, what ails the Wali?"

thought I, as I looked up to hear a member of the Sultan's suite romancing, *a propos* of his travels abroad, on the provocative beauty he had encountered. The implication of the "sin of the flesh", wholly suppositious though it was, had made benign those Pharisaical features that had taken on a cold intolerant expression at the thought of the "sin of silver".

We had intended an earlier start than usual that afternoon, to make Musana'a by sunset, and the beach was already agog with excited preparations. Here, Badawin leading strings of camels were returning from watering; there, others were tightening a girth or giving their saddles a final look over. "*Fallah! Fallah! Juwad!*" — shouts of "Get ready" came on all hands, but just on the hour appointed for our move a horseman had come galloping up bearing a sheaf of telegrams. The translations fell to me, and my puckered brow, or some such betraying sign, soon brought the Sultan to his feet. "What's the matter? What has happened?" A serious situation had, indeed, developed in another part of His Highness's dominions. Gwadur, on the Makran coast, was the scene of a disturbance. The substance of the cables was that a Sunni mosque had been desecrated with human filth. The Baluchis to whom the mosque belonged, suspecting the Luwati, the followers of the Agha Khan, had retaliated on the meeting-house of the latter, whom they do not regard as Muslim at all. A riot was reported to have ensued, one man had been killed and others injured. Terror was said to possess the town and immediate help was asked for.

I looked up. The Sultan, visibly disturbed in mind, was waiting for me to speak. The intelligence was communicated. Should we cancel our camel tour? Should we send troops from Bait al Falaj? Should I myself return and proceed to Gwadur? But against this, the State gunboat was undergoing a refit at Bombay, and the mail boat made only a fortnightly call. We cogitated, and finally sent orders to State representatives in Muscat and Makran, and a reassuring message to the Agha Khan's council at Karachi, and decided to halt for the night and await news of developments before deciding upon a precipitate move in either direction.

ON TREK WITH THE SULTAN IN THE WESTERN BATINAH

DAYBREAK. We were at Barkah still. But the shock of yesterday's news was already softened by accommodation of the mind, and now a fresh batch of telegrams, arriving during the forenoon, was to banish all misgivings.

In the light of to-day's news, yesterday's appeared to be of an alarmist kind. The situation was in hand; it could be dealt with by delegated authority, and no longer threatened the possibility of our having to abandon our tour. We could rest during the heat of the day, and then resume once more the saddle and the northward trek.

Our course lay along the shore towards the pink island of Suwadi, and though the afternoon sun shone full in our faces, the contrast with the dark shades of the date-grove was not unpleasant. The surf came hissing up the beach, and our flanking camels splashed joyously through it. Passing behind the island, we found that the date-grove had receded, to leave a shingle frontage of a mile or more. Here on the edge of it was a small gravelike mound into which were struck some dozen or more straight sticks wherefrom fluttered rags of red and white bunting.

Barkah Fort

"What strangeness is this?" quoth a white-turbaned old chief amongst the retinue.

"A holy man's shrine," was the reply. "Fishermen are wont to visit it and adorn it thus, and bring little gifts of flour and dates."

"Have they turned Hindoos?" was the cynical retort, for a pure Monotheistic conception is the dominant feature of the Ibadhi creed as of the Wahhabi, and here was a Shi'ah or Shafi affront. "Out upon symbolism, for the shadow becomes the substance in such minds as these" — that was the attitude.

There was a cavernous harbour behind the island where a dhow and many fishing craft were hauled up on the beach. Here is the only shelter along the exposed Batinah shores where refuge may be sought from the howling northeasters of the winter months.

As our camels were now floundering in the soft sand, we abandoned the attempt of cutting off the wide detour which the coast here makes, and made once more for the beach to the west of the island. A long stretch of shining strand, purple red from innumerable little shells of this colour, made perfect camel going, and beside and above it ran a sandy strip studded with innumerable crab castles, miniature Eiffel Towers of solid sand thrown up by the hole-boring operations of these small white crabs. Here the beach usually seethes with them as they run this way and that at great speed and finally dash blindly down to the sea, to crouch under a great curling breaker and so disappear from sight. Various small spiked shells tumbled clumsily about on the edge of some cast up sea-spume, but crouched as our great camel army loomed up and thundered over them. Fifteen vermilion flamingos took lankily to wing, followed by two black jack, grown old in an habitual reluctance to be disturbed. Gulls and red-legged *dik al bahr* followed the jack, making a long line low over the sea which would on closer acquaintance reveal bright duck-like plumage.

The sun was sinking and the distant beach before us took on the look of an English seaside resort in summer, with two hundred and more seemingly fair bathers. These proved to be Women and children of the fisherfolk — Baluchis, Jadgalis, and slaves mostly, who wade out gathering their evening meal of *dauk*, a small white shell-fish. Unabashed by our presence, the young women continued to ply their modest calling, but as we passed, we saw, in that pink light, shiny clinging garments moulding many a beautifully rounded young body.

The sun sank red in a bank of haze, and a well-defined eclipse showed up a mountain silhouette — perhaps of the Hajar of far-away Shamailiyah — the sparkling blue-green sea paled first to silver, and then assumed a leaden deadness, and the sails of fishing craft changed slowly from pink to black. Even the gay voices of the Badawin were now stilled by the solemn night, and only as we approached the old town of Musana'a did the distant flashing gun of welcome rouse them to their shouts of *Allahu Akbar*. The starry sky, lit up by the moon rising behind us, now changed to silver mirrors the little patches of water that lingered in beach depressions or wadi channels. It was fascinating, indeed, from one's jogging camel to look down and see mirrored Venus moving straight in her course before one, skipping from pool to pool, or sailing serenely across a lagoon.

"How many men have shed their blood for these sticks and stones," said the Sultan on the following morning, as we sat in shady *burza* beneath the old crumbling turrets of Musana'a fort. "Time indeed changes the value of all things."

A 'reformed' Slave Trader

The early hour was scarcely suitable for a philosophical discussion, which in any case would have been cut short when three Awamir tribesmen, newly arrived, came across and knelt before His Highness in prayerful petition. This was a daily occurrence. On hearing of the Ruler's arrival, every tribesman from far and wide — it was immaterial whether they were his subjects or not — came to pay homage and enjoy the royal bounty as a matter of right. Now of all tribes, the Badu Awamir, whose roamings, incidentally, lie beyond the Sultan's borders, have, by general consensus of opinion, the ugliest reputation. They are held to be desperate raiders, who neither pray nor fast, and by the Hadhr of Oman, often their victims, their room is preferred to their company. The simple request of these three representatives was to be shown their *sabla* (bivouac) by the Wali, but in reality it was a gesture, so that all men should see they were now in enjoyment of the royal patronage.

Looking first at the kneeling Badus, and then at our old astrologer friend, Saif bin Ya'rab, the Sultan turned to me and said: "O Wazir, there was once strife between these men."

"Who were the victors?" asked I, somewhat hastily.

"Upon the chestnut let the saddle-blanket remain," came in an undertone — an Omani equivalent to "let sleeping dogs lie".

The arrival of these oddments altered in no way the nature of our camelcade, essentially Badu in character, deriving from pastoral elements of the Bani Umr and Muqabil from the blue Hajar far away. To such as these men the settled lands of the Batinah could not cease to be the object of wondering admiration; it represented to them vast, incalculable wealth.

The crescent plain, which here is Arabia where it is washed by the waters of the Gulf of Oman, does, indeed, for such a littoral, teem with men. Its two hundred thousand souls comprise Arabs predominantly. Gulf Arabs that is, then Baluchis and Jadgalis, with a considerable negro element from the old East African dependencies, and mixtures of these elements in all proportions.

Man may live in three ways. He is fisherman, or date cultivator, or shepherd (Badu). The last named is poorest and proudest. Pure of blood as natives here go, the Badu regards himself as the salt of the earth. To him agriculture is a mean occupation, sailoring or fishing unspeakable lowness, wherefore it is vain for the follower of such avocations, rich though he be, to aspire to the hand of the Badu's daughter. Here the Badu, like his counterpart elsewhere, lives almost entirely on milk. Meat and rice, the diet of the rich, may come his way once in a moon, if as often, though to wheaten bread he is no stranger, for the neighbouring Hajar grow wheat in plenty. Content to raise camels and flocks — the latter chiefly black and brown goats, for the familiar white sheep is rare in Oman — his only contribution to the common stock is butter, unless one considers transport, for it is his camels and donkeys that do most of the caravaning of the country. His only dwelling is the shade of the acacia, the camel's-hair tent being here unknown. He lives a life of perfect simplicity and ease, but also of watchfulness. A rifle is ever in readiness in his hands, for he is suspicious of any intrusion, and he regards no man as his peer.

To his despised neighbours who go down to the sea in ships, the term "Ichthyophagi" applies as much to-day as in Strabo's time, though curiously enough they who fish are as often as not comparatively recent importations from the Makran coast. Their chief prey is that somewhat incongruous pair, sharks and sardines — the shark for its fins and tail, which command a price beyond that of prime English beefsteak in the China market; the sardine to be exported, generally to India, for the lowlier purposes of agriculture. Sharks' meat, red and rank, is eaten (as I know for my sins) fresh on the coast and salted for sale in the interior. Sardines also have their local uses, as manure for the gardens, and fodder for men, oxen, and camels. The whale and turtle are not unknown, but fishermen do not go in pursuit of them, though turtle eggs, which seem to be laid in hundreds in one sand-hole, are favoured in due season when fishermen go off to the beaches of the low-lying islands to dig up these edible eggs and so cheat nature's heat, which would otherwise turn them into more turtles. Morning and evening, men attend chiefly to their fishing, and, like all the other sons of these climes, rest in the noonday. And so, as one passes, one sees drawn up on the beach a mass of various forms of craft and tackle — the *shasha*, a frail wicker cradle-boat, nets of every mesh, and ingenious cages of our lobster-pot order. Here is a fisherman who, if he can be persuaded to take you out to his favourite coral beds, will point out exquisite sea anemones and other glorious fauna of the deep; and the visitor will surely not come home without dolphin, squid, and seerfish, *barracouta* and horse mackerel.

But it is from the labours of the date cultivator that the country derives most of such wealth as it has, though he is in a numerical minority. These unending palms of the Batinah must be numbered in several millions, and it is the surplus of their produce, sent overseas, that brings back to these shores rice, coffee, sugar, and spices from India and East Africa, and the piece goods of Manchester and of Japan. Diminishing rainfall in the interior in the last decade has not so far affected the Batinah, where sufficient fresh water is to be found but a few feet below the surface and within a stone's throw of the sea, and where tens of thousands of oxen daily work at the wells. Day by day, from the rising of the morning star till two hours after sunrise, and again from the hour of afternoon prayer to dusk, these water-wheels up and down the land send out their old whining noises.

To the Westerner with his partiality to crude-oil engines, centrifugal pumps, and cusecs, all this appears a lamentable waste of resources. "Scrap the oxen and these archaic water-wheels," says he, "install modem plant and. *Eureka!* you double the output, improve the standard of living, and make a fortune for somebody." This probably is true, but whether the change is desirable, who shall say? More production is a Western slogan, and in highly industrialized and over-populated societies is bound up with human welfare, but where standards of life are different, is there the same compelling need for industrialization? If Westerners with their centrifugal pumps are more contented than these simple garden folk with their water-wheels, they contrive to conceal the fact; if they are pitying, it appears to be wasted pity. Here may be ill-nourished and poorly clad bodies — a low standard of life, in short — but here also is a sublime religious contentment, so far unexposed to the cold blasts of Western doubt which seems to be the handmaiden of progress: and no man starves.

With the cycle of the year, the even tenor of men's ways is disturbed for a brief few months, for if one pass in June or July one will witness the flow of two tides of human migration, and if a few months later, their ebbing. Now is the pearl-diving season, when men stream northwards to the pearl banks on the Trucial coast a hundred miles distant. Fishermen and sailors go actually to dive, and they who hoist and lower them into the depths may be gardeners or even occasional Badus, who have joined the pearl fleet for this season of feverish activity. Dhows, *badans*, and other craft of every sort, their decks swarming with prospective divers will already have set forth from these ports, or passed along this coast even from far-away Socotra, and the Batinah now denudes itself of camels too to carry its own quota of many thousands in this vast migration. Even the local Holy Man is taken, for when the exhausted divers emerge from the sea and complain of head or bodily pains, *jinns* (universally believed in) are the cause ascribed, and it is the

Holy Man's role to read over the victims appropriate passages from Holy Writ.

Now, also, is the season of the ripening date, and the occasion of another migration, the migration to the date-grove. Not only does the populace of local towns move out bodily, but from the far distant Trucial coast as well, an army of women, veiled and well dressed in black and gold *abbas* (cloaks), now journeys south- wards to the Batinah by the returning caravans, to sojourn while their men are absent on the pearl banks. Three months hence this process will be reversed, indicating that date and pearl harvests have been gathered.

To-day was the first day since setting out that we had not been in the saddle, and. the Sultan in his white robes, followed by his private bodyguard, strolled leisurely along the beach, while I spent a pleasant hour reading the much-criticized Palgrave, the English Jew- Jesuit Arabian traveller who was ship- wrecked off this coast in '67. The moon rose in the form of a monstrous yellow Chinese lantern over the sea, and put an end to my reading, and I closed my book with the feeling that Palgrave's narrative, perhaps the most fascinating in the whole realm of Arabian travel literature, abounds, so far as Oman is concerned, in inaccurate detail, but that the picture he gives us is true artistically. Palgrave's medium is the brush and palette, so to speak, not the camera.

Near Wudam

Suddenly the voice of a boy singing arrested us, and the Sultan, who had now returned, ordered him to be summoned for our entertainment. He turned out to be a Baluchi slave lad of seven or eight years, very poor, but bright with native intelligence, and endowed with a good voice. We gathered in a small select circle on the moonlit beach, and the caroller, kneeling in our midst, poured forth his young heart in a stream of melody. A solemn *Nashid*, in an ancient metre of Arab *Nabat* (the words pronounced colloquially to the extent of muting final vowel sounds), told of valiant deeds. Although of great length, it was succeeded by another, and still another.

"Do you know a *tahawrib*" asked the Sultan; and the youngster, nothing loath, gave us a merry chant of the cavalier.

"How does he remember it all?" I asked, admiring the prodigious feat of memory.

"A human gramophone," was the answer. "He's picked it up from the roving fighters."

A dish of dates was now brought to the youthful entertainer, who devoured them ravenously, while the Badawin round about were childishly amused and wonder-struck, as one of our number played his electric torch on the scene.

The interlude over, I asked for a sea chanty, and the boy galloped off a jaunty boat song, though at a *tempo* to break the heart of any oarsman. Its theme was of local colour — a fight between a gharfish and a cuttlefish.

A 1780 Maria Theresa dollar, the silver currency common in Oman, pressed into one small brown hand, and a large chunk of dates into the other, sent the boy cheerfully on his home-ward way. I awoke with the first streak of dawn to the strains of last night's songs, and learnt that the boy, returning to gather the refuse of our camels to sell to some local gardener, had once more met with marks of royal favour.

Shouts of "*Juwad! Juwad!*" (To your saddles!) filled the air, the guns of the fort boomed their parting salute, and we were once more clattering merrily along the shore, a vast army of men and beasts. Curious one's passing impressions of this vigorous moving body as one rode along a part of it. Generally some predominant feature filled the mental picture. Sometimes a giant clockwork of a thousand criss-cross legs, long, wooden-actioned, indistinguishable camels' legs; or perhaps a shuttle of taut reins and horizontally shoulder-slung rifles; or the Badus themselves, bowing behind the humps — small, lithe, fierce brown men, with long pillar-like necks set on square, flat shoulders, and small clean-cut heads, bearded, and, maybe, of much refinement; or a sea of billowing humps; or long camel necks crowned by giant heads, that from behind seemed all eyes and foreheads, nodding gently at this pace in contrast to the clumsy jogging bodies to which they belonged.

The sea was a limpid blue, the sails of becalmed *badans* flapped listlessly in the still air — a sudden contrast this to the wind-lashed, white-foamed sea of yesterday, when craft of every kind, their sails bellied out to the wind, went flashing by as if in triumphant abandon. Here the beach was thickly shell-strewn, and here for the first time I noticed faint outcrops of rock lodging into the sea, while on our other hand were high green banks, gorse-covered, where a few sheep grazed, and brown butterflies tumbled and played.

Wudam, where I dismounted for an inspection, is a typical fishing village. At least that is its particular significance here. This name applies also to the date-grove behind and to another non-fishing village beyond, a vague system of nomenclature common throughout this Yal Sa'ad country. Where I now halted, it consisted of perhaps a hundred reed huts, and, on an eminence close by, the inevitable mosque, its white-cemented exterior sparkling in the morning sun. Before the village, deserted at this hour by its inhabitants, whose tiny craft studded the far horizon, were crude goal-post devices of three palm trunks, for drying; fishing-nets, and a pair of primitive giant scales stood over against the woodstack. Derelict craft, relegated after long service to desuetude, littered the beach. Here was one, perhaps in its day the pride of some dim-eyed old villager, who, if he could be roused, would tell of how together they had seen many a shark-fight of doubtful issue.

We drew rein outside the old Arab town of Suwaiq for the preliminary camel racing. To gallop a camel is no easy feat, and to the natural disabilities of her ridiculous cow-hocks and ungainly size, her own unwillingness must be added, but it is almost *de rigueur* amongst Badawin for the new arrival to show the villagers who have turned out to welcome him, the mettle of his mount, and his own riding prowess. Two camels go racing down the straight together, one rider, according to Cocker, having his outstretched cane across the other's shoulders, and as he leans back almost horizontally over her quarters to show off her unmanageable strength, every eye of the admiring watchers is upon him — much as at a race meeting one watches, lynx-eyed and with a single mind, the doings of the incomparable filly on which one has had a modest punt. The Sultan on some occasions led off with this ceremony, and to-day he handed over his sword to me, as was his custom, to indicate that this was such an occasion. Away he went, accompanied by his son in the most approved manner, and Badawin *a deux* followed at suitable intervals. I had turned my camel's head away for the moment, to avoid the scorching sun which was playing on my back, a certain cause of heady fever, when suddenly I heard a commotion, and turning, saw a young camel and its driver had made a heavy fall in the sand. "*Inkassar! Inkassar!*" (Broken! Broken!) shouted an excited Badu at my elbow, as a dozen others quickly dismounted, and, dashing across to where the young camel lay prostrate, ran their hands over it with the air of practised anatomists. Fortunately her young rider, standing by, was unhurt.

"Her near fore is broken below the shoulder," said Saiyid Sa'id to me after awhile; "and she will have to be destroyed."

"The leg bone of the camel is as brittle as the gazelle's," added a shaikh, "and it is vain to set a broken bone." And then the guns of the old fort of Suwaiq — there were none when Sindbad the Sailor came to neighbouring Musana'a on his voyages — boomed out their welcome insensible of the little tragedy of the beach. We had camel flesh for dinner that day.

The assembly followed a hearty breakfast, and a very amusing assembly it was to prove. No sooner was the Sultan seated, than a bent man, ripe with years, came and knelt before him. He looked important, venerable, like a stage bishop, large of head and heavy of jowl, with blue eyes, and a quality of nose that is commonly associated with power to command. Closer view strengthened the first impression. To this rather masterful appearance was added a voice of exceptional depth and resonance, yet the manner seemed gentle and restrained. Slowly untying a knot in the corner of his headdress he unrolled a sheaf of papers, and the manner in which he held them to his eyes showed that he was almost blind. I was moved by feelings both of admiration and of pity.

"What is thy case?" said the Sultan.

"I have been cheated of the inheritance of my slave," came the answer.

"Thy slave!" said the Sultan, as he leant forward to eye the petitioner more closely, and to smile as he recognized an old acquaintance. "Tell us thy story."

The old man started on a low persuasive note, but as he continued his mood grew angry, his voice became impassioned. Twice the Sultan interjected questions, but the old man, unheeding, continued until his voice bellowed as though the whole assembly of two hundred Arabs were deaf, and justice were likewise hard of hearing.

Vastly amused at the man's temerity. His Highness, turning to me, whispered that here was none other than Karam, the arch slave-dealer, the notorious Baluchi buyer and seller of the sons of Adam: Karam who had spent four long periods of incarceration in Jalali fort, at Muscat, for his nefarious activities. In an audience whose religion gives divine sanction to slavery. Authority must needs lend patient ear to the alleged grievance.

"What is the ruling of thy Holy Law on this matter? What sect art thou?" asked the Sultan: for this may have some subtle bearing. Baluchis in their own country are generally of the Hanafi persuasion, but not infrequently adopt Shaft tenets when domiciled in Oman, and *Shar'a* Law, as between the sects of Islam, sometimes has slightly conflicting bearings. Thus according to Ibadhism, the State religion, a slave may not, as under certain orthodox Sunni sects, divorce his own slave wife: this prerogative vests in the master by whom the wife is provided. But *Shar'a* seemed to be unanimous in its ruling that the slave, being property, is not himself permitted to bequeath by the ordinary Islamic laws of succession, that is to say, the slave's wife and children cannot inherit his property at death — this reverts to the master, who is the sole inheritor. Petitioner's claim seemed sound enough, therefore, according to Islamic Holy Law, provided that the slave at decease was his; but the Sultan's patience was already exhausted, and one felt his sympathies to be all the other way.

A shaikh sitting next to me whispered jocularly: "This fellow has always possessed a human 'stud', and has lived by rearing slaves as other men rear horses."

"Tell me, Karam" — the Sultan was again addressing the old man — "How many slaves have passed through your hands?"

"*W'allahi*" (By God), "not more than a hundred head," came back the unabashed reply, as though the speaker referred to cattle.

"How long since you last sold one?"

"I call God to witness, I've done no buying and selling for twenty years."

"Enough," said the Sultan; "I will give you a decision on my return journey."

"Not now? Then I'm done for., I'm rapidly losing my sight, and this is the answer you give me," murmured Karam with an aggrieved air, as he retired gropingly to his place in the circle, screwed up his documentary evidence once more into the knotted comer of his flowing headdress, and tossed it back into its accustomed place over his shoulder.

"I can wait for an answer for twenty days. Then I cross over to Baluchistan," was his parting shot.

This Yal Sa'ad wedge of country in the middle Batinah has always been notorious for its slave-dealing activities. It has profited by its position opposite the Makran, a happy hunting- ground for young slaves for the Trucial Coast, and it has in consequence naturally rebelled against the Muscat connection. whereby it is brought under the British treaties of 1845 and 1873 for the suppression of the slave-trade.

Without in any way attempting to justify so inhuman an institution, one may be allowed to point out that the domestic slavery of Arabia is not the slavery which makes the blood of the twentieth-century humanitarian run cold: there are no whips and scorpions about it; it has little in common with the unpitying harshness of our own Industrial Revolution or the slavery of the sugar plantation. Slavery in Arabia is almost wholly domestic slavery — I do not speak of the pearl fisheries. The slave is the household servant, the court scullion, the tribal coffee-maker, his master's bodyguard. He receives no wages as such, it is true, and therefore is spared the horror of wondering where next week's are coming from. As part of a rich man's household he enjoys security of tenure, is generally well fed, well clothed, and is found a slave girl to wife by his master before reaching the age of twenty. Among enlightened masters his lot would perhaps compare favourably with that of the casual labourer of our own enlightened industrialism. The laws of the Prophet enjoin mercy towards slaves, and the slave — the domestic slave of whom I speak, that is — if not treated properly makes himself such a nuisance nowadays that his master is glad to be rid of him; though it is quite true that abuse of the system in the past has seen young children torn from their mothers' arms to be sold to a highest bidder in a distant land, with never a hope of meeting again.

But the slave, with the Arab, is by no means a class without rights. If he has ability, his master will advance him to the highest position, will reward and manumit him. Burton in his *Pilgrimage to Al Madinah and Meccah* relates that the high dignitary, the Pasha of the Syrian caravan by which he made his way to Damascus, had been the slave of a slave; Bin Sa'ud, I seem to remember, at the time I served in Trans-Jordan, sent a slave as governor to neighbouring Jauf; and here, in Oman, the Generalissimo of the late Sultan's forces, and the *de facto* ruler of two provinces; virtually the power behind the Throne, was a slave.

The Arab, democratic in his social habits, is aristocratic at heart, as his honoured past naturally makes him. But while attaching much importance to his lineage, and following an hereditary principle in the tribal governance, his attitude towards the slave is yet susceptible of the orientation shown by the three instances I have quoted.

The afternoon was wearing on as our column threaded its snakelike way through the palm-grove to the village of Batha [19], whither we had been invited as guests of a loyal and powerful Shaikh of the Yal Sa'ad tribe, Hilal by name. Turning towards the setting sun as we emerged a good half-hour later on the far side of the date palms, we were soon brought to a halt by the rumble of an old muzzle-loading gun on our front, and a regular fusillade of welcome-denoting bullets. The dull beating of drums and the distant glint of steel marked the sword dance, and as we advanced a little towards the open, the villagers retired to the sides to make a corridor for our camel-riding display.

"Come on, Khabura," "Come on, Bani Umr," old Rashid, our Baluchi master of ceremonies on these occasions, shouted to our Badawin, who seemed for the moment to hold back. "Here we are" was the response, and in a flash, two Badus were racing away in a cloud of dust down the straight, the great cow-hocked brutes flinging their hind shanks in such spread-eagle fashion as to show, unmistakably, that Allah never intended them to gallop.

At length our host dismounted, to lead the Sultan's camel in himself, and we all proceeded to a gaily carpeted space, to sit in the public gaze for the halwa (Turkish delight) and coffee of inescapable custom. Before us was the shaikh's fort, its every window and roof lined with women, black-garmented and un-veiled; behind us was the mosque, ample but of unpretentious mud; and around us were the rude palm dwellings, for the time blotted out by swarming crowds of villagers. These, largely negroid, were a villainous-looking lot, every man and youth armed to the teeth, and the stranger might be pardoned the uncharitable reflection that, with their inflammable minds and religious fanaticism, he would dislike having to depend upon their mercy in a tight corner. Four hulking slaves, sporting new brown *disha dashas* (shirts) for the occasion, waited upon us. It took two to carry each of the enormous clay dishes of sweet-meat slung in a mat between them. Custom requires the thumb and two fingers to enter the gelatine-like mass, sometimes hot from the cook, and the dish passes the round of the assembly. A basin of water follows, and one twiddles one's sticky fingers in it, not without wondering what Number 30 down the line is likely to twiddle his in.

"A scorpion! a scorpion!" shouted someone, as we were about to retire, and my flashlight disclosed something worse, a pale crab-like *Abu shabak* which we forthwith killed.

The creaking of distant well-rigs woke me before light flushed the sky, and I was astir when the first dawn was saluted by a *Mu'edhdhin's* call from the mosque:

"God is Great. God is Great." "There is no God but God." "There is no God but God." "I bear witness that Muhammad is the Prophet of God" — and so forth. We were riding down the palm-fringed wadi towards the sea. "*Allah yajl qadrak,*"[20] said I to Shaikh Hilal, by way of introducing a subject of doubtful propriety, "Have you any Zutis?"

The Shaikh laughed. "No! by God! never a one throughout the whole Yal Sa'ad *dira*" (country), said he.

The Zatut are a curious gipsy caste, the most despised race in Oman. Of obscure origin, they rank lower even than slaves. They may not marry or give in marriage, outside themselves. Prolonged halting on their part is obnoxious to tribesmen, who invite them to pass on; thus they are doomed to wander. They have one distinguishing occupation — circumcising. It is curious that though it is a religious custom that requires the Omani boy of six years and the Omani girl of ten to be circumcised, the performance of the rite is a menial task which no one will undertake save the Zuti man or woman respectively.

"And if they come among us," added the Shaikh, "they may stay for three days and no longer."

"But what of those living permanently in Matrah?" I asked.

"God save you! the people of Matrah can please themselves," said the Shaikh, "but as for us, *W'allahi*! our religion will not permit us even to make concubines of their women, though, I call God to witness, they have some fine upstanding wenches."

The Zatut also are barbers, bloodletters, auctioneers, and workers in iron, though these socially degraded callings they share with Baluchis and Biyasara.

The Biyasara are another curious human stratum of Oman society, also of obscure origin. Literally the word means "half-caste", but it is singularly inappropriate in a region already of much racial corruptness, for the male Baisari may not marry outside the caste, a custom that must have preserved considerable race purity. Arabs, however, will take their daughters freely to wife. The Biyasara are generally fair skinned, and though they may be looked upon askance, their activities are not, like those of the Zatut, limited to menial tasks, for Biyasasra are often met with in positions of trust, and may be men of rank and property.

"Was not Shaikh Rashid al Aziz, the Chief Judge and Qadhi of Qadhis a Baisari?" said Shaikh Ali al Khalili to me, "your colleague in the Council of State, the most learned man in all Oman?"

"Whence are these Biyasara?" I asked.

"God is the knower," he replied. "Prisoners, maybe, of the Arabs in the ancient days, but being Muslims were not made slaves as would have been permissible with non-Muslim prisoners of war."

We resumed our journey along the beach where boats had been drawn up and beflagged for our passing. Four dhows lay in the offing, one other had just got under way, a large two-master, her semi-lateen sails giving from one angle a semblance of butterfly's wings.

Dhiyan we reached at nine a.m. Shaikh Khalid, a venerable old shaikh who was not to be blamed for having lost one of his eyes in combat, though the other's loneliness did not serve to make him prepossessing, made a charming host. But such is the custom of the land, a servant may intrude upon occasion to petition even against our host himself. One is struck also by the other side of the picture — the worrying role of the leaders in such primitive societies. The Arab chief has scarcely any privacy. There are no set workaday hours for him when his men may seek justice as in a Court of Law. He is the victim of his high calling, and whether he walks in the morning, noon or night or is a guest at a meal, so long as he is visible and abroad men have a right to demand his ear.

"*Habab*" opened the kneeling petitioner — the use of which word denoted him to be a slave, a Zuti, or a Baisari.

"Well, what is thy case?"

"The Shaikh owes me blood-money, *Habab*, and when I ask for my dues all I get is blows!"

Now the Quran to the Faithful is not only a New Testament but also a book of Leviticus. It embodies a code of civil law which Muslim theologians have built upon with the traditions and experience of the Ages to evolve a *Shar'a*, or Holy Canon, which governs the jurisprudence of settled Arabia. Crime is theoretically punishable -by the *lex talionis*, an eye for an eye, and a tooth for a tooth, though in practice this is seldom carried out. The Sultan, it is true, has before now cut a thief's hand off, the offending hand, and the judgments of the Wahhabi Sultan Bin Sa'ud, one understands, are habitually governed by the same precept; but for murder, the supreme penalty demanded by this law is in Oman seldom imposed by *Shar'a* authority, though it may well come, indirectly, as a result of a blood vendetta. *Shar'a* usage has come to sanction instead the payment of blood-money, and this varies with localities, sects, and Qadhis. Here a murderer expiates his crime by payment to the relatives of his victim twelve hundred rupees in the case of a Shi'ah; eight hundred, and four hundred, respectively, in the case of Sunni and Ibadhi. Among the marsh Arabs of Mesopotamia, I remember, "blood-money" took the form of a woman; the murderer not infrequently was made to hand his sister over to be wife to the next-of-kin, and a rather miserable time of it she usually had. Compensation for bodily injury, not necessarily of a fatal kind, is also provided for by *Shar'a*, though not every Qadhi is accepted as an assessor, and this in fact was the nature of the present petition.

The slave continued: "I was struck by so and so" (naming a tribesman of Shaikh Khalid), "and so went and petitioned the Qadhi and the Qadhi awarded me ten dollars."

"Was it not paid to thee?"

"No, *Habab*! and when I appealed to the Shaikh for help, he ordered me to be beaten. To the 'Alim I went again, and he awarded me ninety dollars for this second injury, so that my claim is now for a hundred dollars. Here is the decision of the Qadhi"; and the kneeling slave handed up with both hands, as is done to a superior, a greasy scrap of paper, greasy but very precious to him. "*Ya Habab*! but I get not justice but abuse."

"O people of the dar!" (habitat), said the Sultan to the circle of local Arabs who had heard the witnesses, "is this Qadhi Shaikh Saif a true 'Alim (interpreter) of *Shar'a*; and is he held among you as one able to assess *'irsh* i.e. blood-money for bodily injury.

There was a murmur of assent.

"Then be it known that this slave's dues must be honoured. Where is Shaikh Ali? where is Saif bin Ya'rab?" he added, inquiring after two principal members of his suite. "Here," His Highness concluded, as they came up, "take this slave to our host, and inform him of our decision."

And so the slave received his dues, and the Shaikh was reproved and told that such goings on were disturbing to the royal conscience, and that the future had better be innocent of them.

High above the shore of Dhiyan was this garden and thick with shade of mango-trees, but fiendishly hot withal. Midday sleep came fitfully by reason of the constant cawing of grey-backed crows, which usually perch themselves on heads and backs of indifferent camels to indulge their omnivorous appetites, and the buzzing of bees that explored every nook of my *sabla*. Both, I suppose, were attracted by syrup-oozing baskets of dates which had been dumped round about for camel rations, and to these, too, I owed a visit of butterflies, gloriously black, velvety creatures with white ball markings, and familiar small brick-red creatures also. Our horses spent their day whisking their long tails to the complete unconcern of pestilent flies, and our lugubrious camels sat up chewing contentedly, or laid their long necks flat with the ground in utter relaxation. Our accoutred Badawin sat in groups, idly, beneath the incomparable shade of the almond-tree, in contrast to skull-capped, bare-bodied gardeners who moved nimbly about their business.

In the corner of the garden was the simple hut of the country, the typical house of fisherman and gardener alike. It is an admirable construction, made entirely of parts of the date-palm. The corner supports and rafters are split trunks, the walls and roofs of stripped palm fronds. The door may be of woven palm fronds also, and there is a window or two in a lighter variety of the same material, widely latticed. The whole thing is light and mobile, costs only a hundred dollars and provides ideal shelter from the sun without checking the cool winds that one hopes will blow. Three or four rooms go to a house, which, if it have a flat roof, is called an *arish*, and if a slantwise one, *gargin*, or *khaima*. Only a few pale, straw, undecorated mats grace so poor a tenement. These, if the occupant is Arab, will be of stout Omani quality, if Baluchi, a rude *samin*, of his own handicraft, wrought of raw reeds that are brought over in sailing craft from his ancient Makran home.

A veiled woman, in loose red garments, emerged and, carrying her child straddled across her hip, went off to the circle of clay pitchers which marked the *biddi* (water-bailing hole). Here played bright-eyed laughing children, the elder girls weighed down with silver ornaments, and among them, one, the Shaikh's daughter perhaps, about whose neck was an enormous gold pendant disc bearing the decorative Arabic inscription of one of the ninety- nine names of God.

We were once more in the saddle. Before us the long ribbon of golden sand lay between a green wall of eternal palms, and a calm sea of purest amethyst. Suddenly, a cable or two's distance off the shore, a shining black mass half emerged from the sea, lingered for a second, flopped back with a mighty splash, sank for a few minutes, and then reappeared to repeat the performance. A great commotion ensued. Hundreds of gulls hovered, screaming and waiting to sweep down upon the monster's re-emergence, attended as it was by a shoal of sardines that vainly leapt out of the water to escape its devastating jaws. It was a young sperm-whale, which I was to see again on the morrow, for this was its regular haunt.

And so on to Khabura. I was up betimes to snatch a sponge, and wander off to look at the Wall's bathing arrangements. There was the usual Arab trough contrivance, placed shoulder- high, that gives a ridiculous little trickle from a small vent, beneath which one must pirouette on the slippery stone slab, if one is to get any sort of bath at all.

The sun had half risen in an amber sky when I returned to my *sabla* on the beach. There, a hundred fishermen were hauling ashore a communally owned net, the vast extent of which was marked by distant bobbing floats, and as their prison walls closed in, multitudes of tiny sardines, gleaming silver in the sun, leapt madly out of the water for liberty, only to be caught up by clouds of swooping sea-birds that followed screaming. In contrast, a lone fisherman, far out, monotonously cast his circular hand-net from the prow of his tiny coracle.

"Come! I'll introduce you to a new delicacy," said the Sultan by way of morning greetings. A servant had just arrived with a dish of freshly cut sugar-cane. It was served as small sticks and was not unlike celery to look at. The art was to gnaw it, to extract what I found to be its sickly sweetness, and then to discard the residue after the manner of the practised gum-chewer. A merest soupcon, however, sufficed me, as my first stick very soon bore traces of bloodstain from gums unaccustomed to encounter solid wood.

Mediaeval-looking Arab craft, in the roads, flying the flaming red flag of Muscat, made the noonday scene gay and pageant-like, but when night came, the sea showed not a single riding-light. This casualness among Arab mariners — who in other ways are skilful and bold sailormen, voyaging to Malabar, East Africa and the Red Sea with no aids save a rickety compass, the starry heavens and their own developed instincts — extends to dispensing with headlights and sidelights at sea, and is a constant cause of anxiety to our own merchantmen navigating these waters.

"Here is an interesting thing for you," said the Sultan to me, as a young camel was passing by. "She lost her first calf two months ago, and ordinarily lactation would need much coaxing and caressing, but she regards this Badu lad, Khalid, as her calf. Hai! Khalid! bring your camel here!"

Khalid obeyed, and in compliance with another order retired backwards from the camel. She, as though by maternal instinct, looked round, and, bellowing, followed after.

"Let's have some milk," said the Sultan, knowing my partiality, and the camel, which would have taken minutes to respond reluctantly to any other milker, sniffed at Khalid and gave freely.

There are fifty breeds or "houses" of the small and dainty, but vigorous camel of Oman, and the Sultan, contemplating a purchase, had a dozen or so trotted out before us, and thought aloud as he ran an expert eye over them. "Of the daughters of Samha" came first, but she was dismissed with a curt "her head is too flat." A good-looking animal of Banat al Uruq, with perfect points, came next, but the *Khizam'a* light nose-ring rein, carried over the top of her head, bespoke an unruly temper. "Look at this," as a third followed. "Isn't she magnificent in front? But look at her quarters!"

I looked, and confess I could see nothing wrong, as all camels had seemed alike to me in tapering miserably away behind. Pointing to a falling away between small projecting bones, the Sultan said: "There! that is a common failing, but a serious one. Beware of the cow that has not filled out there after calving."

We were disturbed by the chanting of an approaching camel party, and all our Badawin formed up in line to receive it with the customary chant of welcome and the sword dance. It turned out to be Shaikh Ghusn, of the Bani 'Umr, whose presence we were awaiting. The blood feud between Bani 'Umr and Hawasinah, the tribe whose habitat was hereabouts, had broken out afresh, and our party's halt was occasioned by the necessity of the Sultan's bringing the temporary Armistice between them to an end and implementing the Peace.

"There is no difficulty about peace-making here now," His Highness said to me. "Both sides are thoroughly tired after two months of mutual fear and bloodshed. Both are in peaceable mood, but as the night follows the day, within a year or two, perhaps before, the fires of hate will be rekindled by some unthinking hothead of one or other of two tribes."

"This of course is an hereditary feud," I remarked.

"It is one of many hereditary feuds whose origins go back into the dim ages. There is a fundamental division of the tribes of Oman into two parties. It is the old, old story of Ghafari versus Hinawi."[21]

"Look," continued the Sultan, "at the ever-smouldering disputes between Bani Bu Ali and Bani Bu Hassan, Bani Yas and Na'im, Bani Jabir and Bani Ruwaiha, Bani.... Have you not heard that the women of the Bani Jabir weep if their men are killed at the hands of any but Bani Ruwaiha!"

The noise of our own Badawin had grown into full volume as the approaching party halted a few hundred yards up the beach in preparation for their camel display; and in another instant, a lean young Badu, sitting well back over the quarters of his ungainly brute — for in South-East Arabia, as distinct from the Najd and Hijaz practice, every man rides behind the hump — lumbered swiftly past, his rein arm carried well back, his bare head proudly poised.

Evening prayers were over, and we gathered for the usual evening reading of the poets. Mutanabbi was always first in demand, in fact, he seemed to have a niche to himself, other poets ranking much below him. But to-night, Mutanabbi's verse was to be displaced by the ribald chantings of a new arrival, none other than Sha'ar, the Court Jester.

Now Sha'ar was an ordinary enough Baluchi regarded statuesquely, but the moment he opened his triangular mouth or made a grimace, of which his mask was the master of many, few were the onlookers not constrained to mirth. Sha'ar, more-over, was not a particularly refined Court Jester. His vocabulary had affinities to that of Billingsgate, and his imagination had depth and piquancy that gave wing to his words.

After an exchange of good-natured banter, Arabian Shakespeares were banished, and Sha'ar ordered to tune up.

"Give us a ballad," said an enthusiast.

Sha'ar obliged with something which sounded excessively moderate; in fact, the performer's plaintive gesture and appealing voice suggested to me that it might have a Love's Young Dream motif, but as verse succeeded verse and action changed, the suppressed laughter of the audience and the sidelong glances to see how the exalted were reacting, made it appear that a certain camouflaged lewdness was an ingredient.

"Enough of that one!" "Let's have such and such." And I, already yawning, excused myself and retired, before Sha'ar came to the end of his latest repertoire.

The morning for our departure from Khabura had arrived. A thick mist hung like a mantle over the sea, as the white disc of the rising sun set our camp astir. Our camels, now three hundred and more, seemed abnormally lethargic, as if they had shrewdly come to know of the long march before them to Saham; the horses, in contrast, moved briskly about their head-ropes to shake off the effect of the night's heavy dew — hardy cattle these, if their breeding did leave something to be desired, for they are accustomed neither to blanket against the dew of night, nor to shade from the burning noonday sun.

The Peace Conference, the avowals, and the pledge, the clasped hands of the disputants covered by that of the peace-maker during the pronouncement of the solemn formula, and the mutual reparations — all was now over, and, leaping once more into the saddle, our Badawin raised their shouts of "God is Great", and we continued our northward trek.

Qusbiyat as Sultan, a Government fort with its warden and an old gun, the relics of former greatness, boomed out its salute at our passing, and the considerable fishing villages of Dil Yal Abdul Salaam, and Dil Yal Buraik beyond, gave an echoing answer with a fusillade of rifle-fire.

This firing is a most fearsome practice. Every villager is armed, and on such an occasion delights to parade and engage in an orgy of war dancing, swings his rifle wildly around his head, finger to trigger, chants himself into frenzied excitement, and as the object of his regard advances, looses off his rifle, in whatever direction it happens to be pointing at the moment. Accidents happen, and there is never any satisfactory evidence forthcoming to show whether the "accidents" are "accidents". Indeed, no less a person that the father of the present Imam — a sort of local Archbishop of Canterbury at least — had been mortally shot in a Hawasinah or "Welcome" when accompanying the late Sultan

Faisal on such a tour as ours, and my exalted old friend, the one-eyed Shaikh Saif, had in consequence spent two penitential years in Jalali Fort. But "sweet are the uses of adversity", as he remarked to me d propos of this episode, for had he not entered a heathen and a wine-bibber, and emerged with a verbal mastery of the Holy Quran and a technique of prayerful prostration surpassed by none? "In the belly of evil is good," said he, quoting an Arab proverb to clinch the matter.

Saham was in festive mood. A genial Governor of twenty stone, Saiyid Saif, proved a perfect host, and our halt for a few hours was all too short. Yet we had to push on to Majaz to ensure making Sahar early the next morning, before the sun asserted itself.

And here at last was Sahar, that old, historical city, one of seven famous centres of the new religion of the Prophet Muhammad to enjoy, in his day, the privilege of a Friday Mosque. To-day, its great fort, the *Qusba*, standing back from the sea, raised its square battlemented tower above the date-grove, the red flag of the Sultan floating squarely above it, and as we approached, the booming of its guns grew loud to the accompaniment of white puffs of curling smoke that shot out across the beach from the gun-gallery below. Here stood a mass of white-robed welcoming figures, who had turned out to pay homage to their sovereign lord, and these, as we dismounted, surged forward to shake hands, or to bow down and kiss the back of the royal hand or lift it reverently to their lips and eyes. The inevitable *burza* followed, and the ceremony of sweetmeats, coffee, and incense. Petitioners came individually to kneel before the supreme seat of justice, with their little but all-absorbing woes pent up, and jealous lest even the first hour should pass without these being laid bare. On rising, these poor folk retired backwards each to his own place. In doing so, one of them, a Baluchi shopkeeper, had placed one hand over the other before him.

"What is the meaning of this?" said the Sultan.

"Courtesy and honour, our lord," replied the man.

"The forgiveness of God," was the rejoinder. "Knowest thou not between Creator and created?" and turning to me, who, innocent of the man's offence, was looking for enlightenment, the Sultan explained:

"That attitude is the Sunni attitude of prayer. God forbid that men should approach me in the same way."

The first day in Sahar was to be a rest-day. Our bodies needed it after a hundred and twenty miles in the saddle, and it meant two immediate joys — joys of contrast. First — for I had been living throughout on Badu food in Badu fashion from the common dish — a cleanly prepared meal at a table with wholesome looking white plates. Unleavened bread soaked in good butter, a variety of chicken stews, fried eggs, banana fritters, spaghetti, and slices of cream cheese — the latter a local fabrication of purest white from the milk of the goat, a little salt to our taste and pitted like Gruyere — altogether a most delicious repast. And secondly, a cleansing hot bath, a hair-cut, and a refreshing change of kit.

The Sultan had gone out in the late afternoon for a motor ride, taking Sha'ar the Court fool with him. I had unpacked my gun to potter about the grove near by in the hope of a partridge — the Batinah only knows the small *see-see* — and got back just as the Sultan's car drew up. It was nearing sunset.

"Behold! O Wazir," 'said the Sultan breezily, as a slave in the back of the car held up a bundle of clothes; and then, by way of explanation — "I took Sha'ar with me, but on our way back induced him to strip and bathe in a garden *haudh* (tank). Unsuspecting, he was soon at a distance suitable to my plan, so I gathered up his clothes and motored off, and Sha'ar is faced with a walk back of two miles stark naked."

"A good thing it's getting dark," said I, sharing his laughter.

An hour passed, but there was no sign of Sha'ar, and slaves sent to the garden, and to scout the neighbourhood, returned with the same story of his utter disappearance

The night wore on, and the Mutanabbi circle forgathered with accustomed fidelity on the first-floor roof of the inner court-yard. After half an hour, a scorpion appeared from a hole in the wall against which we were sitting, and the pause necessitated by its destruction suggested a change of authors. A volume of collected Arab Proverbs of Oman by Dr. Jayakar was produced and propounded.

"Learn it in the face of the wolf", ran one. I looked up with an air of "I haven't got it yet", and, repeating aloud in Arabic, "Learn it in the face of the wolf", confessed myself no wiser. Thereupon the Sultan said he would tell the story — animal stories are legion amongst Arabs, by whom they are beloved, of course — and I would then understand.

"Once a lion, a wolf and a fox were gathered round a dead ox. Said the lion to the wolf, 'You share it between us.'

" 'Very well,' said the wolf, and began to tear off the haunches and the most prime part of the ox for himself, gave the forelegs and the head to the lion, and said what remained the fox could have! The lion, incensed at his own miserable share, gave the wolf a resounding whack in the face, and gathering up all the shares into a common heap, turned to the fox, and said, 'Now you share it between us.' The fox agreed to this and, proceeding, awarded the haunches and the prime parts to the lion: for himself he took the forelegs and head, and what remained of tripe and inferior inwardness he gave to the wolf.

"The lion was now amazed at the fairness of the distribution, and the remarkable sense of equity thus shown by the fox, and turning to the fox in approving wonderment, said:

" 'Where did you learn this wisdom?'

"Said the fox to the lion: 'In the face of the wolf.' "

No sooner was the story ended than ear-piercing screams from the beach shattered the stillness of the night.

We all jumped up.

"Sha'ar!" said everybody together laughingly; and soon an absolutely naked and infuriated Sha'ar came bounding up the steps, laying about him with a stick wherever a teasing slave appeared, and avowing that he was disgraced, and could never look his fellow-man in the face again — adding a rider that he had barely saved his shame by wading waist-deep along the sea beach for two miles or more. The slaves mocked and the Jester vowed vengeance.

Incongruous was this circus-entry upon the stage so recently occupied by the classic Mutanabbi. And now the Sultan waved the naked Fool into an adjoining room to don his clothes. No clothes were there, of course, and there next issued shivering entreaties and threats in turn, which were a continued source of amusement to us outside, but brought no redress. Suddenly the whole place rocked with mirth as the Jester triumphantly announced that he had committed a nuisance in the royal apartments.

It was two hours before the vituperation of the brazen tongue was stilled, and the last, comparatively innocuous, remark that I heard, as I fell asleep, was addressed to a mocking slave: "Out upon you: misbegotten of an uncircumcised mother!"

A HOLD UP— A CAMEL JOURNEY ACROSS THE OMAN PENINSULA

TRANS-OMAN! This was the pleasant prospect now ahead, and as Khuwara bore me to the caravan of my old friends, the Bani Ka'ab and Muqabil, that now left the beach to plunge into the date-grove at Sahar, H.M.S. *Lupin*, by the courtesy of whose Commander I had voyaged from Muscat, signalled "Good luck", and steamed out to sea.

On the Batinah Coast

The way in front of us was very much the unbeaten track, for Sir Percy Cox, and Samuel Zwemer, alone among white men had accomplished the journey before.

An old shaikh had caught up with me. He held a letter in his hand, a letter not addressed to me, but one he had received from a Trucial chief, and his secretive manner conveyed that it was of no good omen. "Read this," he said, "and he who is silent is wise."

It read:

After salaams, and the mercy of God and his blessings. My brother has just returned and has told me of the kind treatment he has received from you. I hope you may not do any harm to the Muslims, but do what pleases them and God. Probably the Nasara (Nazarenes- Christians) will come to you and ask you to do for them something which will bring bad consequence for you and us. I advise you before anything happens, and request you to keep the honour and dignity of Arabs. Do not be deceived with worldly gains, which ate not lasting. It is said that fire is better than disgrace.... Also inform Shaikh *fulan* in case he is sent for.... Show this to no one. I write to you because I know you are the only man to keep secrets. "Victory is from God and Conquest is near. Salaams."

I handed the letter back to its owner with a forced smile, for I had already sensed that my journey into the interior was going to be anything but "roses all the way". The hospitality of the Arab is, of course, proverbial, but not so the hospitality of Arabia, Unknown, remote Arabia is not only not hospitable: it is positively hostile. Man here is insular: he resents intrusion, suspects it, and fears it. He is easily alarmed, too; and, alas! news of my visit had preceded me. The Badu, faced with a stranger's arrival unheralded, is often well disposed, for is not the *fait accompli* indeed "the will of God"? But for the traveller to depend upon this "bouncing" method of progression is by no means safe. One has to remember that the Badu conceives himself to have a perfect right to put a bullet through one, capture one's camels, and, with the easiest conscience in the world, ascribe that, too, to the will of God.

We had crossed the spacious *batha* of Sallan, and now turned through a park of wild acacias where a single distant gazelle shared a startled view of us with innumerable blue jays and doves that flew from tree to tree near by. The oasis before us, dense with palms, was Auhi, and here we halted for the night close to its little Sunni mosque bordering the plain. Shaikh Ahmad, a gracious but now visibly withering old man, produced an enticing dish of fresh young mangoes — for the season was mid-May. The Badawin themselves disappeared into the gardens with shameless deliberation, and soon the sound of snapping branches and the gentle thud of falling fruit showed that they were treating our eighth commandment with their accustomed levity. Light of hand were these tribesmen of the Bani Ka'ab, wild men from over the hills — their habitat was the northern Dhahirah beyond these blue Hajar to our front. They were men I could ill afford to be contentious with at so early a stage, seeing that I was to trust myself to their hands. Was it not the Bani Ka'ab, indeed, whose precarious attachment to the State I had secured but a year before, when, their activities culminating with raids on the town of Shinas, they had carried off two slaves, sold them on the Pearl Coast, and, as if that was not enough, had returned to paint the place red by setting fire to the garden fences of those they wished further to intimidate! Hardy liegemen these, too recent converts to change their nature; and looking around their brazen faces I was obliged to smile and wonder what new devilry was stirring their brave hearts.

I twitted old 'Ubaid, a chief amongst them, over their questionable ethics.

"What, then, is a man to do. Sahib, when God sends drought into his country, and he has nothing to set before his guest?" he said.

Here, indeed, was a conundrum. But too recent was it for me to forget the Badus' descents by night upon the Batinah in quest of food, of cattle, yes, and of young children of manumitted slaves: too recent the terror I had seen in the faces of a simple, unoffending, settled folk. But the semi-barbarous must be impatient when hunger calls and rifles are at hand.

Still, like pirates who unflinchingly walked the plank, man in this condition of life cheerfully faces penalties. Within living memory one of the more recalcitrant of the Bani Ka'ab sub-shaikhs planned a little too bold *coup*, and fell into State hands at Sahar. There, there sat in the scat of the Mighty a Wali of slave origin. Now this Wali thought it an excellent thing to make an example of his prisoner; he had, therefore, one side of the shaikh's hairy face shaved completely, one eyebrow, one moustachio, and, shame of shame! half the beard. Two buck slaves were then produced to assault the shaikhly victim in public, who was forthwith put upon an ass, led through the streets, and so set free. He fled back to an incensed tribe. Their honour had departed. Rifles were thrown into the air in mad consternation, and all kinds of vengeance vowed. But the Wali was a man who had faced far worse than this, and Bani Ka'ab enemies, many and powerful, saw in him a great ruler come upon the earth. Therefore Bani Ka'ab's fury spent itself vainly. A month's truce ensued. But the action rankled in the tribal heart until the passing of that Wali's spirit, which Allah had predestined for the next year.

Across the plain were the blue, eternal Hajar, and as if to mark where they were cleft by a deep green gorge that would give access to our passing, the Haura Burgha, a pink, conical peak, stood, a perfect sentinel, amid low sloping foothills. On this hot, vast plain lived the fox, the gazelle, and the wild ass, amid mirages that played tricks with the imagination.

Date Palm Frond home (Barasti)

Here, preparatory to the crossing, we rested on a little eminence beside the ruin of an old mosque. Now the *Mu'edhdhin's credo* was followed by the bowing ranks of the Faithful and their low reverent prayers. The crossed hands and the loud *amins* showed the worshippers to be. orthodox Sunnis, for Ibadhism has been left behind to the south, nor does it again flourish in these provinces of Shamailiyah and Dhahirah. With the last *amins* of the worshippers, the cawing of innumerable grey-backed crows, the rippling foliage of mango-trees, and the pleasant babble of water of the *falaj* could be clearly heard. Occasional camels, their front legs hobbled below the knee so that they might not stray, grazed contentedly on the tufted thorn; and a young shepherdess, with a water-skin that supplied her wants all day, followed her black flock that skipped over the *falaj* channel. It was a delightfully pastoral scene.

Who would imagine, then, that here was a battlefield of all the ages? Yet it had known the tramp of Persian armies, and flashed with the glint of their spears and bows and arrows; it had resounded half a millennium later to the triumphant shouts of the fanatical devotees of the New Faith; and again, only a hundred years ago, to Wahhabi hordes come to spread their light at the point of the lance.

"Falaj as Suq," my companions announced, as we halted after an hour and a half's ride at some black unimposing surface remains of an old habitation. Near by, the dark bleak hills were to attract my attention. "What is this?" I asked, pointing to a series of small stone mounds that lined the ridge on our left hand.

"Oh! those are 'Bait al Jalil'," they replied (houses of the Days of Ignorance, i.e. the period that preceded Islam).

We dismounted to climb and investigate. The prospect from the top of the ridge showed the surrounding hillsides to swarm with these archaeological remains. The *bait al jahil* consisted of a small circular mound built up of loose, rounded lava stones, big enough to need no binding. About four feet high, it measured eight to ten or even twelve feet in diameter, and was sometimes half roofed over. The wall thickness of about two feet, wider in one axis, left an interior hollow narrow cell scarcely capable of accommodating more than one man lying prone.

"Houses of the Days of Ignorance!" I pondered. What manner of Lilliputians, then, were their occupants! No; these were no houses. Yet they must come down from some dim antiquity, else tradition would have preserved a more plausible explanation. Nor, apparently, was their function military, for they commanded no particular field of view, they often faced inward as well as outward of the same ridge, and they were so clustered together as sometimes to screen each other. The least improbable view I could form was that they may have had some religious, after- death significance: they may have been ancient prototypes of Towers of Silence. Yet such a theory was perhaps difficult to reconcile with their vast numbers, and I noted that their long interior axis had no common orientation.[22]

Bait Jahil

I had left the camel by an ancient water *falaj* system, and, as usual, a stone dropped into one of its black manholes showed it to be dry.

"Well, Salim, who built these old water *falaj*?" I said, turning to a fat old shaikh of the Muqabil. Salim was by no means a Buddha in figure, yet I must remark his corpulence if only to draw attention by contrast to the universal and invariable leanness of his Badu companions.

"The builder?" said Salim unhesitatingly, "why Sulaiman bin Da'ud" (i.e. Solomon, Son of David).

"But surely King Solomon did not live in these parts; and look at the work involved. It is the work of centuries."

Bait Jahil

"Allah ya'sallamak" (God save you), said Salim as if to pity my unbelief. "The Prophet Solomon came here on a carpet that was borne on the wings of the wind."

"Then what manner of men were they who laboured at these waterways — Arabs, Persians, or who?"

"God save you," returned Salim, "not men like you and me at all, but Afarit; these also, I bear witness, of God's creatures."

"And are these Afarit about nowadays, Salim, and have you seen them?"

"Of course they exist. Sahib, but it isn't all men who have eyes to see them. They live in the earth and in the air, and it is only *Mutawwas* (religious leaders) who have power over them, but the Prophet Solomon, Peace be upon him, he was their master."

These *falaj* about which I inquired are subterranean water passages of ancient construction. Prodigious labour must have gone to their tunnelling, which sometimes carries on for a matter of fifteen miles. The springs of water at their source in the mountains may be as much as thirty fathoms below the surface, and manholes at frequent intervals along their course grow less and less deep as the gentle descent of the *falaj* beneath brings it gradually to the surface in the plain, where the oasis springs up. Of such was Auhi: of such had been Falaj as Suq. The whole plain is hereabouts honeycombed with *falaj* — there are probably a hundred of them, though for the most part they have been dry these long centuries. The name Da'udiyat, i.e. David, popularly applied to a region of them would appear to lend colour to an ancient tradition of the tribe of Israel in Northern Oman.

Auhi Oasis

We had arrived at Haura Husn, a steep island hill, commanding the debouching valley below and three miles short of the fairy peak of Haura Burgha, and I halted to climb to examine the ruins that crowned it — the fallen debris of an ancient fort. A low-pointed arch still stood, and the traces of many circular towers, a square tank — presumably a water reservoir — hewn from the solid rock, and an uncemented straggling wall edged the perimeter. Nothing more. Not a solitary dressed and ornamented stone remained to bear witness to the artistry or the skill of the builder. If this was the capital of the Persian Viceroys in the centuries before Islam

— as has been suggested by Colonel Miles, on the strength of local tradition — Jamsetjerd was as nothing beside those noble memorials left by the Persians of the same centuries which I remember at Ukhaidhir, in the desert to the west of Najaf in the Middle Euphrates, and at Umm Shita, in Moab across the Jordan.

Haura Husn

Here, to Jamsetjerd, had come Amr bin Al'As, the Prophet's personal messenger, famous in Arab history, to demand the allegiance of Oman to Islam: and there is a tamarind-tree beside the fort at Sahar under which, according to legend, rested the famous general-to-be, he who was destined to bear the flaming sword of the new religion through Syria and Egypt, and to plant the flag of a Puritanical Islam over the corpse of a degenerate seventh-century Christianity.

And here the story is told of how the young ambassador encountered an old Jew at the top of a mountain, for local history places the Sons of Israel along these western slopes of the Hajar for the space of a two days' march east of Haura Burgha. The Jew was a learned and travelled man, who had visited the Yemen and was acquainted with Mecca.

And he inquired, "How is 'As bin Waiyil?" not being as yet aware that this was the young stranger's own father; "and how fares it with Walid bin Mughira?" — asking after the father of him who in time was to become the "Sword of God". "And you say that the man Muhammad of Bani Hashim of the Quraish is more than these? Then verily and indeed a great son has come forth from the Arabs."

But Amr was not to be deflected by soft words. He had his stern, divinely ordained mission to carry out, and turning to the old Jew he said; "Now must you elect to embrace the new religion or to pay me that which is due from the Unbelievers. Else is there no recourse but to the sword."

The Jew, being steadfast, said he could not forsake the religion of his fathers, but he could pay *Jiziya*. He did so, wherefore his sons and his sons' sons continued to live in the land, as the Jewish cemetery in Sahar still testifies. Only when the land became very poor and hungry did they leave it. It is within living memory that the last remnant of them turned their faces towards the flesh-pots of Bahrain and Baghdad.

The flat gravelly *sih* (plain) was left behind as we reached the steep seaward slopes of the mountains, and now across twenty miles of serried heights, rising to 3,000 feet and more, our camels, bred in these stony wastes, were to carry us onwards and upwards. Barriers to trade and communication are these complex folds of the Hajar range, except where a cismontane wadi threads its tortuous way down to the plain. Only seven or eight such gorges exist in the great length of the Hajar, [23] and Wadi Jizzi, by no means the least of these, here opened before us and signalled the night's halt.

A Watch Tower in the Wadi Jizzi

It was midnight. The camp-fires, surrounded by sprawling bodies of sleeping Badus, flickered out. Suddenly the stillness was disturbed by a faint voice from the direction of the wadi. There came to the ears a chant of much charm — not the chant of galloping order of the day's march, which is colourless because of its limitations within the narrow compass of a minor fifth. There was *nuance* in this midnight note. A long tremolo wail, lasting, it seemed, some minutes, carried the first syllable of some brave line, followed by a torrent of words each with a note of fractional interval descending the scale.

It was the song of the Caravan. The object of this *Wanna*, as it is called, is to reassure the surrounding countryside that here is no enemy raider on the prowl, and still more, perhaps, to fortify the caravaner himself at this dark hour, when, God save you, *jinns* and *afarit* are abroad.

We pressed on in the morning up the wadi, but near Millaiyinah I loitered behind to investigate an archaeological find, an early example of the application of the principle that water finds its own level. For here, to be sure, when the ancients should have been building elaborate bridged aqueducts — the last Persian dynasty was expelled in the early eighth century — was a system where water, flowing along the bank twenty-five feet above, was passed by way of a conduit down through a masonry pillar, thence under the bed of the wadi, Shahabat al Hisn, and so up a corresponding pillar on the other side, to be carried on at a similar height on the far bank.

I caught up with the column at Burj as Shukhairi, the little fort in the bed of the wadi that marks the frontier of the Muscat State. Beyond it I should be an interloper; but even here as I dismounted I was to hear murmurings that the welcoming fusillade was of doubtful character, that bullets had pinged so close above the heads of some of our party that they had dismounted in the belief that discretion was the better part of valour. Here was the warden of shady character — one destined for those other shades before the year was out — who had just spent two months' imprisonment in Jalali fort for accepting bribes to countenance the passing of raided slaves and camels from the Batinah.

"Impossible to go on, your honour," he said; "the wadi ahead is hostile" — and in token thereof he flourished a letter from the shaikh of the Shuwamis tribe that straddled the head of the valley. Shaikh Hamdan forbade further progress without his prior consent; but he came in at my next halt, in response to a messenger, and after a heart-to-heart conversation I found him amenable enough. But his amenability was qualified by a rankling bitterness. And no wonder. In days past his tribe had offended authority, and he and his father had fallen into official hands. Hamdan escaped, but no one saw his father again, for he, poor wretch, had been pushed down a well: and dead men tell no tales.

We forged on next day, and reached the narrow, winding Wadi Shumash, than which Nature could not have designed better ambush. Suddenly the column was brought to a stand-still. There were excited shouts to the front, for Shaikh Hamdan's men, who were dismounted and had run at our side, suddenly darted ahead, scaled the top of a small rise, loaded their rifles, and covered us. Some two or three minutes of confusion followed, and their shaikh and I then went forward to ascertain the trouble and to reassure them. The shaikh explained to me afterwards that the object of their hostility was a certain Arab element of my escort, but I thought I detected horseplay intended to weaken my resolution to push on; in consequence our arrival at Hail was delayed until well past sundown.

There is, properly speaking, no single river in the whole of the Arabian Peninsula, but here is near approach to one. In the upper reaches of the mountain gorge is a spring of perennial running water, whence derives a shallow crystal stream, some twenty feet broad, that meanders — except when it is a mighty torrent in spate following rains in the winter season — from side to side over the rough pebbly bed that stretches a hundred yards or so across the wadi. On either side rise considerable hills, through which an affluent issues to join the main stream.

Here and there massive fallen boulders lie strewn in the wadi bed, and against them, in patches of sand or shingle — the detritus brought down by the floods — profuse oleanders of a pale hue bloom, together with the inevitable slate-grey *ashkar*, a shrub poisonous to man, but of which the little purple star-flower, when met with in the plains, is popular with the shimmering black sugar-bird and the gazelle.

Here also is met the mountain *falaj*, of a different order from the tunnelled system of the plain. It is carried out of the main bed in a surface conduit of gentle descent along the side of the wadi bank; in time it gradually gains height over the wadi bed as this latter falls more steeply, and so at intervals, where the height gained allows gravitational irrigation and the light soil is sufficient, date-groves and villages spring up on the hill slopes. Stepped terraces, reminiscent of Palestine, are made pleasant by the sound of running water, and by the colour and fragrance of vegetation beneath the palm shade — yellow corn, millet and maize, green lentils, red chillies, sesame, cotton and tobacco. The little brooks are moss-embanked and fragrant with maiden-hair and wild flowers; and in the night, pomegranates, mangoes, and lime-trees shed a blended scent, and bullfrogs and crickets keep the air a-humming.

Hail, one of these hill villages, was greatly excited by our coming. Its shaikhs sought an interview at once, but it was late and I was too tired. On the morrow there was a hurried conference between them and the shaikhs of my escort, for Hail had received instructions from the Na'im shaikh of Baraimi to impede us. (I had, however, already sent emissaries to Baraimi overnight.) The local villagers, friendly enough at heart but having to yield to *force majeure*, would have been justified in staying their hand against the answer to my messengers.

But I had no intention of halting, and with the morrow's dawn pushed on out of the main valley into the tributary Wadi Ubailah, and thence reached Najd, the Pass on the Divide. Here I was obliged to camp, for my own Arabs declined to proceed into the habitat of the Na'im unless or until the latter sent a satisfactory invitation. And now, a little impatient, I and a young Badu rode on a mile or two and climbed a small hill, whence we saw afar off the city of desire low in the shimmering red sand beside a hog-backed mountain — Jabal Hafit.

"What are these diggings?" I asked, as we rode past some ancient excavations in the red rock.

"*Allahu A'lam!*" (God is more knowing) returned the Badu.

"Men say it is where the heathen dug for minerals in the Days of Ignorance.

Possibly an old copper-mine, I reflected, for the Hajar is credited with such workings a few days' march south, and perhaps — who can tell? — this ancient land, known as Mazun by its Persian masters, was in yet earlier times the land of Magan whence the Sumerians obtained their copper — the copper of those vases and implements four thousand years old and more, that grace the Museums of Europe and the New World. [24]

My Baraimi emissaries now came galloping up. From their agitated expressions I knew that all was not well. They dismounted and handed me a letter signed by the youthful shaikh.

It ran:

Salaams upon you, and the mercy of God and his blessings. Your letter brought by the hands of Shaikhs Ali and Hamdan is understood. The Wali (Abu Sandan) was not present in the place... but on his return he saw it and does not agree to it.... You suddenly wrote to us about this proposal. We did not know of it. These places are reckoned to be in the hands of God and our hands. This is a disturbance from you. These places are within the territory of Ibn Sa'ud. It is better and safe for you to return. We fear the opening of the hole of trouble. He who knows things is not to be made knowing. He who gave you this privilege is not frank with you. These places belong to Al Hamuda and after them they belong to Ibn Sa'ud. This is all that has to be said. Salaams. Dated 13th Dhu'l Qa'ada.

A Falaj in the hills behind Sahar

But before I had come to the end of the letter, my camp was in a ferment. The returned escort from Baraimi had lost no time in imparting to their fellow Badawin an alarmist version of their hostile reception, of the arrival of a mission from Wahhabi Najd, and of a war-charged atmosphere. They saw blood. A new situation in the Dhahirah had indeed supervened. The Dhahirah rang with news of the visit of a tax-collector from Ibn Jaluwi, Bin Sa'ud's Viceroy in the Hasa, and many of the Dhahirah tribes were paying tribute — a course which, rumour had it, they were obliged to take from motives of expediency, and which they had taken once before in the last ten years.

The principle of "No Taxation without Representation", the notion that if you pay rates you ought to get Police and Drains for it — these are Western conceptions. In the primitive societies of the Peninsula, a man does not have to worry his head about what positive benefits he will receive in lieu of his payments. There are none. Payment is ordained by religious law: the Ruler has a Divine Right to a tenth of all the increase — zakat or tithe. It is the application of "Render unto Caesar the things that are Caesar's". Nor do any hair-splitting polemics decide who Caesar is. This is done by Caesar himself. In a fatalistically and realistically minded society, the test is whether the exactor has power to exact or something worse. If so, then the Will of God has declared itself. In the tribal consciousness another's capacity to bring pressure through neighbouring tribes, by the simple device of ensuring or denying the fruits of raiding, is a strong determinant in the payment of zakat and of much other action. It is an insurance premium, and by no means signifies a voluntary or lasting acknowledgment of sovereignty, though lip service may be paid at the moment. And so, when the phantom had passed, and a year later I was to meet the authors of the solemn letter, there was a good deal of merriment displayed.

But to revert. I read the letter a second time. The unhappy truth was dawning. The Dhahirah tribes were in no mood to let me through, and my own Bani Ka'ab escort were equivocating, for, vis à vis the tax-collector, they occupied the invidious position of a minority of one; and who could measure the dark penalties of default?

And now the immediate upshot, as, thwarted, I stood on that sunbaked pass, was that their shaikh, in whom all my hopes rested, begged me to abandon the journey and to return to Sahar, while his excited tribesmen loaded their rifles and swarmed up the hills to picket the heights against the Na'im's coming after us. Of this latter eventuality I had no fears, though it was with a sad heart that I heard of the Wali, Abu Sandan, the sponsor of the youthful Na'im shaikh and the virtual shaikh himself — incidentally a slave — that he had picketed the wells at Khurus against my oncoming.

The way through Baraimi, at the very threshold of which I had arrived, now seemed blocked; but I drew comfort from the reflection that the Dhahirah after all is a spacious province and Bani Ka'ab country contiguous with the Na'im. But then, alas even the Bani Ka'ab in the present temper had closed their doors, despite their partial commitment in having escorted us thus far, and despite also the friendly loyalty of the shaikh himself to me.

Yet a friendly disposed shaikh is not always sufficient in Arabia, though it may well be half the battle. His is no blind and weak follower who has been used to saying *Ai wallah*, and running off to do the bidding of an Ottoman official. Here is an indomitable, individualistic tribal spirit, and the shaikhly leader must have the psychological understanding of a modern democratic political leader, who, I imagine, is likely best to maintain himself by making the general consensus of opinion his own.

I had not, however, come so far as this to turn back now. Shuwamis territory of old Shaikh Hamdan lay on our flank: so why not, I thought, side-step there? But now Hamdan's timorous soul had become infected with this notion of our evil star, and he kept us out of his village for one night. Not until the following morning was it that we crawled dispiritedly into Kitnah, and then like half-drowned rats.

Kitnah! Here was a typical mountain village — another Hail.

The pebbly wadi-bed, the date-palms that rose above it on the rising banks, the gurgling streams and the terraced vegetation, the rude wicker huts of the villagers, the shaikh's plastered fort, and the mosque rising hidden behind — all these were familiar. Here veiled women, unlike their sisters in the Batinah, were not disinclined to talk to one, and the children, unfrightened, came prying into one's tent. Only the little girls were shy — delightfully attractive creatures (at a distance) with their olive skins, big almond-shaped eyes, and mop of black, bushy hair, hair that was bobbed but for a row of tiny plaits at the back of the head.

Working under their shady palms, the men are generally stripped to the buff, showing their scarred bodies, scarred with hot irons — the universal medicine, for in Arabia, remote from towns, there are no doctors and knowledge vests in aged experience. The surgeon's knife is, as might be expected, unknown, but they possess an uncanny knowledge of the setting of bones. The juice of a few herbs and cauterization are the means for coping with most fleshly ills — especially cauterization. Few men here are unable to show a red-hot iron mark over the spleen, for mosquitoes are legion and malaria is rife, and another over the base of the skull at the back of the head — this they avow an infallible remedy for Oriental boils. Children of nature are these people, whose wants are few and primitive. Reserved at first, they suddenly unbend, and would know of the Great World outside, but their own immediate wants transcend all other considerations, and these may be summed up in two words, ammunition and aphrodisiacs. Shameless beggars are they, too, for anything that they see.

I observed the usual morning and evening *burza* when escort shaikhs, their chief men, and a few of the villagers assembled round my tent for *fuwala* and coffee, an exchange of greetings an< the local news. With the Badu the passing of the coffee-cup is supremely important; the ridiculous trickle, enormously strong though it be, innocent of milk and sugar and barely covering the bottom of the small characteristic cup, seems almost a solemn rite. Should a hungry Badu arrive, let him be greeted, a few dates passed to him and the coffee-cup, and he will regard his treatment as honourable. Kill the fatted calf instead, and give him rice, the richest food in his imagination, and at the same time withhold the coffee-cup, and he will regard it as an affront. Offence too, by those unwitting of the code, is given by keeping a shaikh waiting in the public view. For though one may jump to the conclusion that he is begging (and probably one is not far wrong), it is sometimes tremendously important for him in the eyes of his tribe to stand well with Government, and in any case he may be trusted to circulate the story of his honoured reception.

Days passed, and Kitnah came to get on one's nerves. It was not the temperature of 115° in the shade, nor that one had more camels that ate their heads off than one could wish: it was the uncertainty of the situation, the difficulty of gauging the possibility of a forward move.

A little more fretful than usual I rose liverish one morning, this Baraimi "hold-up" heavy on my heart, and turned on my escort and upbraided them quite unjustifiably for having a finger in the pie.

An old Muqbali Arab in the corner looked up amused, and said with some felicity, "Flesh to the spell-caster; but curses upon the *mutaituwa*" (the local song thrush) — which Omani proverb requires a little elucidation. It is based on a widespread local belief in magic. Certain people, especially old couples, are suspected of having the power of changing themselves into animals and of being able to spirit one away. Possessors of the power are supposed to forgather in some appointed place to perform human sacrifice and feast on their victims, and it is the innocent *mutaituwa* bird which sings at this time, and thus brings unjust curses upon its own innocent head.

The old Arab, with the love of his race for turning the tables by some apt quotation, was typical of his kind. This Badu of the Hajar is easily identified by his *qushura*, dangling at his belt over his dagger — a flimsy, light-coloured strip of hide he wears for sandals to cope with the sharp-edged rocks.

"Well, Hamud, who here casts spells?" I asked.

Hamud laughed. "You will find no dark magic in this valley, *Al hamdu lillah* " (God be praised).

Someone had shouted for water, and as the bowl went round, each man, except the first, deliberately spilt a little on the ground before drinking. "Some survival of a cult of libation", I thought, but no one sitting round knew of any significance beyond custom. Yet superstition is rife. Men sometimes attribute their sickness to a visit to some jinn-haunted place, whereupon, if they would mend, an old lady or a virgin must go to the spot and place some offering there — a chicken, perhaps, or flour, an egg and a little fire often sprinkled with incense.

One grew philosophical. Patience! That is the essential quality for Arabian travel, and I took heart from the reflection that nearly thirty years before, in this very country of Oman, Sir Percy Cox had, metaphorically, sat on a man's doorstep for six weeks before obtaining entry. Kitnah had known me but for a fortnight. It sufficed: the fickle tribal mind had come to see the stars thus set in their courses, for on the morrow was to loom once more the thrilling prospect of the onward march.

Mahadha Fort

Trans-Oman. We were in the saddle again and moving north to Mahadha, the seat of the Bani Ka'ab. At first to the north-west lay the Divide. Beyond it the secondary ridges had no longer the steep and precipitous face which the sea-facing slope of the Hajar presents to the Batinah. Their ruggedness and dark colour suggest immemorial weathering, and as we rode past them at night they threw against a moonlit sky fantastic outlines.

The water-shed was now westward, the ultramontane wadis — except for the Wadi Samaini, which ultimately reaches the sea at Al Ajman —

were merely shallow, dry watercourses which extinguish themselves in the sandy desert to the south-west.

Here are broad-surfaced depressions, wrinkled by numerous shallow watercourses, and studded with acacia *samr*, their scraggy branches stretched outwards fanwise — reminiscent of a conventional Japanese decoration — as if resolved to collect the utmost dew for being cheated by a rainless climate. Here is a popular breeding-place of camels; here, too, roam many wild beasts, the untamable ass, an occasional shorthorned ibex — though he prefers the mountains to the south — and the panther, that yearly takes his toll of camels. The panther's guile is interesting. He climbs the jungle trees and lies in wait upon their upper branches for the half-light of dawn, when the camel, with her long neck upstretched to the most succulent fodder at the top, becomes an easy victim. Suddenly he springs at her head, brings her heavily down, and makes short work of her. We killed a three-foot snake one night in camp, a venomous creature of a kind with which the mountains teem. Fox and hedgehog are eaten by these Badus, but I saw no jackal here — nor, for that matter, have I ever seen one anywhere else in South-east Arabia.

Now before us, amidst mountainous country, lay the oasis of Mahadha, with its fort on the fringe of the palm-grove fronted by a bare plain. The rolling of drums and the sword-dance made a pleasant reception, and for the four days of our sojourn the drumming never seemed to cease, a contrast to the practice of Oman Proper, and even to that of some of the Batinah towns, where Walis of an ascetic order impose the Ibadhi proscription of music save for purposes of war and festivals.

The sword-dance was to be brought to a close with the *azwa* or battle chant. All the villagers, armed to the teeth, with rifles, swords, daggers, and flags, range themselves into two facing lines. Then to the rhythmical roll of the drums one line advances, the other retiring to conform, blades are brandished, and loaded rifles thrown in the air, caught again, and fired. After a dozen paces or so in one direction, the reverse movement takes place, the bodies swinging with each forward step and each foot alternately being made to do an extra step, giving it a curious war-dance measure. A few minutes of this ensue to the accompaniment of the village women ululating from their quarters, and then the end files suddenly turn inwards to make a circle. Into the centre of the circle steps an old and doughty warrior and begins to chant the *azwa* — in his hand his own drawn sword, which with a flick of the wrist he makes flash in the tropical sun. Moving round the inside of the now halted but gently swaying circle with the same tripping step and looking into each man's eyes as he passes, he shouts the praises of war and the glories of the tribe. Those assembled respond militantly. Whilst this was in progress the shaikh [25] took me by the arm and led me to my appointed chamber in the fort.

Shaikh Salim had begun to smoke his small clay pipe, or, rather, to take a long inhaling whiff at it, and then lay it aside, as is the manner of Arabia. I was taken a little aback by this, as I had thought him a Wahhabi. In reality, however, only the Na'im tribe of the Dhahirah and certain elements of the people of Sharjah are in these parts nominally co-religionists of the Najdis, and even then their Azarka in practice at all events, allows them to smoke. The rest of the Dhahirah Badawin except the Ibadhi Daru are orthodox Sunnis.

"But surely no tobacco is grown in your lands. Shaikh Salim?" I asked.

"No," said he, "it is a curious relic of the veto on tobacco when the Wahhabi came and laid waste the country. Inherited fear is a deterrent still." And Jau, as the northern half of the Dhahirah is called, has lived under an intermittent menace for a hundred and twenty years and more, though since the local tribes have come to be armed with rifles no Najdian invasion has been attempted, but instead only an occasional visit of late years by the tentative tax-collector. "The People of the West," said the shaikh (Najdis are invariably thus referred to in Oman), "first came four generations ago, the desert port of the Badawin succumbed to seven hundred of their horsemen and this brought the Bani Yas (Abu Dhabi and Dubai) and Na'im (Baraimi) promptly to their knees. Ten years later, the great Sultan, Sa'id bin Sultan of Muscat, had capitulated to them and Oman was paying 45,000 dollars in yearly tribute. But the Egyptian invasion of Najd from the Red Sea under Muhammad Ali brought respite for forty years. Then back they came and established themselves in Sharjah. That was seventy years ago. There are men among us who still remember it. This very fort was in their hands, and they took my grandfather away in chains to Najd, where he embraced their strict tenets and became a holy man. Eventually they let him come back, but within a year he had joined the victorious rebels who finally freed this province of their men. Never since then have we of the Bani Ka'ab acknowledged their overlordship."

"Oh! the brave music of a distant drum!" I mused.

"To-morrow, *Insha'allah* (God willing), Ali will climb with you to the top of Jabal Mahadha," said Shaikh Salim, by way of changing the subject.

Ali was a fine upstanding Daramqi Badu with long, braided locks that fell about his shoulders, but he had misbehaved, it seems, in that he had murdered his cousin during the holy month of Ramadhan, and was in consequence living it down in the bosom of another tribe.

Jabal Mahadha stands above the village a good 1,700 feet, and it took us nearly two hours to climb it the following hot morning, but we were well rewarded by the view from its summit, which is 3,400 feet above sea-level. In spite of a mist, the white forts of Baraimi and Jimi flashed in the sun, and Ali in answer to my queries pointed out beside them the district of Uqdat. [26] To the north-west lay a considerable plain, and to the west golden sands stretched away to the skyline.

We descended. It was the day decided upon for our departure. Our course lay across these golden sands which from a height of 1,500 feet slope imperceptibly away to sea-level at the Trucial Coast. Sixty miles broad here, this Ar Rami is a spur of that inhospitable Rub' al Khali that lies provokingly unexplored south- wards almost to the verge of the Indian Ocean. [27] Our journey lay past Jabal Faijah. Red, sandy undulations thirty feet high were relieved by stunted shrubs, and in depressions many ghaf acacias grew, thickly trunked, and twisted with age. I was disappointed to hear no singing sands. [28]

Here only the Bani Qitab, of braided lock, wilder than their sedentary brethren of the early part of the journey, and distinguishable by the stockingette they affect against the great heat of the sands, eke out a precarious existence with their camels and flocks, unless, indeed, be counted the little sand- lizards which run off to disappear into the loose sand dune on one's approach, weaving elaborate and beautiful traceries in the sand as they go. A hare with its ears well laid back leapt off at our feet, and was bowled over clean — a great shot — by a Badu using a dum-dum bullet, the vicious variety quite generally in use, to judge from the cartridge-belts of my own escort. Heavy dews made the June night unpleasant, and water drawn from Jifr al Halais at a depth of 20 fathoms was as bitter as gall.

Bani Qatar women and children

It is a poor land. I had recently been joined by a Shaikh of the Awamir, who said he would not change his hungry and thirsty existence plus his liberty for all the fleshpots of a settled life and its bondage. But the borderland of starvation makes man barbarous, and he told me an illuminating story.

A Badu saw a wayside Arab carrying a small bundle over his shoulder. And the Badu was hungry unto death. Imagining the bundle to contain money or some other valuable, the Badu levelled his rifle and shot the man dead. Rushing up to open the bundle he found not treasure at all but only date-stones, the poor provender intended for the dead man's cow. He was overcome with grief, not, indeed, for having shed innocent blood, but from the remorse of having wasted a perfectly good round of ammunition.

The lanky towers of Sharjah edging the low skyline now in sight looked like lighthouses on the rim of the sea. As we approached the town in the early morning, a cavalcade rode out to meet us, and the shaikh's tower boomed a welcome. We arrived to find a feud had been raging. An ex-Shaikh of Sharjah had abortively attacked his successor in office. The latter had celebrated his success by drawing red-hot needles across the eyes of six hapless prisoners, an operation which killed one and blinded the rest for life. This had happened only six days before. [29]

I dismounted on Sharjah beach in the fierce heat of a June forenoon. The Peninsula was crossed, and Sahar lay twenty- two days behind me.

One of H.M. ships, spick and span as she might have been at a Spithead Review, lay off the shore. In ten minutes I had felt, learned, and tasted the luxury of electric fans, the latest Test Match news, and the amenities of the ward-room.

ON TREK WITH THE SULTAN THROUGH THE SHAMAILIYAH

Sahar Fort

SAHAR IS POLITICALLY the second town of the Sultanate. This ancient seaport, the wealth and importance of which were acclaimed by early Arab geographers before Muscat was as yet heard of, was the mart of those early Persian masters of the land, Zoroastrians, to whom came the ultimatum in the vanguard of the spirit-moved Arab armies that were to expel them. "Give up your heresies and accept Allah and his Prophet." Sahar, where every Pretender to the Throne has since established himself, has, when the land has been divided in its allegiance, been a capital itself, and privy to every Machiavellian crime which ambitions to a Throne inspire.

Sahar Fort

Beneath the great battlemented tower is a vault that holds the murdered remains of Saiyid Thuwaini, the Sultan of Palgrave's day. In a chamber upstairs, while the Ruler slept, it was his own son Salim, kneeling but a few yards away, who had levelled the fateful matchlock at the old man's heart; nor was the public conscience such that the murderer could not thereupon succeed to the Throne and rule for two years till a Pretender arose.

But to-day Sahar is but a shadow of its former self. Gone are even the sunset glories which Palgrave saw, maybe through rose-coloured spectacles, sixty years ago. This Sultanate Port of the Dhahirah has ceded much of its commerce to Dubai, the young and flourishing pearl centre, and has fallen upon lean years indeed.

In the cool of the late afternoon I accompanied the Sultan along the beach beyond the tottering north-east buttress of the old town wall, for the usual *burza* ceremony.

"Of your bounty upon us, our Lord." This was the invariable formula as a long procession of Badus rose from the circle, one after the other, came and knelt, uttered the formula, and, retiring backwards for a few paces, betook themselves to their places. Such is custom. To a European eye it seems to be a shameless cadging for money, *rukhsa*, the Badus name it, when leaving after enjoying hospitality for themselves and their camels, and the recipients, who in any other but a primitive form of society, would scarcely conceive of their services having merited the slightest recognition, do not scruple to grumble publicly that the reward is small and their expenses are many. For the rest, the *burza*, except for a legitimate petitioner or two and the coffee-cup, drags on in gloomy silence.

We wandered back, around the edge of the moat that flanks the old city walls, and turned in at the back of Sahar across an earthen ramp — a, portcullis in olden time — through a gateway once pretentious, where a rude column or two still stands, but otherwise a heap of ugly brick masonry. A small, square, shallow burnt-brick is a feature of Sahar architecture: it is found nowhere else in the Batinah, nor is it any more made here, its manufacture being popularly ascribed to Jews.

Camels on a Batinah beach

The city walls, now crumbling, flank the gateway and nm irregular courses, and their equally slender buttresses are all of this small pale brickwork. The way through the town lies over an eminence on the west side of the fort — a *tell*, and perhaps the site of an earlier fort, though the present construction which is fast decaying must itself be of considerable age, for its walls betray three different periods, and a doorway superscription at the entrance gives name and date to a restorer Lutfullah 1211 A.H. The headquarters of Government, it is the residence of the Governor Saiyid Hamad, a brother of the Sultan, who is a great figure in the land, and a charming host. Here and there a few of the older houses are of burnt brick, but the bulk of the inhabitants to-day live in their unpretentious palm-thatch *arishes*, which are screened from public gaze by lanes of tall mud walls that pass between, or by avenues of palms.

A strong wind had sprung up, and beneath the blue sky were long filmy wisps of white cloud. I was sitting on the roof about half an hour before sunset. The gathering clouds below the setting sim were lit up in golden splendour. Midway up the western heavens appeared a curious and most beautiful phenomenon. A solitary, long, white cloud suddenly developed a perfect opal of astral light, occupying perhaps half the apparent area of the sun, in relation to which it was a hand's span above and slightly to the south. Vivid at first, its reds and blues and greens gradually paled and changed, and in the course of ten minutes it had been swallowed up in the cloud and was no more to be seen. The sun set in a golden crimson, and thus an hour passed, while overhanging palms changed to black feathery plumes profiled against the starry night.

Mabruk was sent for again to report progress. Mabruk, I should explain, was the slave coffeeman, and our butcher on the march, who had that morning complained of sprained wrist, which he attributed at first to lifting a heavy bucket over- night. He was a man of twenty-two stone, and, incidentally, was a great favourite of the Sultan. At Muscat, if guests at the Palace were to be diverted with slave dancing, the elephantine Mabruk, whose mastery of steps dated from more slender years, was usually introduced to add piquancy to the ballet.

"Well, Mabruk," said the Sultan as the monumental black approached, "how is thine arm?"

"Better, *Habab*," and the slave lifted up a swollen arm normally huge but now the size of four, and a limp hand grown to equally alarming proportions.

"The treatment seems wrong," said the Sultan. "You must go to Muscat and let the doctor put the bone back."

"No! No!" prayed the man. "It is nothing (this with the slave's habitual fear of the surgeon's knife). It will be all right in a day or two. I do not want to go to Muscat. Let me have a reading of the Quran."

"What else have you done for it?"

"Fomentations, *Habab*. The white of egg, the leaf of *sidr* (jujube), and salt."

That evening the slave wished to come again.

"Well! what is it, Mabruk?"

"o Master!" said Mabruk, "thy servant, Saif bin Ya'rub' who reads the stars, tells me it is not a sprain. It is the evil eye."

"Well, what then?"

"Only a reading will avail."

"Come," said the Sultan to Saif: "This is your diagnosis, so you must carry out the treatment; but I had rather the man went to Muscat."

Mabruk was adamant, and he and the reluctant Saif withdrew for the reading of Holy Writ and its curative virtues. [30]

The Dawn,

In the name of God, the Compassionate, the Merciful,

Say: I seek refuge in the Lord of the Dawn,

From the evil of what He has created

And from the evil of the utterly dark night when it comes,

And from the evil of blowing on knots,

And from the evil of the envious when he envies.

The Men,

In the name of God, the Compassionate, the Merciful,

Say: I seek refuge in the Lord of men.

The king of men.

The God of men.

From the evil of the whisperings of the slinking (devil).

From jinns and men.

The Allies,

And Allah turned back the Unbelievers in their rage: they did not obtain any advantage, and Allah sufficed the Believers in fighting: and Allah is Strong, Mighty.

The Pen,

And those who disbelieve would almost smite you with their eyes when they hear the reminder and they say: Most surely he is mad.

In the Hajar Mountains

I turned to a shaikh close at hand: "Do you believe in the evil eye?"

"Yes, I do," said he, "and so does every man present. Do you remember the camel at Khabura? Well, I was admiring its paces when it fell"

Here was self-confession, for a peculiar idiosyncrasy of the cult is that the possessor of the evil eye has merely to admire and not to will harm.

Saif now returned, and, not to be outdone, adduced a number of instances, all duly authenticated by the credulous assembly. He and a companion, it seems, were travelling, and wanted meat. His companion had drawn his knife and gone in pursuit of a solitary goat in their path, but the goat had leapt into a tree as if Fate had intended it to escape. His companion, the notorious possessor of an evil eye, had merely to look up at the creature admiringly for it to come tumbling down at the very point of the knife. [31]

Saif came to me on the following morning, and I asked him how he had come to know that Mabruk was the victim of the evil eye.

"I read the sands," replied Saif, "and so I came to know that she is a woman of fair skin whom we passed on the way."

Musing on the admiration theory, and regarding Mabruk's black monstrous shape, I wondered what manner of beldame this could be.

Saif was now to unravel to me the riddle of the universe. Alone among all these Arabs, the science of geography was his, he began. Saif's science, I soon gathered, attached no particular weight to a latitudinal equator. Its guiding principle was a longitudinal equator. This passed through Rum (Constantinople) and Iskanderiya (Alexandria) and Mecca: west of the equator was *terra incognita*, east of it the *diras* of the Turks, the people of Pars (Persians), the Arabs and the Indians, the hub of the Universe, so to speak, and the home of True Believers.

The mysteries had all been revealed: only one remained. "Where is the iron wall of Alexander of the two horns?" A vexed problem indeed! and I took refuge behind a limited understanding.

Turning from science to science I asked: "In which is to be placed more reliance — the stars of, the sands?"

"The stars, God save you, are less informing, but exercise a direct influence: the sands merely answer questions."

"But come, Saif, what of Mabruk's arm?" I said, "for men say it was not the evil eye, nor the bucket cither, but a snake bite!"

"God is the Knower," replied the astrologer royal, without a suspicion of discomfiture.

Still, no one read the poets better than Saif. He had the histrionic sense and a dramatic manner, which, I am sure, would have brought him fortune had Hollywood, and not Sahar, been his mentor. Every evening his after-dinner reading on the roof was eagerly awaited, followed by antics of Sha'ar the Jester, and concluding with certain lyrics of Mutanabbi, to restore the sober note. The latter was not mere chanting of the poetry; classical Arab poetry is normally rendered as a chant, but this particular form of lyric verse was actually sung.

A general chorus followed each couplet, and I was curious enough to record three of these *Murdads* which, unlike the camel chanties, are susceptible of European notation.

A heavy dew fell that night, but it was the *Mu'edhdhin's* call to Dawn Prayer, and not my wringing wet bed-sheets that awoke me, and I rose to see the date-palms around the house enveloped in mist. The call for coffee from an inner room signalled the end of the dawn reading of the Quran, a morning parade at which the whole of the Sultan's entourage must daily attend, so that I joined the party at its conclusion. Through the open doorway the faint mist hung like a frail curtain of falling snow, turning everything one beheld through it to a milky white. "Typical monsoon weather of South Arabia," remarked the Sultan. "Thus is Dhufar for three and a half summer months. It is a blessing: there will spring from the earth a green carpet.

A messenger came in at this moment. "Our lord," said he to the Sultan, "Shaikh Ubaid, 'our servant, salaams, and does not want any castor oil after all."

His Highness, who always travelled with aspirin, and drugs of the more explosive sort, looked up. "Why not? He asked for some on his arrival yesterday!"

"Your servant says that one of the *Mutawwas* (religious leaders) will write across his shoulder from the *Aiyats* (verses of the Quran) which treatment he prefers." (The shaikh had arrived with a rigid tummy and a headache he had had for two days.)

Such is the holy pharmacopoeia of Oman.

Meanwhile, downstairs, Mabruk the slave coffee-maker, sat nursing his stricken arm. I looked in on the groaning wretch as I went out for my morning ride. Thrice had the changes been rung on his treatment in a week, for the ointment and the reading were now reinforced by a new cure. The arm looked as if it had been dipped into a flour-bin — except that it was the parade ground of all the flies in the neighbourhood — an appearance it owed to the treatment of white bone of the Indian *sambhur* with a little white of egg. This *adhm al ghulb*, as it is called, is stocked in every local bazaar, and its powdered application is held to be a specific for swellings and sprains.

It was the night before our departure. The Sultan and I had been on the roof to enjoy the cool evening air when a slave appeared with the first fresh mulberries of the season. A refreshing sight they were in their cone of large green overlapping leaves — like rhubarb-leaves — and one sighed for English raspberries. Above in the pale sky following the course of the recent sun was the yellow crescent of the Dhu'l Qu'ada moon in fascinating combination with bright Venus and twinkling Pleiades, a tiny group of sentinels a little aloft. The sea had receded, to expose a vast expanse of shallow beach, where some men say once stood old Sahar. Fishermen will tell of palm stumps and house foundations where now water stands three fathoms deep at flood some four cables off the shore. Of this theory, however, the Sultan is dubious. "There," said he, pointing to some slight mounds north of the city, "there was old Sahar."

It was time for bed. No readings to-night, against an early start on the morrow.

Morning came, and the beach was soon agog with Badus and camels, and loud with the brisk noises of a stirring camp.

"Well, how is it this morning?" I asked of Mabruk, whom we were leaving behind.

"Easier, your honour"; but groans belied the words. "Sayyid Muhammad bin Hilal has read over my arm."

"Another reading?" I queried, "and by the Wali Muhammad of Shinas?" for only is there virtue in the readings of the Pious, and Muhammad was, alas! notorious for his lapses in the sacraments of prayer and fasting.

"Ah! not a religious reading," ventured an amused bystander. "Muhammad is famous for his snake-bite cures."

The magician came to see me before we left. "Whence and how these powers of yours, O Muhammad?" I asked.

"*W'allahi*, Sahib, 'tis true, and I will tell thee, though to none else would I divulge the secret, for I paid forty silver dollars to come by it from a shaikh of Tiwi'."

"What is the formula, then?" He wrote down for me in his phonetic Arabic, the following jargon;

Harmaki? Barmaki?

Come out of the wound

(Victim's name) son of (Mother's name)

From bone to blood

From blood to flesh

From flesh to skin

From skin to hairs

From hairs to the earth

Sultan Ahmad.

"There is no might and power except in God the Highest, the Almighty."

A curious blend of pagan beginning and Muslim ending, but why the mother and not the father's name?

"Where the patient feels squeamish about bringing his mother into the picture, 'son of Eve' will do," he volunteered; and added: "But there is a rite, too. I must take a lime and cut it across the middle so as not quite to sever it and it holds together by some skin only. I then open it as far as possible to 'read' over it the formula seven times. Then I close it and squeeze, so that the juice runs freely from each half to the other. Next I sever it, give one half to the patient to drink of its juice; the other I take and rub down the affected limb seven times — the action always being downwards never upwards. The victim of a snake-bite, if thus treated at once, promptly vomits and perhaps a good deal of the poison is brought away. Be that as it may, cure is almost certain. I have cured many, and, *ashad!* (I bear witness) the snakes were poisonous ones."

Here was non-praying Muhammad, would-be Rationalist, the scorner of the cult of *Zars*, yet unshakable in a belief in his own poor superstitious powers, to which, indeed, many of those assembled bore witness.

Within a week came news of Mabruk's death.

"Kismet," said the Sultan. "It was predestined. There is a day and an hour written for each one of us, and from which there is no escape. *La haula wa la quwwa illa b'illah*" (There is no might and no power except in God.)

The road into the Shamailiyah lay before us to the north. I found myself in a strange saddle, for Khuwara was slightly lame — why I could not tell. But Shaikh Dahba, my old friend of the Awamir tribe, was at hand with a hot branding-iron, and what Dahba did not know concerning camels his world considered was not worth knowing. Cauterization is as widely applied to suffering camels apart from their tribal *wasms* (distinguishing marks) as to suffering man, and, sure enough, Dahba's singeing application to her shoulder did the trick, for two days later she was fit to ride again.

The deep shade of the date-grove gave place to the wide sandy *batha* of Sallan. Here in the bright sunshine the glittering sea spread away on the one hand, and on the other the faint blue mountains of the Hajar lifted themselves beyond the scorching yellow plain. Then back once more into the palms, which now grew thinner as we edged gradually inwards, through dusty lanes wherein cows aimlessly wandered, or loaded asses were driven before their poor masters passing to and fro on their petty affairs. Now came a wide stretch of salt plain as we crossed behind the sandy ridge of Harmul to the palm-groves of Liwa — a plain destitute of trees but thick with the willowy tamarisk bush, where grazing camels looked up to watch us fixedly. Great, immobile brutes they were: one could imagine them thus sculptured from cold stone.

"Liwa," said Saif, riding at my side. "This tottering old pile is the work of my forbear, Ali bin Hamdan; a little offspring of ancient Sahar was this Liwa," he added, "which had a name ere the word Shinas passed men's lips."

Liwa to-day is still seat of a Government Wali, though it is but a small date-grove village some miles back from the sea. Drums and glinting swords, rifle shots, and a swaying, chanting multitude now barred the way to further progress until the Sultan should dismount and honour their poor habitation. Hence we sat at the gate of the fort, the Seat of Justice, for salutations, *fuwala*, petitions, and more salutations. Two Badus had ridden up and I was soon to hear that one was blind.

"Blind?" said I to the Sultan. "Incredible! How, then, can he manage to ride his camel?"

"Ride? He can gallop it, probably," returned His Highness. "These two camels have probably been brought up together, and one will not leave the other. So long as his companion is with him, a blind man has no difficulty in carrying on."

Here the old wali interjected "And what of Abdul Rahman of Al Riyaisa, then?"

"*W'allahi sahih!*" (True! by God) said the Sultan, smiling.

"Who may that gallant be?" I inquired.

Abdul Rahman, it seems, was a famous camel-thief, and a brave and honoured son of the Riyaisa tribe. But his raidings into the Shamailiyah became a terror, so that a trap was set for him, and one fine night they caught him. Now the tribe that would have suffered by this little nocturnal visit used a method of reprisal by no means novel in these sinister parts.

"Bring a sharp clasp knife, somebody," said the shaikh.

"Put it in the fire, Ahmad, and make it red-hot. Now lead forth the brave and hold him down."

Four tribesmen leapt to their master's bidding. And while one stalwart held open the victim's eyelids, another withdrawing the scarlet blade from the fire, drew it across the pupils of the wretch's eyes.

Thus returned Abdul Rahman to his tribe, blinded for life.

"But do you think that cured him of camel raiding?" said the Wali. "No, by God! No! Two years later in the dead of a moonless night this same tribe had ten camels taken. Abdul Rahman had paid a return visit — God is the Knower — the thieves were he himself and his son. Abdul Rahman still lives, by the grace of God, an old man now." [32]

We left by leafy lanes that led past Nabar — a place of pilgrimage to local Shafi sectarians, for the shrine of a Saint Shaikh Mas'ud sanctifies it, but it is a poor and rude building, in no way comparable to the blue domed shrines of the Shi'ah sectaries of Iraq. On we went by shady glades between palm-grove and the acacia jungle which for a mile stretched towards the nearing mountains. A spacious parkland this, and in the distance spread a yellow carpet of what ought to have been buttercups, but turned out to be tufts of *harm*. Slender bee-eaters with their long green tails perched on branches overhead, bright blue roller birds, strong on the wing, flew from tree to tree, and the beautiful crested *hud hud*, with its brown-white throat and black-barred wings was enchanting as it made off, followed by its mate. The Arabs say that this is the bird that brought tidings of the Queen of Sheba to Solomon.

By a large stretch of salt plain, devoid of a blade of vegetation, we came to Shinas, with its humbled old fort standing gaunt across the waste.

This plain becomes a sheet of water with the spring tides of the equinoxes. At normal times, also, the gently shelving beach before the town is exposed for a distance of half a mile as the tide ebbs out, becomes a temporary lagoon with the flood, and is covered almost to the edge of habitation at high water.

But here was Muhammad bin Hilal, the wali, the hero of many battles, and a worthy man despite his snake-bite cult. Muhammad's last exploit had been to walk into an armed and rebellious village single-handed and arrest its erstwhile shaikh. Insomnia, or a conscience, made Muhammad more wakeful than any man I ever knew, and in camp, if one woke in the early hours, and looked around, one could always see the red glow of his old clay pipe. It was said that Muhammad's walking abroad at nights kept in their beds most other men given, for less valid reasons, to such practices. Certain it was that Bani Ka'ab and Bani Qitab tribesmen, who in time past swept down from their mountains and took a toll from the villagers' comparative prosperity, had since the arrival of this forceful character thought twice and reduced their demands. Mankind in such wild environments may be divided into two categories, and Muhammad belonged emphatically to the category of the man one would like to have with one in a tight corner. [33]

There was room inside the fort only for the Sultan and his entourage, so our Badawin camped in the plain under the old walls. With such limited accommodation, His Highness and I had to share the same roof of the guardroom in the fort precincts, and there we slept as well as a heavy dew would allow.

I was now to observe my companion at prayer, in which he was always most punctilious.

The Muslim prayer is a set one, of course, ordained in the Quran, to be prayed five times a day, at dawn, noon, after- noon, sunset and an hour and a half after sunset. The different sects of Islam are to be distinguished by such superficialities as the position of the arms in prayer, the introduction of *amins* (amens) that are not in the original, and the nature of the modified observances on the march. Washing of hands and feet before prayer are necessary, and after sexual intercourse the washing of the entire body — else is the prayer of no avail.

"Wherefore the purpose of laying a cane across the head of the praying rug?" I asked.

"That," said my royal companion, "is to save the prayer from lapsing in certain eventualities."

"How?" I asked.

"As you know, we may pray only facing the holy city of Madina, where our Prophet is buried. But if any one should pass across our front within forty paces we must start all over again, for the prayer has lapsed. This also applies if, within the radius, comes anything unclean, a dog, a woman in her courses, or a man who has not yet washed the greater ablution. This cane, then, is a token of those forty paces, which thus placed saves my prayer."

"Many of the Badus on the march," I observed, "use their rifles."

"The Shi'ahs," he returned, "rely upon a small stone brought from their holy town of Karbala, and this they carry with them, avowing it to partake of the holiness of the soil of Paradise."

"How, then, do the Badus manage about their ablutions in the waterless sands of the desert?" I asked.

"Thus" — and he patted the earth three times with his open palms, brought them down over his face and beard, one closely following the other, and, patting the earth again he stroked his forearms alternately. "There, that is all."

We were on the march again through palm-groves raised high above the beach. Beneath their shade vast areas of tobacco, at this stage like giant lettuces, spread away on both sides, for the Shamailiyah is the great tobacco-producing area of South-East Arabia, whence the smokers of Dubai and Bahrain draw their needs, and the semi-illicit wants of the Dhahirah of Wahhabi tradition, and the wholly illicit ones of Ibadhi Oman, are supplied. But in the latter place Persian opium and Indian bhang, a much worse decoction, serve, to a limited extent, the purpose of soothing men's hardships and weakening their brains. Alcohol is unknown to all save a handful of town dwellers with Indian associations, and I have never yet seen an Arab drunk. His religion in proscribing alcohol is surely greatly knowing, for he is of an ultra-inflammable temper, and he invariably carries his lethal weapons.

As we jogged chanting along, now and then about these fragrant lanes there came a refreshing whiff as of rural England; picturesque low banks of acacia thicket, wild hedgerows in contrasting greens, and, half hidden in unsuspected nooks, a rustic stile or two; vivid green *ma'awarah* bushes, a deadly poison to the sight, and from which men shrink, the *asbaq* that resembles it, a prickly-pear variety of cactus the Arab calls "the jinn's palm", the fern-like "scorpion tree", the podded seeds of which provide boys with pawns for their sand games and the sage-green *ashkhara* — all these were conspicuously present.

We had reached the thriving young tobacco port of Abu Baqara. The usual reed shelters had been arranged facing the sea for our reception amid innumerable boats drawn above high-water mark along the sloping beach. A curious feature of this small place was that it seemed to unite in itself representatives of every considerable sect of Islam. The merchants of Persian origin were either Shafi or Shi'ahs, the Baluchis, Hanafi here; Malikis and Hanbalis were represented in Dhahirah factions, and Ibadhism by the occasional Omani. The free and full inter-sectarian use of mosques not only here but also throughout the country was marked, and provided a lesson in toleration which Christendom should learn, if it would follow the spirit of its Founder.

Night was drawing on, and the sea had reached within a few feet of us. The temptation to go in for a swim was compelling, despite the presence of sharks in these waters. But the shark seems to dislike inshore shallow water, and also brown bodies seem not to whet his appetite — at least divers on the pearl banks and fishermen along the Batinah coast seem fearless in using shark-infested waters. So, soon, we had a dozen slaves swimming off with their merry shouts to form a ringed bathing pool which brought us splashing in. The water was beautifully warm in the tropical starry night, and so brilliant with phosphorescence that one came out with bathing suit bespangled. Bathing parades were henceforth popular, though our escorting Badus from the interior would not indulge, holding that a bath causes a month's fever.

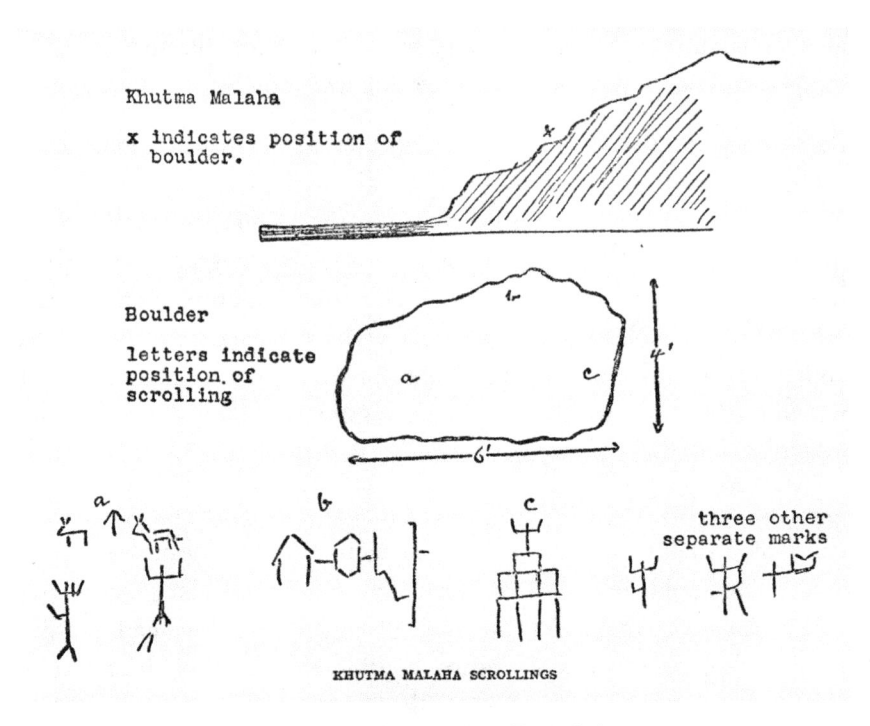

Khutma Malah scrolling (Rock Art)

Next day we moved along the beach to Murair, where the great coastal palm-grove comes to an end, the mountains ever closing in on our left hand. Here the Sultan and the main body rested, but the young Heir Apparent and I, with half a dozen Badus, pushed on to explore Khutma Malaha, where the Hajar, swinging round to the coast, puts an end to the great crescent plain through which we had come, and marks a frontier with Trucial Oman. Actually the main Hajar runs on to strike the coast just short of Khor Fakkan, an older frontier to the north, but here, at the Khutma, two spurs ending in bluffs run out from the range and project themselves into the plain at right angles to the sea beach, which is but six hundred yards or so distant. From this point north to Daba is the habitat of Qawasim elements, a lateral extension of the Pearl

Coast tribe which threw off Ibadhi Government allegiance in the eighteenth century, and achieved this advanced frontier in piratical days from the great Saiyid Sa'id bin Sultan himself. At Daba starts once more Sultanate territory of Runs al Jabal, giving to the intervening wedge the nature of a Qawasim corridor. Its two small towns, Kalba and Fujaira, once tributary to Sharjah and Ras al Khaima respectively, but now virtually independent, had just before our arrival been fighting an old feud, and their shaikhs had recently come to join the Sultan's party for the purpose of inviting him to settle their dispute. Thither we were marching, and needs must the shaikh of Kalba leave overnight to precede us to his own town and prepare for our reception.

Saiyid Sa'id and I climbed the Khutma and looked down upon the oozy black mangrove swamp that here lines the shore. A notorious place this for slaves from the settled villages, coming to cut firewood for their masters, to be pounced upon by Badus from the Dhahirah who delight to lurk here for the purpose, and carry off their prizes generally to the rich markets of the Pearl Coast.

I made a discovery here. On the face of a large broken boulder, about six feet by four by three, that lay half-way up the Khutma, I noticed some scrollings. Rude and superficial and isolated — I could find no others, though we continued the search — they might have been, I thought, the dagger work of some Badu at the time of the Frontier Delimitation Conference a hundred and twenty years ago and contemporary with the little loose stone wall that, starting below, runs out seawards fifty yards or so to make the frontier. Curiosity led me to record them. Later I came upon a record of Sabaean inscription discovered by officers of the East India Company's surveying ship Palinurus in 1834 Hasan al Ghorab in Hadhramaut, and an odd design beneath one of their inscriptions recalled to my mind these scratchings at Khutma. [34]

Moving northwards we were already in Qawasim territory and without the pale of Muscat's jurisdiction. Halting in a plain studded with scrub and acacia we found a delightful camp three miles or so behind Khor Kalba, a spot to the south of Kalba proper — which place was faintly discernible by the outlines of palms alternating with gaps of blue sea and filmy mirage. A few crested larks, songless creatures, attracted notice to themselves by their dusty sand-baths, and the *qa-ta'ing* of distracted thirsty sand-grouse, that came in zooming clouds, denoted a scarcity of water in the neighbourhood. For miles, indeed, there was only one well, that now within our midst, and hither tribal women from the neighbourhood had come to draw water. Our innumerable Badus, a thirsty host, stood in detached groups round about, impatient to fill their water-skins. One fellow to whom the slow trips of the solitary *dalu* (water-bucket) spelt unbearable suspense, and who had stood here too long, he thought, with his empty *qirba* (water-skin) under his arm, suddenly grasped the well rope and disappeared into the inky watery depths. Having reached bottom and filled his *qirba* he now shouted to be drawn up. The women at the top, however, said "No"; and soon the whole camp tittered over the ridiculous situation the Badu had placed himself in.

"Come up the way you went down, Hamdan!" were the laughing Badu jibes shouted at him from above.

Hamdan was drawn up only when he had agreed to give his water to a woman waiting to depart, and to take his turn for water ration with everybody else. His emergence was greeted with the ironical shout of *Allahu Akbar* which was taken up, one after the other, by every tribal group in the amused camp. But nobody blamed the action. It was an inbred impulse which was perfectly understood. To me it was an interesting commentary on the stem war of survival which the son of the desert must wage with his surroundings and on its implication of "the devil take the hindmost".

There was nothing noteworthy in Kalba itself, which was of a piece with every other town along these Arabian shores, except for the deep entrenchments along its north side and a new watch-tower in the palm-grove close by, evidences of a recent action with the men of Fujaira. The bone of contention was a boundary. and Fujaira ambitiously desired that Kalba's place in the sun hereabouts be restricted to her four, walls, though they were both content with a curious boundary arrangement between them to the north, where their respective seaboard territory alternated in the manner of a chessboard, Khor Fakkan and Zadna, two squalid little fishing villages, belonging to Kalba in a stretch of Fujaira's barren rocky coast to Daba.

The Kalba Fujaira Peace Conference - Shaikh of Daba, Shaikh of Fujaira, Sultan Taimur, Saiyid Said (standing), Shaikh of Kalba

This Khor Fakkan had a murky past, for its now spacious innocence of encircling harbour had been a famous pirates' lair, whither a British Naval Expedition under Sir Sydney Smith in the days of the East India Company swept in upon it, burnt the pirate fleet, and sent the pirates scurrying up into their mountain fastnesses. These were gallant days, when a merchant- man must be well armed if she would sail these seas. For the Qawasim pirates, in their frail, swift craft, swarmed these coasts; they would spot her hull down, rapidly overhaul her, and launch their attack like a cloud of hornets. Many a rich prize was taken, many a fair ship has paid the price of blood or gold that she may pass on her lawful occasion, and, strange thought! our own authorities in India, but four generations ago, were driven to consider the means of buying immunity from the forbears of these lowly offenceless fishermen.

We had left Kalba in the afternoon for Wadi ar Ras, the historical boundary of the disputants and now the recent casus belli, and halted there for the night. On the following day we; made Fujaira, climbing amid broken and uninteresting country behind the plain that stretched to the sea. Fujaira's character was different from that of the Batinah village in that it stood back against the mountains. Its open spaces and an unusual preponderancy of mud dwellings were also notable.

The old fort of the shaikh stood on a considerable eminence, and was in a sick and sorry condition, for only six months before it had received attentions from H.M. ships. At that time the "Amir of the Gulf" had called upon the shaikh to surrender a young Baluchi slave girl he had recently acquired. As the young lady considered the present shaikhly home an improvement on her past hungry freedom, and as she excited the manly admiration of her lord to boot, she decided that she would not exchange the new amenities for the old. So the shaikh, being of like mind, returned the answer that the slave girl was dead. Nor would he agree to come off to the ship and discuss this or any other question. The old shaikh of Fujaira, it seems, alone, perhaps, amongst the shaikhs of this coast, except his Shihuh neighbours, was averse from paying calls or showing much amenableness to authority of any sort, so the ships after giving him notice to evacuate his village, as slave treaties could not be repudiated with impunity, replied with their guns, and the shaikh and his villagers betook themselves to their mountains until God had again swept their horizons dear. It was a privilege, therefore, as an Englishman, to find myself the shaikh's guest so soon after the bombardment; and he, a thorough sportsman, was not in the least embarrassed in taking me over his fort, and into the tower, now considerably shot away, nor did he seem to bear the slightest ill will. Four well-set-up sons, the noblest family I met in these parts, followed at a distance, and the virile old chief of seventy-eight, who gave the impression of being a thorough-going megalomaniac, confided to me that he was taking his twenty-fourth wife to wed that year, though I gathered that the little "dead" Baluchi coquette was still about, ready to light the old man's pipe for him.

The Peace Conference did its work, and the Sultan set his seal to the agreement by which Kalba and Fujaira were to live in future amity. The occasion was one for a feast, and the Badus, anxious always for a pretext for fete and gala, were racing their camels. Suddenly one Badu so engaged took a heavy purler, for his young untrained mount deceived him in its paces by a fatal camel trick of heading in one direction and turning in the other. He lay motionless — I thought dead. His companions near at hand rushed to his side. Stunned, bruised, and a broken collar-bone — that was all. Everyone mumbled an "*Al hamdu lillah*". Their treatment of the accident was novel to watch. A six-foot pit was hastily dug like a shallow grave, and fire was introduced to heat it and then taken out again. It was then bedded down with large sage leaves of the *ashkhar*; next was introduced the Badu himself with his head just above ground-level, and more of the same leaves were then placed over him, and so he remained for a space.

We left the following day to return to Khor Kalba, so I had no opportunity of gauging the effects of the treatment, but I met the man a year later riding his same camel, and he told me smilingly that a knuckle to his collar-bone was all the hurt he could show for the experience.

From Khor Kalba we headed for a saddle in the hills behind Khutma Malaha, for it was decided to visit the small mountain tribe of Wushaihat above Shinas. In two hours we had come through bleak broken hills with scrub and stunted acacia trees to a wide shallow wadi, Qaur, on the opposite side of which amidst a few tall palms was the village of Aswad. No song or sight of bird had gladdened our way. Only a few sand-grouse and doves were content in this dying *falaj* oasis, and we passed on the next morning through hillier country of similar desolation, save that the acacia were now taller, and one heard of water and villages beyond the hills.

As we rode along, the Sultan drew my attention to one of our newly joined Badawin, from whose saddle was dangling the head and neck of a dead camel calf, stuffed to look alive except for its staring, deathly eyes — altogether a gruesome sight.

"A *bau*," explained His Highness. "The Badus carry such to encourage easy milking."

"True," said the Badu who had now drawn close up for me to see it, "my camel lost her calf some months ago, and this is her *bau* which, when I milk her, I put before her nose to sniff, and so she is deceived into ready generosity."

We had arrived at the village of Ajib, the Wushaihat shaikh's residence. Here, at the entrance of the settlement, were pleasant fields of tobacco that led on to thick palm-groves lining the sloping banks above Wadi Hatta. A long flank of the hill, open-spaced, was crowned by the fort and a mosque that looked pleasantly down into the volcanic wadi below. Our reed shelters had been erected above the flowing surface stream that ran half way down this clearing, from one palm grove to another, and in its course was a large five-foot-deep trough, which was soon cleaned out and filled with cool spring water. I refreshed myself with a swim.

The next morning the Heir Apparent and I were up at crack of dawn to go off and visit yet another boundary of the State, marked by a small tower, Wujaja, two and a half miles up the tortuous valley. A great place for a watch-tower this, for the high cliffs close in to the narrow gorge, massive boulders encumber a small ravine with its splashing mountain waters, and leave only a narrow way beneath the battlements for man and beast to pass. The entrance to this mountain tower is small, characteristically placed ten feet off the ground, and accessible only by means of a rope drawn up by the defender after himself. We spent an hour listening to an account of an attack, by my friends the Bani Ka'ab, on the post twenty-five years ago, and watching the more innocent activities of a praying mantis.

The day for our departure from Ajib had come and we were once more in the saddle. At first was a joyous sight of green terraced gardens, beneath lofty palms that clothed the left-hand slopes above us as we passed down the deep valley. Now and then an extra tall palm-tree obtruded itself from among its fellows, and, unlike them, no clustered fruit hung from under its sprouting fronds: for date-palms are male and female and four or six male trees will be found on an average in each garden of two or three hundred females. But bees and Nature's processes are not availing, and in due season the young fruit must be pollinated artificially from the male pod, the gardener spending his days scaling every palm.

Leaving the wadi-bed a few miles farther down, we moved up to the red pebbly bank, its rough undulations studded with the *sidaf* shrub beloved by camel and Badu alike, and thence descended into the plain towards the sea, where the going became smoother and the wadi had lost its trough character, breaking up into a number of characteristic shallow scourings. Thence into the coastal palm-grove we journeyed, and so towards the booming guns of Shinas fort beyond.

The night was lit up by the flashing of rifle fire, for this locally made Martini-Henry refill leaves a stream of light behind: it makes a report like a squib, too, and, what is worse, stinks like one. To one who wants to discover himself to his enemy at night I can recommend no better medium.

"But what can you," says the Badu, riding at my side, "when new European ammunition costs a rupee for three rounds at Dubai or Abu Dhabi, whereas you can get ten of the local sort for the same money if you will only bring your own empty cartridge cases," Wherefore it is that one sees Badus diving like cormorants after a *feu de joie*.

And so to Sahar by our beaten track. June was approaching, and all that that means in these latitudes — tropical heat and glare. The Sultan arrived with a slight fever. Most of our party, indeed, had one thing or another, while I, a European, seemed — *As shukr l'illah* (Thanks to God)- to survive the camel saddle as well as most, for I escaped without even a headache.

TREKKING SOUTHWARDS HOME

Muscatwards! And the *aiya* (holy verse) must have flashed through the hearts of the Faithful:

"Verily, He who has made the Quran binding on you. He will bring you back to the destination"

"A snake! A snake!" shouted the last of our Badus to arrive into camp as they dismounted at sundown under a *sidr* tree. But it had disappeared before I could get over to the spot.

Here was Qusair, that lay under the Hajar mountains, back behind Saham, for we were taking another line of country, on our homeward journey — a small palm oasis this with scarcely more than a dozen villagers to work in its fields of sugar cane. The fort gave the impression of having seen better days; indeed, its doors and roof vaulting suggested an earlier and better period than many of the Batinah forts. Beneath it ran a swift *falaj*, its water teeming with small fish, which in no way diminished our desire for a dip after our woefully hot ride.

Bani Kaab

The Sultan and I were up before the sun, and, with a few Bani Umr *shikaris* and two camels, set off with our guns through the open scrub. Soon after passing a decayed village, Ruwaidha, on our right hand, he dismounted for distant rifle-shot at a slinking fox, and thereby startled some gazelle, our real object, which here, however, seemed to move in threes and fours only, in contrast to twenty and twenty-five head usually met with in Central South Arabia, owing, I suppose, to their having been shot out more by locals for the pot. It was a barren morning, and we were returning by way of Falaj Sahami, where sand-grouse were coming in to water, when halting half an hour over the brook, nine couple of grouse and three dove fell to one gun. A hot morning this, and the *falaj* was too warm to afford much comfort.

A subordinate Customs official, not very suitably named Good Jesus, awaited my return at the fort, and having transacted his business, we bid adieu to Qusair, and struck across the stony plain to Khabura.

"God is great," went up an ironical cheer, as a Badu, having slid off his camel and run crouching to a bush, fired and missed his mark — a gazelle, which, alarmed, went steeplechasing over the scrub, all feathery lightness and grace.

At Khabura the Sultan had convened a *majlis* (assembly) to put the finishing touches to the tribal peace, and I sent for two recalcitrant shaikhs who had been languishing in leg-irons too long for their past misdeeds. Their dungeon lodgment, like the rest of the fort, we found falling to pieces. Its mud walls, founded, like those of all the Batinah forts, upon sand, were never intended to contend with the centuries, and I questioned the wisdom of spending more money on their poor wrinkled faces. Outside our camels sat cheek by jowl round a mountain of lucerne, paragons of behaviour, eating one of the other in such dignified toleration as to put the race of horses and dogs to shame. On their backs and heads swanned feasting crows, the two mutually enjoying each other's society.

We were now a much diminished company on the march, for many of the Badu escort had received their *rukhsa* (parting present) and had departed blessing the Sultan and the day on which he was born.

In Wadi Dhiyan, a long tenuous valley, darkness descended, and a dozen camp-fires began to lick the night. The sky was cloudy in parts, and a great ominous circle surrounded the young moon and foretold a heavy morning dew.

"Shall we send for the incense-burner to dispel the mist?" said the Sultan.

"*Allahu Akbar*" came from Saiyid Mahmud on an ascending note, by way of clinching the matter.

A white haze hung thick in the valley, as on the morrow our host of phantom figures rode out. The sun rose a mere blaze of light at first, but before its increasing majesty the mist was to melt away. Meanwhile the going was cool along the edge of the palms, where little columns of blue smoke issued from lowly homesteads. Tom-toms and the tripping sword-dance announced our arrival at Khadhra, a garden village on the inward edge of the grove some two miles, perhaps, from the fishing village of the same name. There we were once more to enjoy the old-world hospitality of our one-eyed friend. Shaikh Khalid.

Dinner, of vast quantities, consisted of piles of rice and the goat (many goats) the whole carcase served of course — head, eyes, and all — and so strongly- spiced, and cooked with all the indifference of the Badu to finesse, that I ate only as much as was sufficient to keep away hunger. The goat is the primary meat food of Oman; it is rated above sheep, which are rare. Beef is a very bad third, though there is no lack of cows, albeit often fish-dieted.

"Say not so, O Khalid! Bounty is not from the created. Bounty is from the Creator."

I confess I thought this a trifle hard on Khalid, who was doing the honours superlatively well. Then came the coffee. Now the coffeeman normally moves round with a coffee-pot in one hand, and a half-dozen cups of the usual handleless shape which admit of their being telescoped, in the other, and these are relayed round the assembly to save time. But to-day there was an unaccountable shortage of cups, only two, in fact. It is also the custom of the country that the first cup from which the Sultan has drunk be promptly taken away — a sign of deference, for no one else may drink from it. Here was a pretty problem, for the time taken in passing the one cup left by this observance from hand to hand round a hundred or more men, would be excessive. "Sit down," said the Sultan quietly to the man who had hastened across to remove the royal cup from the assembly. An embarrassing moment it was for Khalid, whose household staff work was not up to scratch, and the old shaikh wilted as two cups went round without more ado.

It recalled to my mind the old practice of tribal Mesopotamia during the War. There a Shi'ah tribesman would never drink after one, on the religious score that the cup had been contaminated by an Unbeliever's lips, and this without bearing the slightest ill will or making the action unnecessarily obtrusive. Often, indeed, have I been afforded guarded amusement to see the coffeeman there with a marvellous sleight-of-hand slip my cup to the bottom of the pack, so to speak. But this is not one of the Ibadhi intolerances a Christian meets with in Oman.

Water Well and Bani Qitab

A Yal Sa'ad shaikh had just entered.

"*Salaamun alaikum*" (Peace be upon you), he drawled out with a characteristic sweep of his outstretched cane around the assembly.

One shaikh whispered to another: "Don't ask after his son. He's absent in Dubai, with a new slave or two, and making his visit profitable no doubt."

The acacia jungle of the Yal Sa'ad country, bordered by bright green fields of lucerne and melons, shaded lanes, and fortified villages sped by, and we reached Wadi Qasim, the limit of the Yal Sa'ad country, where we were to rest during the noonday. The usual monster clay dishes of the local Turkish delight, a full load for two men, coffee, and delicious fresh-cut melons were set before us, and thus refreshed we retired to our palm-frond *sablas*, and for midday siesta.

Here was to appear again Karam the Baluchi, blind Karam, the hardened old slave-dealer, who turned up for a decision about the alleged last of his numerous African entourage. Karam could have been but one amongst a large Makrani contingent present, for many were they who wore the *wudar* (a garment that serves for blanket by night) over the shoulder, a dress habit, peculiar in this part of Arabia to Makranis, Shihuh, and Ahl al Hadra.

Here also we were joined by three yellow-beards — not the henna beards of Iraq where a white beard stands for wisdom, surely a prerogative of the Prophet! — but a canary-coloured variety so tinted for rational reasons. They proved to be the Badu Shaikh Muhammad, of the Bani Bu Hassan tribe of Ja'alan and two followers, who had come by way of Sharqiyah and brought letters to the Sultan from the interior Chief. Shaikh Isa bin Salih. Not only their beards but also their faces were stained yellow, giving them a jaundiced appearance, and, as though to complete the colour scheme, their clothes were smeared too. This colouring is called *wars*, a vegetable product of the Yemen, made into a paste by mixture with the oil of sesame and judged precious by standards of poverty-stricken Arabia. Its use is widespread in the Ja'alan, in the Sharqiyah, and to a less extent in the mountain regions of the Dhahirah. In the latter place, indeed, on festive occasions a cup of *wars* may circulate with the coffee-cup that the assembled may anoint themselves. Its addicts claim its use to be healthy during hot winds — a preventive of the skin's becoming dry and cracking.

A Halt in the Batinah Coast

Also here present was the dear old Governor of Barkah, whose religious susceptibilities involved his every sentence beginning with *min fadhal Allah* (Of God's bounty). He came with news of a small tragedy attending our salute, for the warden of Musana's fort had looked down the barrel of his gun at the worst possible moment, and was *hors de combat*. Poor wretch! the whole of one side of the face had been lacerated, and was blood-raw, and one eye, the condition of which was doubtful, would not as yet open. That accidents of this kind were so rare most astonished me, for Arab saluting guns are invariably old muzzle-loaders, and the Arab, more casual than most, is apt to ram in a new charge of gunpowder before the burning residue of the last discharge is cleared, and ascribe the results to the Merciful and the Compassionate.

On we went to Sib and its pleasant gardens, to enjoy the semi-luxury of the Wali of Matrah's house, and to hear again the inharmonious double-wheeled water-hoist.

But we were not to linger here. The following day we left, skirting the palm belt to its end at Hayil, the site of our camp when journeying northwards, where poor old Mabruk was wont to prepare our dinner with so much skill. Hence, through bleached salt-bush, we struck across to the beach where patches of drying sardines glistened in the sun and groups of fishermen looked 'o their nets. But now, stretching before us was a beautiful sweep of pink shore ending in a promontory that pointed to old Fahl, alone in his sea; and beyond, the high black peaks where Muscat lay hidden. On past the little isolated palmeries of Ghubra and Ubaidha, we turned in and floundered across some sandhills to our camp of Khuwair, set about with *sidr* (jujube) trees.

An incongruous figure appeared at the morning *burza*, a Hadramaut Badu of the Karab tribe, black and broad of face, with a tattered handkerchief of a *musur* (headdress) under which a wealth of long, narrow raven plaits fell about his shoulders, his short skirt to the knee and big bone distinguishing him unmistakably from the Omanis gathered round. A pleasing virility in his gutteral accent went with a supreme self-assurance, and the Sultan recognized an acquaintance of Dhufar, whence he had come.

The Finish

"How are this year's rains?" asked the Sultan referring to the monsoon in his remote South Arabian province.

"*Khair* (Good). They came on 15th of Ramadhan. *Allahu Alim!*" (God is the Knower).

"*Al hamdu I'illah* (God be praised), and what of my garden at Mahmudiyah?"

"Black! I bear witness," returned the Badu, by which he meant green, as is the Badu's wont to describe new foliage and a generally flourishing condition of the springing earth.

"Where are you journeying, o Ali?" asked the Sultan.

"To Dubai, *Insha'allah*."

"*Insha'allah*", which is the Arabic for "if God wills", is a phrase that the Faithful use immoderately. The future is in God's hands, and vain is man to express himself without due heed of the fact. Indeed, to say definitely that one will do something without adding this rider is held to be an affront to Allah. On this subject the Sultan told me this Arab folk story.

"When God first sent down the birds from Paradise into the Garden of Eden he did so at nightfall. And they all sat roosting and waiting impatiently for the morrow and discussing their new surroundings. Said the hen, a little more vocal than the rest, 'To-morrow I shall fly.' Said the others in unison, 'And we shall fly also, *Insha'allah.*' And when morning came the eagle was first into the air, then followed the vulture, and, God bless you, the crested *hud*, and so all the others down to the humble sparrow. All save the hen, for the hen opened its wings and flapped and flapped but nothing happened: fly it could not.

"And the reason? It alone among the feathered creatures sent down had forgotten the will of God, had omitted to say *Insha'allah.*"

This was the day for our entry into Muscat, and we sprang into our saddles with light hearts. Our camels were lively with the shouts and songs of their riders. Out of the dunes of Khuwair our long column wound past the mangrove swamp that leads to the palm-grove of Wataiyah, on into the mountain gully towards Ruwi, and thence past Bait al Falaj fort. So we descended into beflagged Matrah, whose folk turned out to cheer and bless the returning Ruler.

Jalali Fort and British Embassy

Now along the new sea road that skirts the rockbound coast to Riyam we went, and so over the Pass that leads down into the blaze of dazzling white houses that is Muscat. Merani's twenty-one guns reverberated along the hills. Badawin chanted merrily as we struggled into single file through the narrow lanes of the town, thronged with veiled and unveiled women and girls in gay dresses who indulged in an orgy of hand-clapping and tongue-wobbling ululation. Onwards we rode, through an ancient gateway to the tiny white mosque beneath the shadow of Merani Fort. Here we halted, a mighty host of two hundred camelry that glittered with sword and dagger surrounding the venerable figure of the white-robed Sultan.

And here our Badus, lean and hungry men shining with the sun and dew of the desert, vied with each other in valiant camel- racing contests past the Palace to the verge of the bazaar, where pallid Banians sit and do their money-changing.

And as I looked upon this scene, of which I was now to take farewell, there came back to me the brave music of Flecker's *War Song of the Saracens*.

ADVENTURE 4

WAR DRUMS IN MUSANDAM

THE ALARM

War-clouds were surely gathering over the Peninsula of Musandam.

Two months and more had passed since its inhabitants, the Shihuh tribe, had become fractious. Disobedience had grown into truculence, and Shaikh Hasan of Khasab, encouraged in his belief that no action would be authorized to bring him to book, fomented tribal defiance, and announced that henceforth he repudiated all authority and would be master in his own house.

The trouble arose in this way. A survey ship, H.M.S. *Ormonde*, had suddenly appeared over Shihuh horizons. She came with plans to make a new survey of that ill-charted part of the world, and to that end a small party, armed with theodolite and survey flags, was to land and ascend a hill as required for the normal purposes of triangulation.

"No!" said Shaikh Hasan after some equivocation, "this land of the Shihuh is ours, not yours; what you say you want to do is of no value to us, and in any case we do not admit your right to land on our shores."

"But," rejoins the Occidental reared to a reverence for the legal position but profoundly innocent of Arab ways, "here is a letter to you from your

Muscat overlords whose jurisdiction extends to these waters: they have given their permission."

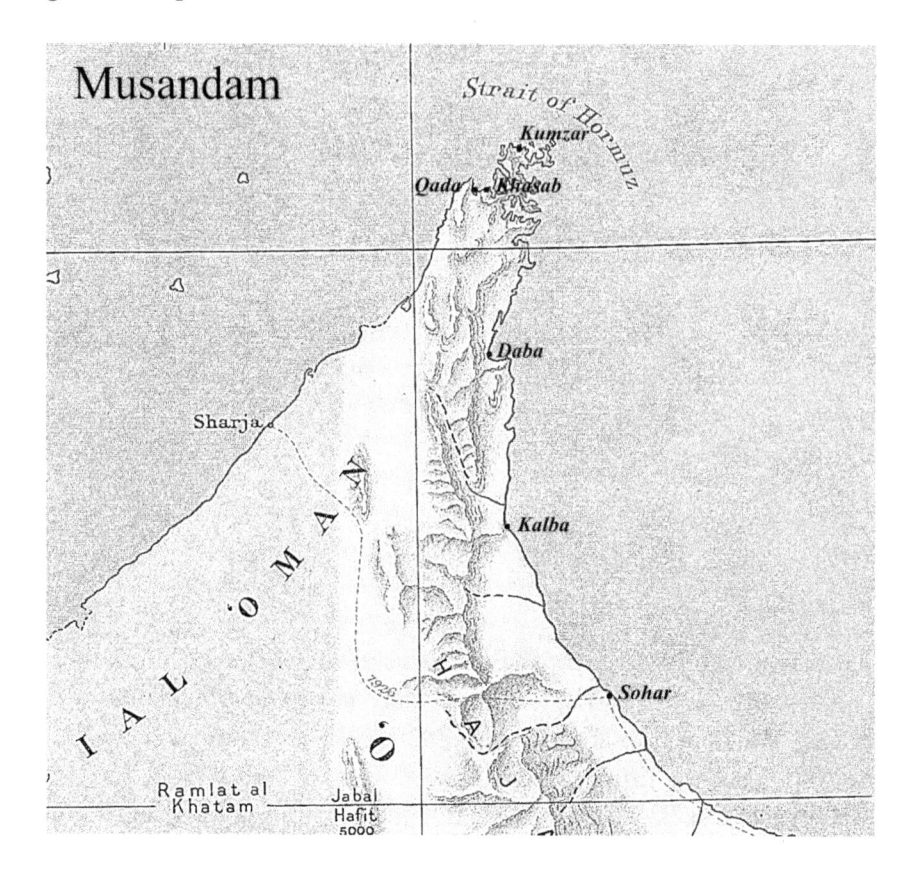

"Very well, then, but we do not recognize the Muscat Government."

And so the fat was in the fire.

Actually, however, the forces at work that made for a deadlock were not so simple as all that.

Musandam, or Ru'us al Jabal, as the whole region is called, is a "fringe" of the Muscat State. It has its own breed of wild men, the Shihuh, who derive from their remote and inaccessible mountains a certain independence of attitude and action. The social organization is tribal and militant, and not unnaturally impatient of anything more than a minimum of government. The "fringe" is characteristic of the far-flung

Oriental State: the old Ottoman Empire had its Kurdistan, India has it's North-West Frontier. Let the Central Authority of Government, for whatever cause, become weak, or be believed to have become weak, and the "fringe" celebrates it with an orgy of uncontrollable self-will. Some ugly situation arises and blood flows. Such an incident is without political basis, in the ideological sense, that is, for "fringes" have no flair for national aspirations. It is born of a certain crude appreciation of realities, an appreciation of the right moment to be up and doing, if the tribe is to retain any sense of worthiness of its fighting forbears. It is usually ephemeral, owing to ammunition running short and an unstable temper. The European may reflect that if he regard his own self-elected government as a "necessary evil", there is really nothing very odd in the reactions to authority of the wild man to whom all restraint, but particularly the restraint of a peaceful order, is irksome. The wild man has no inherent respect for law and order, rather the reverse. Equity and justice as abstract considerations leave him unimpressed, and as for the soft ways of civilized life, and the instruments of it, he despises them. Men who have spent a large part of their lives handling him, learn to appreciate certain of his qualities, learn also that he reverences force before all things, and that in the long run he is amenable to one form of persuasion, namely, the threat of compulsion, and, failing that, its reality. Suspend the fear of penalties, and he will give you a run for your money, if not for your life.

Now for the Shihuh tribe, in the month of January and the year of grace 1930, the fear of penalties did not exist.

"Local unrest is largely nourished from outside," I was told by a neighbouring chief, perhaps the most enlightened of the Trucial hierarchy. In post-War years, Egyptian, Indian and Iraqi news-papers devoted to politics have come to circulate in Oman and are the medium for the news of world unrest -a contagious germ — the medium also for the trumpeting of the civilized world's renunciation of the sword — a declaration, my "Pirate Chief" held, that induces a contrary disposition in a lower intelligence actuated by self-interest, not, alas! an enlightened self-interest, as witness the chart-making obstruction.

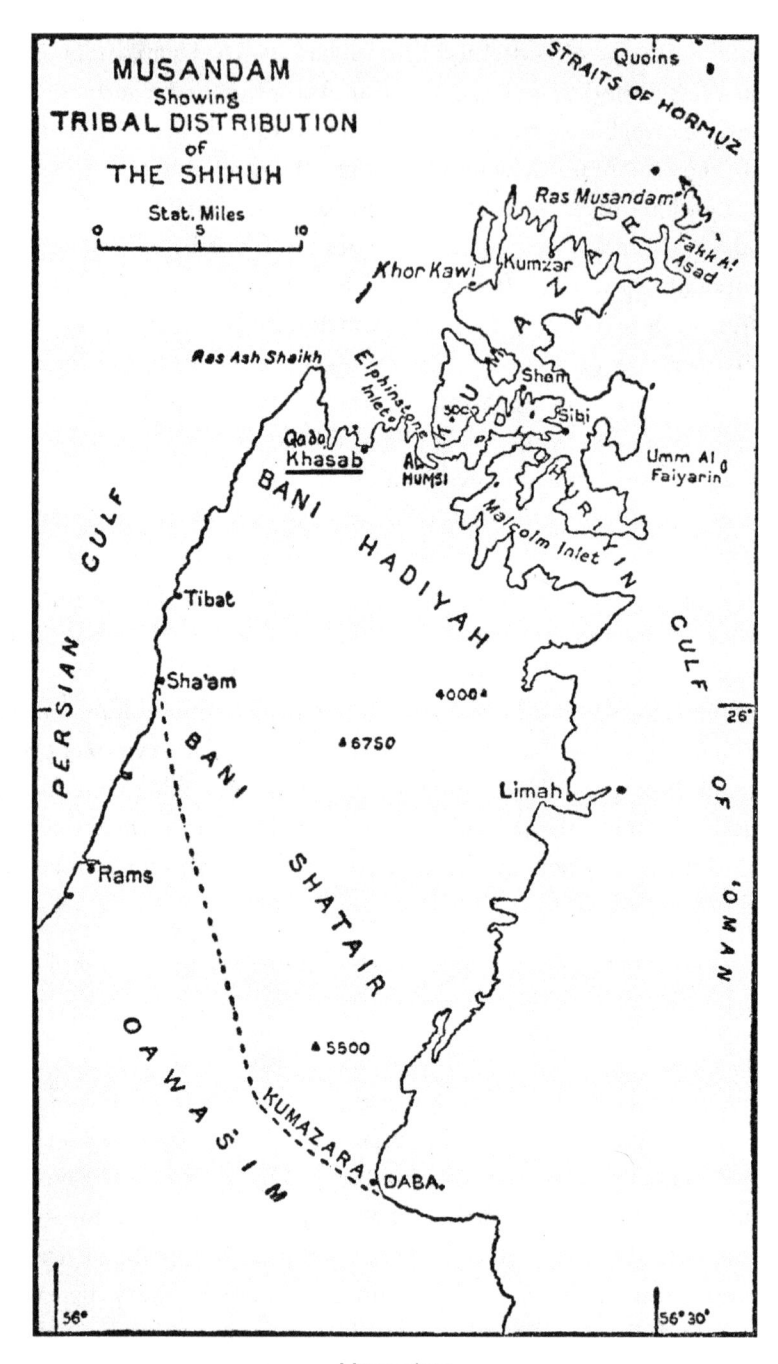

Musandam

Another source of opposition to H.M.S. *Ormonde* lay in a deep-rooted aversion to the foreigner, an aversion to him not so much qua foreigner as *qua* infidel. The religious exclusivism of tribal Arabia explains, perhaps, why the number of European travellers to have penetrated it usefully can almost be numbered on two hands. The Shihi habitat is so forbidding, however, that no European has ever dared to penetrate it at all, and the Hindu shopkeeper, who for centuries has been established in the neighbouring Sultanate and Trucial Oman ports, has here never found a footing. For the primitive tribesman, fanatical in his Shafi'ism, divides mankind into two categories (a) the Muslim and (b) the infidel — the wheat and the chaff, so to speak. The notion of a charitable toleration for Christian and Jew on the score that they are "people of the Book" is a refinement for theologians. He has never heard of it. Enough for him that the personnel of H.M.S. *Ormonde* belonged to category (b). A less fanatical shaikh than Hasan might have weighed the consequences, but Hasan felt his own pious reputation at stake. He was credited, indeed, with cherishing amongst his own followers a heresy-purging campaign after the model of the Wahhabi movement in Najd, with himself in the role of Imam; and matters were already advanced for compulsory attendance at midday prayers in the village mosque, and a public flogging for the delinquent. Could anything be more humiliating, then, than to acquiesce in contamination of their soil by infidel feet, or pollution of their mountain air by infidel survey flags?

He would challenge them, assured in his own mind that no ill could befall. Had they not renounced the sword? Had not his *mutawwa*, too, administered to him a sacred potion? No ordinary potion this — a glass of water over which were recited some verses of Holy Writ against snake-bites or bodily disease — but one the particular virtue of which insured him from the consequences of his acts for the round year.

The low tower where the shaikh lived was almost obscured from the sea; only its yellow battlements lifted themselves above the waving palms. It stood half a mile back, deep in the date-grove that skirted the edge of the cove, and round about it in a clearing were the rude houses of the villagers. Here was the objective of a small, mysterious party of men that landed from a newly arrived dhow one dark night towards the end of

January. None beheld them — unless the ramshackle old fort midway along the front kept a ghostly watch. Gaunt against the sky this fort stood, a frail memorial to Portuguese adventurers of Drake's time. Three centuries had passed since Admiral Ruy Frere da Andrada reared it for the base of operations against the dazzling prize of Hormuz, that lay just across the Straits to the northward. Below it, the tide rapidly ebbed, to uncover a thousand yards of beach; and the dhow, now high and dry, lay listing over upon its gently shelving bosom.

Khasab Fort

Stillness brooded beneath the great encircling amphitheater of mountains where nestled the sleeping village, save in that mean wartower, where in a dim, candle-lighted garret a party of six men sat plotting.

Offshore H.M.S. *Ormonde* rode at anchor hopefully awaiting permission for the prosecution of her humane task, and quite innocent of the barbarism that was frustrating it.

The following day the cat was out of the bag. Two letters had come to light: one was from Salih bin Muhammad, Shaikh of Daba, and was addressed to Shaikh Ibrahim bin Muhammad, Messenger of the Council of Ministers.

After salaams and the mercy of God and his blessings. Your honoured letter has reached us and the contents have been understood. Particularly with regard to the arrival of the man-of-war at Shabus and Khasab. Be informed, my brother, that we will not give our places to anybody absolutely, neither to the weak nor to any- body else. As for you, 5'ou are not a king over us so that you might discover our conditions, and we wish you to postpone the interference. And if King Saiyid Taimur arrived in the land of Muscat we will follow on his tracks to see what his Ministers are doing in this matter. That is what had to be said and salaams.

Dated 28th January, 1930.

(Signed) Salih bin Muhammad as Shihi.

The other was from Hasan bin Muhammad, Shaikh of Khasab, and was addressed to Saiyid Nasir bin Khalfan, Wali of Khasab, and Shaikh Ibrahim bin Muhammad bin Juma', Messenger of the Council of Ministers.

After salaams and the mercy of God and his blessings. The tribe in general and particular have been informed that you are desirous of placing a flag in the Ru'us al Jabal. This is absolutely impossible, and never obtainable from them neither as a favour nor with a price. Do not trouble us with a thing that we cannot endure. We apologize to you. Do not expect the friends to accompany you to-morrow morning to the places you desire. We warn you against it. Be it known to you. It is our desire to assist you to procure what is required so that you may be advanced by your good service with the Governments and officials, 'but muchness of water will spoil the flour'. Pardon us.

[Signed) Hasan bin Muhammad ash Shihi.

These two letters spoke with a single voice and bore the same date. But they had a greater significance: they issued over the signatures of the two rival and important shaikhs of the Shihuh tribe. Daba and Khasab stood for elements racially and linguistically distinct. Blood-feuds divided them, and, ironically enough, the keeping of the tribal peace between them was the *raison d'etre* of the Sultanate Wali at Khasab. A house normally divided against itself, they joined hands only in the face of a common enemy, such as was provided by the neighbouring Qawasim tribe — *Joasmees*, as they were known to the British sailor of the period, a race of bold pirates who had in the early days of the last century been a menace not only to the Shihuh tribe and to the Sultanate, but also to British merchant ships passing on their lawful avocations. It was from the suppression of this common enemy that the Shihuh-Muscat connection dated. Then the ties were the strong ties of mutual self-interest. Now with the passing of the Qawasim menace they had grown feeble. The link of sentimental attachment which survived, whatever the *de jure* position might be, would clearly not bear the strain of an act of disservice to Shihuh interests and sentiment, and the Shihuh regarded Muscat's part in authorizing infidel chart-making activities as nothing else.

Here was the upshot. A tribal pact had been solemnly and secretly sworn. The landing of any party was to be prevented: the Sultanate Wali must quit Musandam.

THE STATE GUNBOAT AL SAIDI'S COMMANDER

It was one midnight in late April. I was being rowed off from the beach at Muscat. My instructions were to proceed to the scene of the troubles and deal with a situation that had reached a dangerous pass.

"*Ub* anchor," shouted the Arab captain.

There was a grinding of windlass, the ship breasting up to her cable, the tinkle of the telegraphs, and now she forged gently ahead; thereafter a muffled thudding of engines down below, and a voice from the man in the chains that at intervals rang out across the black waters.

Al Sa'idi, a small yacht of 150 tons' burden, white hulled, with yellow funnel and masts raked jauntily, flew the red flag of Muscat. I had armed her with a three-pounder Hotchkiss gun, and two French machine-guns. Thus she constituted the Muscat Navy; a euphemism, perhaps, still she served her purpose as patrol ship, for which I had bought her from the Royal Indian Marine some four years earlier, since when she and I had explored every nook of the South-east Arabian coast for a thousand miles.

Shihuh Men

Captain Rashid emerged from his bowed meditation behind the lighted chart stand.

"North 25 west," said he gruffly to the helmsman, as he rang the engines full ahead, and the flash of the lighthouse perched on the flanking cliff of Muscat harbour darted round to *Al Sa'idi's* quarter, there to poise steadily over our wake winking as we made for the open sea. A son of Muscat was Rashid, a giant of a man, and a "character", too. Whenever I think of the old Muscat gunboat, I shall always picture her redoubtable commander. Captain Rashid, arrayed in his inevitable tunic, a flamboyant creation of his own in which he had indulged a rich Oriental taste. There was in this tunic a profusion of gold braid in Arabesque invention everywhere that deserved what it received, the accompaniment of a clanging gold sword — a *tour de force* that would win the prize at any ceremonial occasion.

Al Sa'idi was not Captain Rashid's first armed command. Before her had been *Nur al Bahr* (a grandiloquent if typical name for an Arab ship, meaning the "Light of the Sea"), until she had outlived her royal usefulness and now, in her old age, and under another flag, humbly plied for trade along the Indian coast. Her ex-Captain's figure had grown to represent a generous 18 stone, and his sixty years had fashioned it into

Buddha-like proportions. From its depths came a roaring voice, that seemed to instil chill obedience in the fo'c'sle rather than' a divine content. Rashid's every action was marked by a certain liveliness. His raised glass contained a miniature tempest always — a fascinating sight — and the shaky hand that gave rise to it was an infirmity, as I have heard him explain over and over, that dated from an affair of honour when he and another brown mariner had attempted to settle the matter with their daggers — the national weapon. Bo that as it may, a strict observance of the Muslim proscription calculated to prevent shaky hands — the avoidance of strong waters, to wit — had not claimed from our hero any very noticeable attachment.

Fate had seemed to smile upon the youthful Rashid. There was the loom of a handsome patrimony. His father, an Arab merchant, like his prototype immortalized in the *Thousand and One Nights*, sailed the seas in his own ships, and Rashid was brought up to the same tradition. These ships in the Muscat of old were as often as not ex-British "windjammers" that had been sold east before the advancing tide of "steam", and it was Rashid's lot to spend his youth as second officer of the full-rigged ship County of Lanark, late of Belfast, [35] a proud craft owned by the master and an heirloom for himself.

To-night he was in reminiscent mood. His mind harked back to those far-off days. He had reached the point where he had had enough of Calcutta, and, having just passed his Board of Trade examination there for "Foreign master, square rig" — a no mean achievement for an Arab without educational facilities in his own country — he had regarded the moment propitious for approaching his father for favours.

Now one of the five great ordinances of the Muhammadan religion is the Pilgrimage (*Haj*). Once a year on certain prescribed days this great event takes place at Mecca. As it is a costly undertaking, only the man of means is able comfortably to face the expenses; for him, therefore, the haj is obligatory once during his lifetime. Yet every Muslim, however poor, hopes for the virtue that comes from its accomplishment. So Rashid made his pious purpose known, and an old man, with a full heart for being vouchsafed such offspring, gave to his son a paternal blessing, six months' leave of absence, and a blank cheque.

Bombay was the first stop. Bombay! what must it answer for! Here were numberless distractions. A halt was cried, a dalliance made, and when at last the youthful traveller decided to move on, alas! the ship sailing for Jeddah and this year's Pilgrimage had left. Ah! but the world was young, and the first-class passenger ticket Rashid decided to take was by a ship bound for the port of Venice.

Venice was found to excel Bombay, and, in due time, Paris to be preferable to Venice. So a felicitous year passed by.

"Think of the educational opportunities, *Allahu Alim!*" said Rashid, as he smilingly recalled his youthful exploits, "And who would spurn the attractions of Italy and France which Pre- destination had so clearly laid at his feet?"

"Unanswerable," I thought.

Yet anyone who had had dealings with his father knew that that otherwise revered person was not a pleasant man to cross swords with; wherefore his own filial conscience began to stir within him. The month drew near for the ensuing Pilgrimage — the next one afterwards, so to speak. He must perforce turn his steps to the east, but would linger for a space in Port Said to fetch a bride, thence proceeding *a deux* to Jeddah. So it all happened; but at Jeddah he was overtaken by the embarrassment of depleted finances. This started him wondering whether the discomforts of the Pilgrimage would, after all, be improving for a young wife. He decided to leave her in a boarding-house in Jeddah, and himself passed on to Mecca and Medina in company with a great multitude in pursuit of salvation.

Thus, after two years' absence, home came Rashid, pilgrim and bridegroom. The blank cheque had been filled in and presented. But what was fifty thousand rupees to his father in those days — and, even so, it formed but a portion of his own inheritance? Nothing could be more logical than that.

He grew to man's estate; the adventures of a worthy middle life had been shared by the ocean and the harem. Armed with the right of facile Muslim divorce, Rashid had taken unto himself seven wives. But deviousness in courtship rather than constancy in the bonds seems to have been his guiding principle. Hence it was that one of the septet — a fair Circassian — had been ordered through the post from Constantinople, while another — her bust, pictorially represented on his enamelled cuff-links, ensured her an evergreen memory — was an Italian bride by whom he had been taken to the altar of Calcutta Cathedral.

Shihuh Sword Dance

Hugging the Batinah coast, we were making a steady seven knots as I turned to my amusing entertainer to say good-night before going below. At sea so long as we were under way Rashid never left the bridge. And if one came up in the small hours for a breath of cool night air, there, inevitably, was a cigar aglow or a cheerful humming to encounter. Rashid's inspiration had come with the years to derive from his ship and his tobacco. He was habitually happy, happy in the bluff manner of his lovable kind. Reduced circumstances he would ascribe to the Divine Purpose, and to the same source an unblushing past and a glorious future.

A spirit courageous, indeed!

IN THE LAND OF THE SHUHITES

"Let go!" shouted Captain Rashid, and the cable rattled through the hawse-pipe as *Al Sa'idi* shook up under reversed engines, and then swung listlessly to an anchor.

We had arrived at the southern gateway of the Shihuh country. The early dawn lit up the mighty Hajar that yesterday we had carried on our port beam, a blue range well back from the sea but which here approached the coast and hence to the northwards formed an ocean escarpment. Below the mountains was the magnificent sweep of the bay, and a date-grove that marched with it. The battlemented towers looked out of their palm settings at points where there were two small settlements. This was Daba, as old a village as can be found in the land, for Pliny, if this be his Dabanegoris Regio, gives it honourable mention, and here, certainly, the ancient Persian conquerors of the land made their last stand under a pagan standard, before the zealots of the Caliphate of Abu Bakr.

An old Portuguese gun in the more conspicuous of the towers — that which stood midway along the front — boomed out a friendly acknowledgment of my flag, the red flag of Muscat, flying at the; fore, and soon afterwards my old friend, the Qasimi Shaikh, came aboard to call. But it was the master of that other tower, his Shihi neighbour, that I had come to see — Shaikh Salih, who could play the strongest hand in the Shihuh and had already put his cards on the table. The Khasab incident was really no affair of his, yet in the nature of Shihuh relationships it was his sworn if passive support that had made it possible, if indeed he was not the instigator.

But I had come not to appraise blame, but to arrange a peaceful settlement if one was to be had, and my secret information that Hasan had already left Khasab on a visit to Salih was the reason of my visit.

Would Salih come off now that I had arrived? Safe conduct was his without the asking. We had met before, and he must know that. Nor was I mistaken. He was coming along even now. And so to the matter in hand. Why all this misunderstanding? Where was Hasan? Would he be reasonable? — and a general line in that spirit. I carefully refrained from reference to his own incriminating letter of two months ago — which was intended to keep the door open.

Shaikh Salih's attitude was not unfriendly, but it was defensive. He hedged. I saw clearly he was not going to commit himself or involve Hasan in compliance with satisfying Muscat demands, until he knew whether Muscat had the means to compel it.

It was my turn again. Could I come ashore and discuss the means of getting into touch with Hasan? Would he, Salih, accompany me to Limah or Khasab to arrange a meeting there?

"Your house" (i.e. his house), was the rejoinder, "is always at your disposal, but to-day your landing is inconvenient." Tomorrow', if God willed, he would come off again and give me his reply.

A hundred belted retainers followed him into his boat, which pulled for the shore to some old sea chanty. Odd men, these Shihuh! shepherds, fishermen, boat-builders and date-gardeners for the most part, when they were not on the warpath. To-day, each one of them bristled with arms, the inevitable Martini-Henry and a curious miniature axe peculiar to the tribe, as well as a double-bladed sword or an occasional spear. By and large the Shihi was an uncouth man, who looked unfriendly. Above us loomed the lofty exclusive mountains which are his home and which account for many strange things about him, such as his speech, a dialect of Arabic spoken nowhere else; or his silence — he is a recluse and a troglodyte, for natural caves provide him and his flocks with shelter. Where the natural caves are inadequate he makes artificial ones, the whereabouts of which he keeps a secret from his neighbours. To this end he hews a pit some fourteen feet square and roofs it over with acacia logs and earth to make it invisible to those walking abroad. A hatchway leads down a flight of steps to a dark interior where the existence of a capacious water tank enables him to disappear from the sight of men for long periods. This is the *bait al qufl*, so called from an inordinately long door-key which is a feature of it.

In his mountains the horse is unknown; the camel in small numbers may find sustenance from acacia jungle in the catchment folds, where, however, rain is never sufficiently copious to support large village settlements or allow cultivation beyond a strip of wheat and barley sufficient for local needs. Even the hardy ass can scarcely cope with the sterile conditions, and the Shihi lives on his forbidding hill-tops with his herds of nimble goats. To him the cow is anathema; he will neither eat its flesh nor drink its milk, and he is said to flee from the feast where beef is exposed — the plough, therefore, is drawn by his veiled womenfolk.

It was the morning following our day of arrival. I waited in vain for Salih's promised visit. The hour was already overdue when a rowing-boat was seen approaching. The white border to its red flag, however, denoted its occupants to be not of the Muscat connection, and it turned out that the Qasimi Shaikh had come off with Salih's messages.

"I am called away unexpectedly by a murder case, and it is inadvisable for you to land" — that was the purport. Rumour was rife that Hasan had already arrived at a neighbouring village, that he was coming to stay with Salih, that he was engaged in rousing the tribes to his banner in the event of punitive action being taken against him. The value of Salih's gesture yesterday was thus made evident. He was running with the hare and hunting with the hounds. In the eyes of Authority he was harbouring a recalcitrant shaikh, and I must give him a word of advice.

I sent ashore my Council colleague. Shaikh Zubair, partly to convey in peremptory language that he who was not for us was against us, partly to discover the present nature of the tribal situation.

"Four bells" had just been struck as Captain Rashid came to report the approach of one of H.M. ships. Arriving from seaward was a man-of-war. Long and low of hull, tall of mast and with two squat funnels, she was a beautiful and dignified model of lead, looking spick under a tropical sun. For me it was an unexpected visit, as *Al Sa'idi* was not equipped with wireless. But we soon established flag touch, and I went over to make my number. She was H.M.S. *Lupin*, the Acting Senior Naval Officer's ship, through which I had to report the situation. Her Captain, with similar instructions of my mission, had come in pursuit. We discussed plans. He would return direct to Khasab to await me. I would leave in *Al Sa'idi* at midnight to make Kumzar at a convenient daylight hour, and there endeavour to wean the Kumazara from their allegiance to the rebels and arrange an alliance against future developments.

But what was the significance of the War Dance on the beach that *Lupin's* telescopes had discovered? It seemed a rather flagrant challenge, they thought aboard.

The explanation was simple. *Lupin's* arrival had coincided with Shaikh Zubair's departure from the shore, and it was for the departing guest that the Shihuh were indulging their farewell ceremonial— the famous *nadabah* or *qubqub* — a tribal war-cry (but by no means limited to war) unique in Arabia so far as I am aware. A dozen tribesmen stand close together in a circle with heads bowed inwards and almost touching. In their midst stands the shaikh, or some person of quality, holding his left arm across his chest as though in a sling, and his right arm bent above and behind his head. Then, straightening and bending his elevated arm, he sets up a curious howl, not entirely unmusical, ascending and descending the scale over a compass of nearly an octave — a sort of vocal imitation of a swanny whistle pitched an octave or two below. Meanwhile his associates, with their hands to their mouths, *mu'edhdhin* fashion, break in at intervals with a chorus of barking, staccato and doglike. The rest of the tribesmen career about in a frenzied sword-dance, throwing their blades high into the air and catching them again with naked hands.

We rounded Musandam at dawn — Musandam, that excrescence on the eastern seaboard of Arabia which spoils the rectilinear symmetry of the great peninsula. A bleak and barren coast, indeed. The sea, as ever, was a seething cauldron, because of the conflicting currents that race through narrow courses between rocky islands and past tortuous headlands into the waisted entrance of the Persian Gulf.

Al Sa'idi swung wildly, and the uncomfortable thought of uncharted perils called to mind the daring of the ancient mariners such as Nearchus, Alexander the Great's captain, who navigated these same Straits of Hormuz under unstable sail, and achieved the voyage from the Indus to the Euphrates through these waters, all of them at that time uncharted.

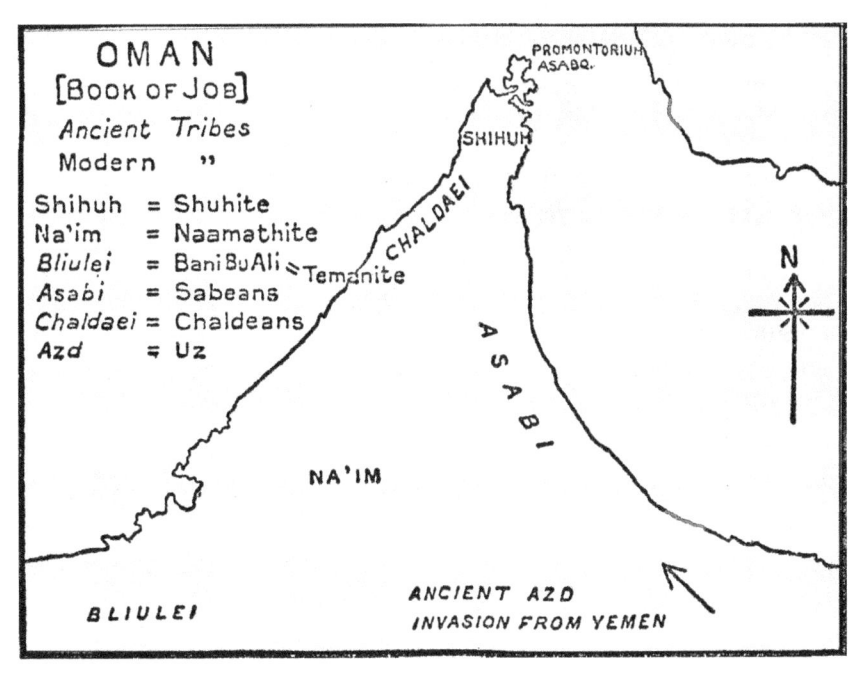

Ancient Azd Tribes in Musandam

"Ichthyophagi" the ancients labelled the inhabitants of this coast, and today the term is still applicable, but whether racial distribution has been much modified throughout the ages is a nice speculation. The Shihuh are clearly a composite tribe with definite racial and linguistic divisions, not only internally but also in relation to their Arab neighbours. As such they are a source of interest and of perplexity to travellers. Dr. D. G. Hogarth held them to be a pre-Semitic survival — a not unreasonable view of some of the remoter elements. The classical geographers are, unfortunately, silent about the Shihuh, as also, indeed, are the early Arab travellers, but the tribe have a tradition (as I was to learn from Shaikh Hasan) of a Sabaean origin, of having migrated in remote times from the land of Queen Belkis. Still, the silence of old writers is strange, in consideration of the supreme importance of the Persian Gulf as an ancient trade route, the prominence this mountainous peninsula must have attained as a landfall for mariners, and the tribal tradition of an ancient Shihuh occupation, a tradition supported by their peculiarities and by their location in this mountainous extremity of the land which would have been the natural asylum for the aboriginal.

Tribal tradition tends, of course, to extravagance, yet it is entitled with ancient tradition — e.g. the Mosaic account of the peopling of Arabia from the five patriarchal stocks of Cush, Jokhtan, Ishmael, Katurah and Esau — to the claim of reflecting, in some measure, historical facts. And here an interesting point arises. The Shihuh, having escaped the notice of historical geographers, has a record of the word having been preserved in the Shuhite of the Book of Job. I have found lively interest in discovering a set of coincidences between the old Biblical book names, and the tribal distribution and geographical terminology of ancient and present-day Musandam and its environs — a discovery that would show this area as providing a remarkably close tribal setting for the story of Job. [36] But let me say at the outset that I advance the theory more from a point of interest than as an intellectual conviction.

"When Job's three friends heard of the evil that had befallen Job, they came to console with him, everyone from his own place, Eliphaz the Temanite, Bilad the Shuhite and Zophar the Naamathite, for they had made an appointment together." Now three of the biggest and most ancient tribes in Oman to-day are the Bani Bu Ali, the Shihuh, and the Na'im. The latter two readily suggest identification with the Old Testament names; and the Bani Bu Ali — the Bliulaie of Ptolemy — derive, on the authority of Miles, from the ancient Bani Teman.

Thus the three kings of the East are to be equated with the three shaikhly comforters who by inherent probability would have been neighbours.

"And the Sabaeans fell upon the servants and took them away.

"The Chaldeans made out three bands and fell upon the camels and have carried them away."

The once popular conception of the Chaldeans as exclusively the people of Chaldea in Lower Mesopotamia, and the Sabaeans as the remote subjects of the Queen of Sheba in *Arabia Felix*, placed the land of Uz in an unenviable geographical position for a valid reason, namely that the story requires the habitat of Sabaeans and of Chaldeans both to have been within raiding distance of their victim. That Sabaeans were found not only in South-West Arabia is suggested by the name still attaching to a quaint people living in the Lower Euphrates where I once served amongst them as their Political Officer. Then there is the historical Sabi of the Persian Gulf with the local tradition I have referred to. The identification of the terms Chaldean and Bani Khalid — the latter a much scattered tribe in Arabia — has been widely suggested. However this may be, the classical geographers make specific references to Chaldeans and Sabaeans inhabiting the Oman Peninsula. Pliny places the *Gens Chaldei* under the Eblitae Mountains on the western side of Musandam, and Ptolemy, not only places the Asabi or Sabi (the prefix being merely the assimilated article) along both coasts, but also shows that they gave their name to the entire area — i.e. *Promontorium Asabo*, as he styles Ras al Musandam. This name is still preserved in the Shihuh village names of Khasab and Sibi.

Thus the geographical requirements of the story of Job would seem to be satisfied in an extraordinarily complete measure by tribal distribution in ancient and modem Oman. The identification of Azd — to which confederation belongs the Ruling house of Muscat to-day — with Uz is another curious coincidence, if not more, but it is only fair to add that the first historical reference I can trace to the Azdite migration is the invasion following the bursting of the dam of Ma'rab. If one remembers, however, that Oman supplied the ships and sailors for the ancient carrying-trade between Babylonia and India and that from the evidence of its theology the Book of Job is held by many to have been written not earlier than the time of the Babylonian captivity, it would appear not unreasonable to suppose that it was Musandam, that most prominent point on the Great Trade Route of those times, upon which a Babylonian author of the Book of Job drew for his local colour.

THE LIST OF INIQUITIES

EIGHT WEEKS of patient negotiation for permission to ascend the hill produced a final and categorical "No". This is how it was put:

From All the Shihuh Community of Qada,

To The High. Glorious, Honoured, and Stately Shaikh Jesus, Son of the Servant of the Kind One. [37]

Peace be upon you and God's mercy and his blessings always. And after be it known to you that the incident which has happened in connection with the English and the subjects of Shaikh Hasan and of Shaikh Muhammad bin Ahmad we have heard about it and now we inform you to be careful, you and the English. And Shaikh Hasan and all his subjects we have nothing to do with you and do not be interferers in our precincts and properties, and the place in which your desire lies is our property and precincts, and whoever of you trespasses in that quarter not one of you shall return. By God! By God! By God! and by the Lord's glory and by the Right of the Proud. We desire *Jihad* (religious war), and kill whomsoever arrives in our quarter and will spare none of them to return. There is no Governor who governs us and we are independent by ourselves and we do not recognize Shaikh nor Governor nor Sultan, and now we warn you with every warning, take heed to arrive at this place. And you, O Shaikh Isa! pardon from you. Be helpful to fend off the enemy with means that will succeed, and this is what is required of you. This is the policy of the infidels and do not bring upon yourself blame. And a hint will suffice the wise. This is what we have told you. We drink the blood and we do not care. It is requested from you to fend off this matter and do not interfere in our precincts and property. Your despotism be upon yourselves and your danger be upon yourselves. Do not blame us and salaams.

(Signed) Muhammad bin Sulaiman,

Shaikh al Badu in Qada.

Such was the letter brought aboard H.M.S. *Lupin* for the Residency Agent — an Arab in charge of British interests on the Trucial Coast, and a much-respected man throughout those parts.

Qada, whence the letter had come, was, therefore, just outside his sphere. It was, in reality, an appanage of Khasab, as were all these villages within the ambit of the harbour, and its shaikh, the alleged writer, a nonentity, or at most a mouthpiece for his master, Hasan. The letter itself came hard upon an early-morning skirmish. The Survey ship, after having waited vainly for two months in the daily expectation of a change of mind ashore, had understood that an accommodation had been reached overnight and that they were to send their landing-party into Qada Cove at sunrise. Not suspecting a trick, they sent off the gig with the Agent's son aboard at crack of dawn. But as they approached the beach, all became agog there. The wadi, strewn with giant boulders that had fallen from the steep containing cliffs and made a perfect ambush, was held by fifty or so armed men, who suddenly emerged, and, holding their rifles above their heads, shouted,

"Weigh! you must not come on!"

The party, still some way off the shore, were somewhat taken aback at the reception, and rested oars.

"But," they returned, "don't you know? Shaikh Hasan yesterday gave us permission!"

Elphinstone Inlet

"Then Shaikh Hasan hasn't the right to give anyone permission to land here, and whoever attempts to do so, we will resist."

It was unfortunate, but things might have been worse. There was but one thing to do if bloodshed was to be averted — turn and go back to the ship. And as the disappointed party pulled away the tribesmen called out challengingly that the Agent's son might land and come amongst them.

A fortnight earlier the Wali had suffered equal humiliation at the hands of Hasan himself. One of the fort *askaris* had gone into the bazaar. There, a slave of Hasan coveting his rifle and dagger, struck him, and secured possession of both prizes — and in the light of recent events and of a shaikh-dominated future these events seemed to portend, none among the eye-witnesses dared come to the *askari's* assistance. The shaikh had thereupon written to the Wali. But there was no mention of the incident or the arms in the letter. Instead, it told the Wali in plain language that his remaining in Khasab was to his own peril, that it were better to hand the fort over to him — the shaikh — and be gone. From that day onwards, indeed, neither the Wali nor his *askaris* ventured into the bazaar. Worse than this, a shaikhly edict had gone forth that the bazaar must henceforth boycott the fort, so that its rationing forthwith became an obligation of one of H.M. ships. And now the day following the Qada incident came Hasan's crowning folly. He placed an armed guard over the well which supplied the fort with water, and issued orders to boatmen forbidding them to take the Wali off to ships.

For those in authority on the spot the cup was full. Eight weeks' negotiating for the privilege of ascending a wretched hill had not only come of itself to naught but had also led to this pass. The Survey ship, returning periodically from small neighbouring surveys, was due to leave for one or other of the Seven Seas, but could scarcely do so with her Khasab plans left wholly unfulfilled. So an alternative hill to the hill of desire, though less desirable, was found in another part of the harbour. It had lately been abandoned by its villagers, and served the purpose well enough. Some three weeks had elapsed since the last of these events occurred when Khasab Cove came to know once more the strident tones of Captain Rashid. It was late afternoon on April 30th when *Al Sa'idi* slid into her berth inside H.M.S. *Lupin* — her first appearance here since the trouble began, H.M.S. *Lupin* having arrived the day before, a day ahead of us in the passage from Daba, according to plan.

"*Aria* boat! *Aria* boat!" shouted Captain Rashid, but before we could get our skiff away. *Lupin's* motor-boat came alongside for me, and within a few minutes I was aboard the man-of-war, immersed in a sea of signals. The situation was no better than had been reported. Ashore the atmosphere was tense. It had long been unsafe for anyone to land. Shaikh Hasan's prestige had grown with success, and was now, by God's will, unquestioned and supreme. Hasan had not yet returned from Daba, where I had left him three days before, so I sent a message after him. In a day or two he arrived, but not, as we soon found out, to meet me. He was adamant. He refused to come off to the ship under safe conduct. He declined to meet me in the fort ashore. Equally he declined to meet either my Council Colleague, Shaikh Zubair, or a member of the Ruling Family, Saiyid Malak, the Sultan's brother, whom I had brought along against such a contingency as this — for the Shihuh were notoriously boastful of their loyalty to the Albu Sa'id dynasty, and fifteen years earlier elements of them had fought under the Muscat banner in the Oman Civil War. Apologists ascribed Hasan's present attitude to fear. He may have been afraid. He acted as if he wasn't. The only effect of his return to Khasab was that local fishermen who spread their nets under our noses every day were prohibited from coming alongside to sell us our morning's breakfast — and Khasab mackerel is not a fish to be despised.

The "fringe" was running strictly in accordance with "form". Hasan's experience encouraged his belief that nothing would happen to him. There was no fear of penalties. The *Mutawwa's* potion was working. He would go on with it.

I now left *Al Sa'idi* and crossed over to join H.M.S. *Lupin* "for the duration". My appreciation of the situation must go through her captain, with whom, therefore, the closest collaboration was necessary. The position demanded immediate action. The Muscat State, left to itself, had not the resources at its command to deal with the situation. And if the situation was not dealt with, a worse one would supervene; for the authority of Muscat in Musandam, shadowy though it may have been before, would then be extinguished, the prestige of H.M.S. ships would suffer, landing of European personnel in future, tribal psychology being what it was, would be attended with grave personal risks, and finally, there might be repercussions of the rebellion elsewhere, for Hasan's victory would be an encouragement for others to play the same game.

The Captain and I addressed ourselves seriously to joint proposals which, as soon as we had drawn them up, would go flashing from *Lupin's* aerials to the distant seats of those in authority. In the time that elapsed before the answer came we set ourselves to explore the harbour thoroughly against the probability of operations.

There is a massive grandeur in this mountainous promontory with its deeply indented sandy coves and placid seas. The light is extraordinarily pure, so that the scenery, grand in itself, seems to take on some ethereal quality. Stratified cliffs reflect patches of exquisite colour in the unmoiled water, and the high hills at early morning and late afternoon are often enveloped in rose- coloured splendour.

On the east side of the harbour is Elphinstone Inlet, a remarkably fine fiord seven miles long, with Ras Sham, a sentinel mountain of 3,000 feet, marking its otherwi.se deceptive entrance. Throughout its serpentine course mountain ridges, scarcely less imposing than Jabal Sham, flank it on both sides. On their desolate slopes appears here and there an incongruous tree, or a flock of goats swarming along precarious ledges a thousand feet above a Dhuhuri village that nestles by the shore. *Batils*, quaint, gondola- like craft, swarm the waters, with here and there a fisherman standing in the prow and using the weirdest measures. He has a coiled hand-line, baited with nothing more than a wad of cotton- wool, winged with two feathers to give it the appearance of a "locust of the sea", as the Arabs call the flying-fish, and his cunning is to fling it out, lasso- fashion, and haul it rapidly hand over hand so that the bait comes skipping along the surface to the undoing of the tunny that abound. These fishing folk would shortly be quitting their nets for the pearl banks of Trucial Oman, for the summer pearl fishery there draws all men from neighbouring coasts. It is this industry — pearl-diving — which, by reason of its arduousness and its rewards, is, perhaps, the greatest single factor making for the perpetuation of slavery in these parts.

The possession of slaves, I may remark in passing, is general throughout South-east Arabia. It would be unusual for a shaikh or person of consequence to be without some "head". They customarily provide the material of his bodyguard — an old tradition — because the slave is held to be capable of exceptional personal fidelity and is, therefore, invaluable when regicide — a fate experienced by many tribal leaders — is being planned. They are, moreover, the instruments for the murder of a rival. Three to four slaves will be found attached to the poorest shaikh, but the possession of double the number is not abnormal. Great Britain's Slave Trade Agreements with the Sultan of Muscat and the Trucial Chiefs of 1845, 1856 and 1873, followed by considerable British Naval activities, practically put a stop to imports from overseas and to open slave markets in local ports, but they have not succeeded in suppressing internal slave usage. This endures from the force of public opinion and the sanction of religion, as locally interpreted.

A Cyclamen/Lupin class cruiser

The Oman slave market is said to have been satiated before the operation of these treaties, and the institution has continued by slave begetting slave. Such manumission as has taken place has not solved the problem; and help has not come, nor is it likely to come, from a more enlightened public opinion such as exists in Iraq or Syria. The religious *Mutawwas*, the chief priests and scribes, so to speak, are, in this illiterate land, still the chief, if not the only, repository of learning and influence, and they regard anti-slave activities as alien if not heretical and subversive. The law of the land is the Holy or *Shar'a* law, perhaps the most sacred and powerful institution in tribal Oman. Its ordinances no authority can defy without becoming discredited, or, indeed, incurring odium. By this law the slave is "property", and on a master's death the slave forms part of the estate, and his or her value is subject to the usual rigid laws of Muslim inheritance. While a change of public opinion has in late years greatly modified the once hard lot of the slave, and to-day there is no obtrusive buying and selling as in pre-treaty days, yet the operation of the *Shar'a* laws of division of inheritance must, and does, entail slaves changing hands on a monetary basis. Local slavery is of two kinds, domestic and industrial. Slavery in Arabia is, generally speaking, "domestic" — a comparatively innocuous kind, which I have already remarked upon, and which has no counterpart in modern Europe, and certainly bears no resemblance to slavery in the European conception of the word. But the slave who is pearl-diver and to a lesser extent date-cultivator, that is to say, the slave of these parts, very largely belongs to that other category which affords points of contact with our own methods of two centuries ago. Such a slave will here be found labouring in his master's date-groves or at his fishing-nets for the greater part of the year. He receives no wages, but is given food and clothing, and in theory it would appear to the master's interests to keep him fit and contented. If the master has no garden the slave is generally put out to cut firewood, or else is liberated to fend for himself in the neighbourhood, custom requiring that he bring a load of firewood each week as the mark of servitude. The slave who wishes to fly makes use of the opportunity thus afforded, but public opinion is such throughout the length of the land that as soon as the runaway is detected, the local shaikh of that part arrests him and returns him to his former owner. The metallic chink of ankle-chains, heard, perhaps, from the bull-pit of a well within the date-grove, is an indication of some such ill-fated escapade.

It is the industry of the pearl banks of Trucial Oman that at once yields the world its choicest gems and illustrates the economics of slavery. The army of men moving annually from the south to its service is made up of individual contingents, often tribal units, and some considerable percentage of each are said to be slaves. For slaves are generally the expert divers, as they have "dived" from their boyhood upwards, and in consequence their earnings are considerably more than those of the freemen, who chiefly do the "hauling up" and other auxiliary work of the pearling fleets. The freeman enjoys the fruits of his labour; the slave's earnings go to his master. The pearling contingent, bond and free, is accompanied to the "banks" by a tribal agent, who enlists them generally with the *nakhuda*, with whom he habitually has dealings, and in order to secure good terms is prepared some- times to give a lien on the future services of the slaves. The *nakhuda*, who has been financed by the pearl merchant, thereupon makes an advance in money and rice (the staple diet of the Omani Arab who can afford it) against the harvest. This the agent takes back to the master, and so comes again at the end of the pearling season to collect the balance of the earnings as well as the human source of them.

Two years had passed since I had last visited Khasab to investigate a slave petition. Two Baluchi lads had been trapped and sold into slavery some six years earlier. They were now traced to Khasab, where Shaikh Hasan denied knowledge of them. That they were in his house was testified by State menials, who prayed that their own names might not be divulged lest they suffer afterwards for their effrontery. One of the slaves had, indeed, escaped to the fort, but no *askari* was bold enough to give him sanctuary; he therefore returned to his master, and had been confined and given exemplary chastisement for his pains. The Council's letter demanding the surrender of the slaves was, as I say, met by the shaikh's stout denial of their presence, and it required but a small stratagem to pass them on beyond official surveillance to a neighbouring village, where their safe custody could be left to an ally until the official memory had grown faint. The petition went unsatisfied. Indeed, to have pressed matters would have created a situation involving the use of force.

Then came the Khasab murder case, an ugly affair in cold blood and with cold steel. The unfortunate was believed to have been an itinerant Moorish doctor who, according to the Shihuh, had failed to cure anybody, though he took their fees. Truth was that among his possessions was a heavy tin box, and this box was vulgarly supposed to contain a horde of rupees. Thus lust of loot had been the motive of the crime. A year had passed since then; but the shaikh considered that the Wali's demand for the surrender of the murderers of an obscure foreigner, coming from none knew where, was unnecessarily squeamish. And so they had remained at liberty.

Such was the dark mood of Musandam.

Sheikh Salih of Kumzaara

A NAVAL BOMBARDMENT

Aboard H.M.S. *Lupin* the days passed pleasantly. Number One spent his time very energetically up aloft selecting targets and making range tables; the gunner went over his various ammunition, and the signal officer evolved a table of signals for use with the Arabic-speaking Al Sa'idi. All this was against the day of battle. For now there was a feeling of suppressed excitement in the air as we awaited the approving word of authority for our stem designs.

The yeoman passing to and fro on his message-carrying duties aft attracted unusual attention. "Was this the signal?" "Was this?" — till one day the keen Signal Officer, cap under his arm, stood to attention in the Captain's cabin. "A signal is coming through, sir," he said; "it is from X, sir. N groups, sir."

"This looks like it," was the Captain's remark.

Five minutes later he looked up buoyantly from the fateful signal he held in his hand.

"Good," he said. "We're for it now," and passed the signal across the table to me.

A Cyclamen/Lupin class cruiser

The British Government had agreed to support the authority of the Muscat State, and *Lupin, Cyclamen*, and *Al Sa'idi* were to proceed with the measures we had submitted. A thrill went through the ship, for the sailors belonged almost all to a post- War generation, and this was to be their first experience of being "under fire" — for it was improbable that the Shihuh would take their punishment lying down. In fact, they had already built a small sniper's tower a night or two earlier on a cliff overlooking the harbour, some 800 yards from our anchorage, and stalwarts carrying rifles came swaggering along the beach each morning, and swarmed up the rocks to occupy it till nightfall. A trifle rash of them, perhaps, as it need last only as long as we allowed it, but it was a symbol of a combative spirit ashore.

And now to the writing of the ultimatum! But there were things that came before that. The Wali's wife and children were in the fort, and must be evacuated before the ultimatum was launched. The fort, too, would need reinforcing, for the Wali's normal garrison of less than a dozen *askaris* would be woefully insufficient, would, in fact, be inviting trouble.

That night I crossed over to *Al Sa'idi* and we weighed and put to sea.

"I want to arrive at Kumzar as soon as possible after dawn to-morrow," I said to Captain Rashid.

If Musandam Peninsula is likened to an anvil, Kumzar is the point where the blacksmith's hammer falls when it falls most truly. I had visited it many times before, and the halt I had made there on my way north from Daba was made in anticipation of this visit. At dawn we were steaming between precipitous, wind-swept hills towards the village that nestled under the precipice ahead. I landed on the sandy beach amidst a hundred handsome *batils* drawn up there uniformly on their even keels, thence through lanes of teeming fisherfolk into the village itself, a closely crowded collection of unpretentious flat-roofed houses. Coming to a certain house, the dwelling of my old friend Muhammad bin Mahdi, I entered. Now Kumzar obeyed four several shaikhs, and Muhammad was but one of them, although the most influential and loyal, for the other three had been sworn to the Pact; they, indeed, with their kinsman, Salih of Daba, had formed the party of Khasab conspirators on that fateful night of January.

"Well, Shaikh Muhammad," said I, "you've had nearly a month. Have you been able to arrange it?"

"All is ready. Your Excellency."

"Very well! I want a hundred men landed in Khasab to-night. It must be to-night, and it must be done with great secrecy, as I'm anxious that Shaikh Hasan should not be provoked into opposing the landing."

"But," said Muhammad, "we can't get there in the time. This Shamal is a contrary wind."

"That's all right; you'll be towed part of the way. And you. Shaikh, I want you yourself to land first, go straight to the fort and embark the Wali's family, send them back in your own boat to-night to be looked after here till the troubles are over. You and your men will remain and report to the Wali in the fort."

Shaikh Muhammad belonged to the old school, and did not hold with the Sultan's enemies. Old personal scores with the Shihuh of Khasab were also known to rankle in his breast. He was, in short, an enthusiastic ally.

"Send Juma to me," he shouted to a slave, and a confidant came in. "Listen, O Juma" — and he poured forth a stream of orders in that strange Iranian dialect that is exclusively spoken by the Kumazara.

I gazed round the poor room with its single carpet and dowdy cushions, conscious that this was in very truth a tomb, that within a few feet of us were the decaying bones of Muhammad's kindred of many past generations. For, like the Dravidians or other ancient races that dwelt in Anau across the waters, these Kumazara bury their dead in their own houses under their living-rooms.

A stream of fish-wives carrying pitchers on their heads lined the wadi-bed as I emerged from Shaikh Muhammad's house. This bed led to the single well the village boasts under the backing cliffs, a well that, local legend maintains, will dry up whenever a dog shall bark there; hence it is that that useful scavenger of the fishing village is not to be seen in Kumzar. Had the barking chorus of their *nadabah* any connection? I wondered. Maybe not, for that war-cry is common to the other and original elements of the Shihuh who have not the dog taboo. I was being treated to a rendering of it as I pushed off from the beach. There also four *batils* were being slid down into the water, a sign that Muhammad had lost no time in getting our plans in train.

It was after the midday prayer in the mosque — this in deference to the old man's wishes — that these four craft came pulling off, each crowded with a party of twenty-five men in all their war-paint.

"Pay out that line," shouted Captain Rashid, as the sound of their rousing chanty grew near, and the warrior with drawn sword, who, standing in the prow, did a kind of pursuing practice as the boat leapt forward, cut his last flashing figure in the air

"Take that line there," said the Captain; and within a few minutes *Al Sa'idi* was steaming out of the blue inlet into the choppy open sea of the Straits of Hormuz with four prancing batils in tow.

It was late afternoon when we dropped them, a few miles off Khasab just out of sight of the beach; there in the offing they must wait for nightfall, and then pull secretly in and land. As for *Al Sa'idi*, she steamed on in innocent loneliness to her berth in the harbour in time for piping down the colours — an observance which Captain Rashid was scrupulous about when H.M. ships lay near him. *Lupin's* launch was already cutting across to us as we dropped anchor to take me over to rejoin. As we drew along-side the man-of-war, there were signs and tokens. The ensign no longer flew over the stem, where it might get in the way of fire of the after gun, but aloft from the peak. The awnings and stanchions had come down. This gave the ship a certain naked appearance, like a sailing-ship with her sails furled.

That night there were to be no searchlights. Muhammad deserved that, I remembered. It was time I wrote the ultimatum.

From The Government of Muscat,
To Shaikh Hasan bin Muhammad, the Shuhite.

We order you to surrender yourself unconditionally to your Government, the Albu Sa'id Government, in the gunboat *Al Sa'idi*, within a period of 48 hours from the receipt of this ultimatum by you. If you do not so submit yourself, Muscat and British forces will bombard property in the Bani Hadiyah area of Khasab by sea and land, together with that of its coastal village dependencies, i.e. Qada, Mukhi, Hana, Fanakha, Al Humsi, Ghassa, Al Harf, and Nadhifi.

And thereafter we shall bombard again frequently, unless you surrender.

No fishing will be allowed, and no other craft be permitted to arrive or leave.

If you surrender yourself, this will not take place, but if you do not surrender yourself, be it known to you that for any damage resulting from these measures you will be responsible.

(Signed) The Council of Ministers, Sultanate of Muscat and Oman.

"To The Inhabitants of the Area of Khasab subject to the Shaikhship of Hasan bin Muhammad

We hereby order you to leave [Khasab] immediately, so that your lives may not be endangered, and do not return until we have made a settlement of Khasab affairs, because your area will be liable to frequent bombardment. Enclosed is a copy of the ultimatum we have sent to Shaikh Hasan.

(Signed) The Council of Ministers, Sultanate of Muscat and Oman.

Thomas with other members of State Council

A small boat had taken the ultimatum ashore. A garrison of a hundred friendlies looked out from the fort and saw her go past, for Muhammad, the Kumzar, had not bungled during the night. A black flag was broken on the mast of a small craft near the beach. It denoted the time of receipt of the letter by the Shaikh, a matter of importance, marking, as it did, the hour, two days hence, when, failing the surrender of the Shaikh, the bombardment would commence. For we were giving two whole days' notice, in order that the town might be evacuated and that there might be no intentional loss of life. And the little villages round about were treated likewise. These, however, were already mostly empty, for their men had flocked to Hasan's standard at Khasab.

"'There is no answer," said the small boat's crew on returning; "Shaikh Hasan took both letters himself."

"Here, take this," said I, handing a duplicate copy. "Take it by another way, and post it up in the bazaar" — for it was necessary to take every precaution in case the Shaikh, for his own purposes, concealed the knowledge from his people.

Twelve hours passed, twenty-four, thirty-six, and never a sign appeared of compliance with the demands. Only the men of Qada ceased to come and occupy their hill tower — very wise of them. As for Hasan, did he think we were bluffing? Had his belief, born of his intuition that we were unwilling to act, now turned into a conviction that we were unable to act? It seemed so. We heard nothing from the shore, except a mocking rumour that the Shaikh had a gun, too.

At dawn on Monday, April 21st, H.M.S. *Lupin*, H.M.S. *Cyclamen* and *Al Sa'idi* seemed like "swans asleep", as they lay at anchor indolently, just as they had done for a month past and more. But movements aboard did not belong to the normal routine. The day of execution had arrived, ensigns flew from the peaks, decks were cleared for action, and voluminous smoke belched from five funnels. The hour was approaching, *Cyclamen* and *Al Sa'idi* were already under way and making for their distant stations, for Operation Orders detailed them for the east side of the harbour that day.

In this middle act I was to be "off". My role was that of spectator only, and I went up on *Lupin's* bridge to witness her application of herself to Khasab.

The main deck below the bridge bristled with men at action stations, and about it shells were arranged in readiness.

Boom!

That was our warning gun — a blank round from a three-pounder aft.

Boom! came the delaying echo of *Cyclamen*, as she lay hidden in the entrance of Elphinstone.

This was the signal for ten minutes' grace, so that possible laggards ashore might take to cover before we began the bombardment in earnest.

Number One, his glasses slung round his neck, scaled the foremast and leapt lightly into the crow's-nest, for his was the important job of fire control.

We looked at our watches. It was time to carry on, but no! Number One was shouting down to the Captain:

"I believe I saw a movement onshore, sir."

"Damn 'em! Why don't they clear out?" — a pause.

"Very well! pass the order," said the Captain, "stand by to fire another warning blank!"

And so ten minutes' more grace was given.

A strong easterly wind was blowing, which swung us at a convenient angle with the beach so that our forward 4-inch gun was nicely bearing.

"Carry on!" said the Commander, looking up from his watch to Number One aloft.

A pause.

Then from the crow's-nest came a slow, deliberate, clear order.

"Number 1 gun — range 3,000 — left 4 — load — fire!"

There was an ear-splitting report. The ship seemed to quiver under the mighty explosion. A tongue of fire, a burst of hot fumes, and the shell went shrieking to its goal. A pause. Then a noise of distant thunder, >and a cloud of smoke rose at the front of the grove that marked the fall of the shell.

"Number 1 gun — down 100 — right 1 — load — fire!"

Again the shock, again the deafening noise, and the hot smell of the bursting charge.

"Good shot!" said the Captain, watching the fall through his glasses, and when the smoke cleared the Shaikh's dhow, lying on the beach, was seen to have a gaping hole tom in her broadside.

And so the targets were taken in the order of the beach first, gradually ranging back into the town — a creeping barrage, we called it in the Great War. Here it was employed for the humanitarian reasons that any men in rear might save themselves. Half an hour had passed, and a haze of cordite smoke hung like a mantle over the stricken village.

That was enough for Khasab to-day!

We were under way.

"Ship going ahead, sir!" said the man in the chains.

"Midships," said the navigator; then, "Starboard twenty."

"Twenty of starboard helm on, sir!" came the voice of the man at the wheel below, and *Lupin* made a graceful sweep towards the cove of Qada hard by.

As we reached the point that marked the hidden inlet, our warning "blank" was fired.

"Slow ahead!" said the Captain.

"Hard a starboard."

"Helm's hard a starboard, sir."

"No bottom," sang the leadsman.

"Midships."

"Helm's amidships, sir!"

"Steady."

"Steady, sir!"

"There are some armed men running along the cliff ahead, sir — there they have dropped, sir!" said the Yeoman looking through his telescope.

"Where?"

"Deep, eight," sang the man in the chains.

"There," said Number One pointing, "shall I turn a Lewis gun on to them?"

"Not necessary, they have not fired at us," said the Captain, mindful of his own Operation Orders, that laid down that every precaution must be taken against the loss of human life.

We crept onwards into the jaws of Qada Cove. Even now, so narrow was it, I thought I could have thrown a cricket-ball ashore on either side, and the cliffs were narrowing as we went.

The objective was partly screened at this point because just ahead the creek took an ugly turn.

"By the mark, seven, sir!" came the measured, sing-song, down-hill voice from the chains.

Then almost immediately, "And a half six, sir."

Whizz! Crack! there was the whiplike crack as an enemy bullet struck the iron ship — a pause — then ping! as another whistled over our heads on the bridge.

"There they are, sir," said the Yeoman, pointing to the top of the hill where occasional puffs marked the scene of desultory firing.

"One of the port Lewis guns to open up on that target," came the order. "Aim above them; it's sufficient to keep their heads down"; and there followed the devilish clatter of machine-gun fire in short bursts.

We were approaching the curve whence the village would appear again.

"Number 1 gun come into action as soon as the target is bearing."

Ping! again — as a bullet whistled over us from another angle.

Ping! Ping! Ping! and I felt myself ducking — a ridiculous thing to do as bullets that you hear are past.

"Hands below off the bridge," said the Captain, and the Captain's Messenger, the Yeoman and others legged down the ladder to cover.

"Take cover, Thomas — there, behind that range-finder."

Number One had his lips against the fire-control speaking-tubes. "Search the rocks with the port pom-pom," said he, and soon the noise was infernal. Every type of gun-fire reverberated between these narrow cliffs. It was a deafening roar. Before us rolled up clouds of smoke from shattering debris in the villages hidden in the palms.

Crack! a bullet struck the bridge, almost at the same time as three spurts of water leapt into the air alongside the ship where more bullets were falling.

"By the mark, 'five, sir!"

"What did he say?" shouted the Captain to the Navigator above the din.

"Five fathoms, sir."

"Hard a port," said the Captain.

"Half-speed ahead — 90 revolutions."

(Had she room to turn? I wondered.)

"Stop."

"Half-speed astern."

"Ship's stopped, sir," came the voice from the chains.

"Tell the after three-pounders to come into action on the turn," said Number One.

"Hard a starboard."

"Helm's hard a starboard, sir!" came from the wheel-house.

"Ship's going astern," shouted the leadsman.

Bang! Whizz! there was merry hell again after the lull occasioned by the swinging ship, and now the after guns began to bear.

"Half-speed ahead — 94 revolutions."

"Hard a port."

"Helm's hard a port, sir," repeated the helmsman.

"Midships."

"Helm's amidships, sir!"

"Deep, six, sir!" came the voice of the leadsman.

The deafening clatter continued.

"That's a good one," I shouted, and pointed to a dhow. The gunner firing a three-pounder himself had made a direct hit, the craft leapt into the air, and settled slowly down on even keel, her unequal masts showing sorrily above the shallow water inshore.

"By the mark, seven, sir!"

"Cease fire," ordered the Captain, "but Lewis gun to remain loaded."

"Deep, eight, sir!"

We were emerging once more into the open harbour, and my three companions on the bridge, the Captain, Number One, and the Navigator, smiled the smile of men who understand their craft.

Somebody took the cotton-wool out of his ears, and we all followed suit and thereby became articulate again.

"That ought to larn 'em," said Number One.

"It is certainly what they've been asking for," I replied, showing no sign of what I was really thinking — and that was *Lupin's* own fine performance of skill and daring and her sporting spirit, and the thrill of pride I felt in the manner our ships go about their occasions.

"Personally, I give the Qadites full marks," said the Captain. "They put up a show. Now when we go in there next time we'll..." and I remembered that the Captain had a flair for going into places. He had, in fact, been the Navigator who took the Vindictive in against the Mole at Zeebrugge.

"They aren't such bad shots either," said the Chief as we came down off the bridge. "Look here!" and he pointed to where a bullet had struck the wheel-house and ricocheted off against the steam-pipe that worked the steering gear and had made a dent in it. That might have been a most unfortunate shot. Another bullet had made a hole in the deck close by, another had holed an after-scuttle, and others had chipped the paint along the ship's side. But there were no casualties. The Sick Bay was empty. And the young doctor, trained to the use of saws and lances and expecting a field-day, stood disconsolate, as if he considered he'd been cheated!

And so *Lupin* returned to her anchorage. *Cyclamen* and *Al Sa'idi* returning to theirs at about the same time. *Cyclamen*'s Captain, a jolly personality, came over in his motor-boat to compare notes and ask us to dinner. He confessed to fewer thrills than we had had —but I thought of his standards — he had commanded a submarine in the North Sea throughout the War. *Cyclamen* had done extraordinarily well, of course, and if we had our Qada, she had her Al Humsi, and there was little in it.

The question was: What would be the reactions of it all ashore? Meanwhile, my Council Colleagues and I would issue letters to Bakha, Lima, and our old friend. Shaikh Salih of Daba, to inform them of the action taken, our objective, and a warning on no account to succour the rebel lest they become no better than he.

But there was a letter from the shore, the first from any insurgent source since the bombardment. Here, then, was what Qada thought about it all.

To Saiyid Malak, Son of Saiyid Faisal, Sultan of Muscat and Oman.

May God save him and keep him and glorify him and protect him and make the Paradise his dwelling and the Peeping Nymphs for his reception, and then we all people and your slaves from before Qada, we inform your high and noble position. O our lord! we are your people and slaves and the dust of your feet from the time of our fathers and forefathers, and now as it is not concealed from you that Hasan had become a governor over us, and to-day we do not want him to be either Shaikh or Governor at all, and to-day we beg your pardon and forgiveness and we are under your orders and command and cannot disobey you. You are our Imam and Sultan, and we want a reply from you soon by hand of the bearer of this letter, and what- ever your commands we are obedient to you and we beg of you pardon. Pity us, O lord! Make us a favour. You are the people who grant favour, and whatever is demanded of us that shall be given.

From all the Shihuh of Qada,

(Signed) Shaikh.

The letter, it was amusing to note, was in the same hand as that other letter of theirs sent eight weeks ago. Then they were arrogant with success, recognized no authority, were "drinkers of blood". Now they had reformed. They were after a separate peace.

"No," I said, "that would never do." These villages belonged to Shaikh Hasan, and up to twelve hours ago Hasan was their vaunted champion. They would follow him to hell, if necessary. This conversion was too sudden as yet. Clearly, if everybody sued for separate peace and got it, all Hasan need do would be to retire to his mountains, wait until the ships had been drawn off, and emerge as Shaikh again with added prestige. To concede to the Qada petition would be a step most calculated to stultify ultimate success. The only possible way of achieving our objective and a lasting settlement lay in Hasan's becoming thoroughly discredited in the eyes of his followers! And so a Council letter was issued to Qada in the sense that there could be no peace until Shaikh Hasan had surrendered.

But there was no compelling reason why he should surrender as yet. He perhaps thought that we might now be content to go away. Our minds ran in another direction. Would he give in? Would he ask to come in and treat? The speed of such action on his part, after all, was likely to be in proportion to the pressure we applied. Considerations of humanity required our giving due notice before each bombardment so that there need be no stampede ashore from the fear of loss of human life. Furthermore, shell-fire on houses chiefly of mud could do comparatively little damage. No! Hasan was not discredited as yet. But it was a matter of time. For the sinking of their craft entailed widespread incidence of loss, and the gradual attenuating of their food supplies must have steadily growing effect.

The "lower deck" were more concerned with the action itself; and wherever two or three hands were forgathered, a post-mortem was held. The findings of some were amusing in the extreme, for I was on occasions an invisible audience. This arose from my occupying the Captain's sea cabin for'ard, where I found myself, alas! well placed for eavesdropping. A downright summing-up came floating through my ports one sunny morning. It was a leading seaman's commentary on the Qada letter, of which a translation had been put up on the Men's Notice Board. "Peeping nymphs!" said he, scornfully, to his pal. "All the peeping them b-s do is along their b-y sights!"

Hasan's stock started to depreciate after the second bombardment a week later. His house had been struck and part of his watch-tower knocked down. The people saw the hand of God in it. An opposition party had already arisen in the town, and there were murmurings against the folly that had brought this wrath upon them. Hasan himself, strong in the faith of his security against the infidel, must, they agreed, submit to what was come to pass. It was predestined; and I recalled the views of the Shuhite of old: "Doth God pervert judgment? or doth the Almighty pervert justice? If thou wert pure and upright, surely now He would awake for thee, and make the habitation of thy righteousness prosperous. Behold God will not cast away a perfect man, neither will He help the evil-doers."

Now came a portentous letter from Daba. It read:

"To The Council of State at Khasab.

Your noble letter to us has arrived, and no news has here occurred to deserve bringing to your notice, and what you have informed us has been understood, particularly about our neutrality. We are, *insha'allah*, obeying the order. The tribesmen have all been informed, also the people of Limah, Aqabah, and whoever depends upon them not to succour. We desire from God and you forgiveness. The faults of your servants have been numerous, and their faults are due to having secured the privilege of your kindness. He who forgives and makes straight the path will be rewarded by Allah, and whosoever saves a Muslim's neck, his neck will be saved from the Fire (Hell) by Allah.

Hasan only refrains from submission by reason of his being frightened of you.

(Signed) Salih bin Muhammad, Al Shihi Shaikh of Daba.

The defection of Daba was thus accomplished. With Kumzar turned renegade before a shot was fired, and Qada flourishing to the world its will to secede, the sworn pact had become a scrap of paper.

Hasan was finding himself despised or rejected. His whip hand had been thought to be the mountain Badus, and, indeed, had a thousand of these marched under his banner at Khasab — and they were available — the disintegration now taking place could scarcely have occurred. But where were the supplies to support them? A wall of mountain barred the interior roads. The harbour even at night was ablaze with searchlights, and not a craft could be expected to live for five minutes. Hence it was that even the two hundred men that Hasan had with him, after a fortnight of operations, now began to melt away to their villages.

The day was May 7th. Our ultimatum to bombard later in the day had been issued at noon, when a large motor-dhow was sighted coming into the harbour. An intermediary had arrived. As elsewhere in tribal Arabia where direct appeals for peace by the weaker to the stronger combatant are deemed to be neither dignified nor wise, so throughout Oman an intermediary is used. He is saving the face of the weak, though in practice he must personally be acceptable to both sides, and judge the moment propitious for his move, if any good is to come out of it. Shaikh Sa'id bin Maktum, of like Hinawi faction with the Shihuh, had sent his factor with a letter to Hasan offering his services as an intermediary, and the olive branch had been avidly grasped.

The motor-boat came and anchored close to us, and my old friend Shaikh Sa'id of Dubai came aboard.

"What can I hold out to Hasan when I go ashore? What are the Muscat terms?" the Shaikh asked.

"Hasan's unconditional surrender," I said.

"Nothing less, Sahib? Nothing less? His life! is there no mercy?"

"As you are the intermediary, there shall be mercy, and Hasan shall have an honourable imprisonment. That I promise you; but as for Shaikh Hasan himself, he must surrender unconditionally."

The Shaikh drank his coffee and went over the side, and the hybrid old dhow of his with its Kelvin engine chugged efficiently for the shore.

The Captain and I paced *Lupin's* quarter-deck and discussed the chances.

An hour later the dhow was back alongside. A craven figure came crawling up the gangway and saluted.

I turned to the Captain: "This is Shaikh Hasan, sir!"

That night *Al Sa'idi* got under way.

Captain Rashid was combining pleasure with duty in transporting Hasan to Muscat. I was sending a letter to the Governor of the Prison of Jalali Fort at the same time. It said: "Shaikh Hasan is a State prisoner, and you will be responsible for his custody for a period of eighteen months."

I landed next day at Khasab to clear up the aftermath. A vast concourse of Shihuh were on the beach to greet me. The first work to be done was to make peace between them and their Kumazara neighbours, who now, as a result of it, filed out of the Government fort. Peace accomplished, I went into the village to inspect the shelled quarters and to speak a friendly word. The villagers were more amiable than I had ever known them. They shook hands without the accustomed fear for their souls, they laughingly pointed to the Shaikh's shot-away tower, they said they were astonished by one thing — our moderation— and they were visibly overjoyed that peace had come. Nearby was a large palm- frond hut, shadowy and gay with carpets. Here they had prepared a feast in my honour.

It was time to go, and I proceeded amid a dense throng of erstwhile rebels to the beach to embark. As I went, they dragged out their poor muzzle-loading gun — they would have it so, though I protested — and fired my salute.

It was mid-afternoon and the hour of prayer as I pulled off from the shore, and looking back I saw them with their lips to the earth in abject devotion. A cry came faint across waters:

God is great!

God is great!

There is no god but God!

There is no god but God!

I bear witness that Muhammad is the prophet of God!

ADVENTURE 5

PAGES FROM MY SOUTH ARABIAN DIARY THE LIGHTER SIDE OF A SIX-HUNDRED-MILE CAMEL TREK, 1927

A THWARTED FLIRTATION

Rub' al Khali, South Arabia's great virgin desert which obsessed Wellsted and Richard Burton as it obsesses every white man whose life is cast in Arabia, was luring me on.

Rub' al Khali! a teasing mistress, that beckons only to forbid. This was to be my first flirtation with her: I cherished no illusions, therefore, of an immediate and final conquest. The heart of the sands could await experience and my present ambition was limited to a preliminary journey through the Southern Border-lands. This was quite enough, for it represented terra incognita or a distance far more than that between Land's End and John o' Groats; and alas I at my first essay I was to find myself thwarted at the outset.

From a study of the map Khor Jaramah appeared to be a suitable starting-place. This lagoon, near to the heel of Arabia that projects itself towards India, was to be my rendezvous. The ancients called it Corodam when Alexander the Great's fleet took shelter here on an historic voyage from the Indus.

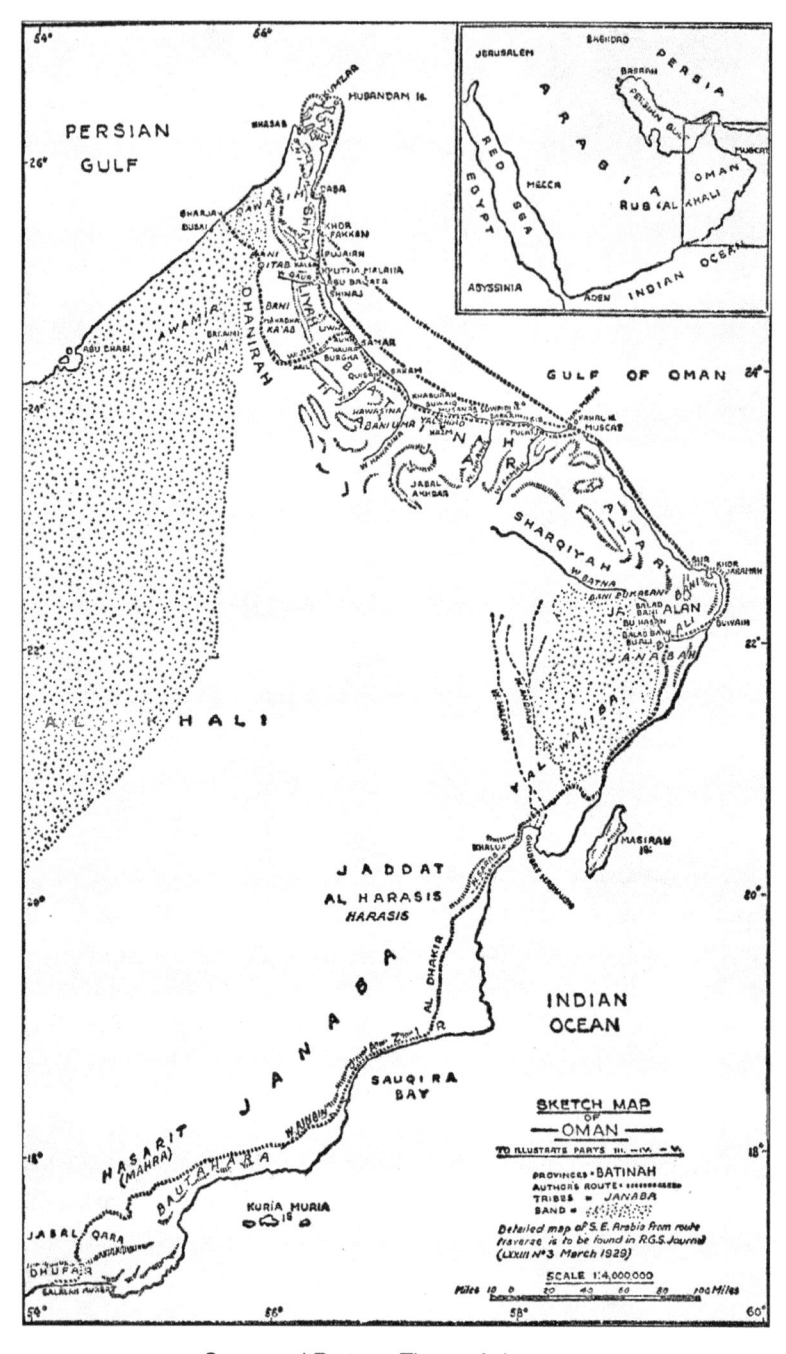

Oman and Bertram Thomas's journeys

I landed hopefully; but where my friends? The shores of the lagoon were innocent alike of caravan or human kind, and after waiting two days in vain I turned disconsolately back. Perhaps Sur, a small port a few miles up the coast, might be worth trying!

Khor Jaramah with Al Sai'idi at anchor

A large two-hundred-ton Sur dhow had come bowling along into the estuary — for Khor Jaramah, though normally deserted, is popular with native craft for refitting before the turn of the monsoon — and had dropped anchor close under *Al Sa'idi's* lee. It was unlikely, however, that she would have news of arrival of camels for me at Sur, and in any case the matter was one to be guarded about, for the Faithful are roused to opposition by any infidel intrusion upon their almost sacrosanct soil. Excitement prevailed aboard the dhow. Her anchor rope had parted, and a slave mariner promptly dived into six fathoms of water to act as human grapple. Amphibious like his kind, he remained below for what seemed an interminable time; then his woolly head emerged and he was hauled inboard. "A *jinn* struck me," he said, as he placed his hand to the side of his face which was affected, and he laid his head back to stop the bleeding from his nose.

"Aren't you afraid of sharks?" I asked.

"*Ketebet* Allah," his companions replied, meaning that man's portion is what God has written; but it was clear that, of the two, *jinns* were the more frightening to him.

When he had sufficiently recovered, his shipmates ordered him over the side again, and after staying a minute below his black naked body came limply to the surface. This time he had achieved his purpose of finding the anchor and bending a rope on, but on being hauled aboard he collapsed on the deck, blood streaming from his nose and ears. We were under way, but still within hailing distance when he came round, and I gathered from our crew that he had had two smacks in the head this time, but whether that was to be accounted for by two *jinns* or only one with a right and a left, none could say.

Dhows in Khor Jaramah

The Arabic word Sur has the same significance as the Greek word Tyre, and if Herodotus wrote the truth when he recorded that a Phoenician informed him that the Persian Gulf was the source of the Phoenicians, Sur is not improbably the home of the fathers of those early merchant venturers of Tyre and Sidon.

There was no caravan here, and it would have been fatuous to think of getting one together at such a place, for Sur has a most inhospitable atmosphere — one that is tainted by internal as well as external antagonisms, and to acquire the co-operation of one faction there is to incur the opposition of its rivals. The State fort which I was to inspect lay remote in a hidden date-grove some three miles from the sea, and for all its author's cunning in building it over the wells from which the village obtains its water, it ministered traditionally but to a feeble authority. On the right of the road that lay between low hills Al 'Ais was pointed out to me as the site of a cave, so I turned off there to explore it. Two of my twelve *askaris* had entered it before and were ready to do so again. The rest counselled caution about *jinns* and snakes, particularly *jinns*, and firmly announced their preference for remaining without. About twenty feet up the hillside was the dark entrance, looking scarcely bigger than a ship's port-hole, and access by it involved lying prone and elbowing one's way in, turtle fashion. Husain the leader carried a *buti* (lamp), for I had come without electric torch or preparation of the kind.

If my companions suspected some occult science, as they are wont to do, by which I could divine chests of buried treasure, I myself cherished a hope of an old wall carving, some flints, or perhaps an ancient skull. A ten-foot crawl brought the three of us into a dark, irregular chamber, some twelve feet by fifteen, of musty smell and insufficient air. There was scarcely room to stand upright. The floor of the cave, choked with debris, sloped violently away, and the roof more or less conformed with it, the whole thing being irregular and rough as Nature had fashioned it. Two other chambers lay beyond, but the hole of access was too small for any but an undersized man, and as neither of my Badu companions showed the slightest enthusiasm for the job, I had to content myself with the thought that the interiors were probably just as barren as was the spot from which we were glad to wriggle out again into dazzling sunlight.

Natural caves are a characteristic feature of this Oman massif, and I heard stories of one, vast and unexplored, lying a day and a half's camel journey distant at Muqil in Wadi Bani Khalid. Though its entrance is as insignificant as that of Al 'Ais, its interior is in vast contrast — a lofty hall that bores into the mountain, some say for a mile and more, for none has braved it to its uttermost length for fear of *jinns* and the alarming noise of rushing waters beneath its floor. The neighbourhood was the haunt of raiders at the time I write of, and for this and other reasons a visit there was inadvisable.

That night I was to see how *jinns*, those Heaven-sent afflicters of mankind, were exorcised; or perhaps I am unjust, for the *zar* is not a fire-wrought jinn but a disembodied spirit, an evil spirit that possesses man and is the explanation of his bodily and mental ills. What to do then but to propitiate it? This cult of the *zar*, though not found in the desert, flourishes throughout the fishing villages of these coasts; and although the enlightened Muslim scorns it as a heresy, and a pious Wali will sternly forbid it in his area on religious grounds, *hoi polloi* have from some dim antiquity clung to its sensuous rites. The temple — though none would dare to call it such in this land of the True Believer — is a palm-frond hut of spacious proportions; fire and iron will not normally be allowed in it, nor will the ceremony be performed on a Thursday or a Friday, lest any of these things render it nugatory. It is presided over by a priestess, or witch, or medium, whichever you will, who is not infrequently an old negress, and who shines in the sobriquet of *Umm az Zar* (Mother of Zars).

On the night of the *rumsa* (for darkness is essential) come the devotees in small parties, perhaps a hundred or so altogether, and usually nearly all women. Throughout the night a stream of fresh arrivals and departures in relays ensures a packed congregation and a sprinkling of new and lively zeal. To each is given a sprig of mint if the season favours. But always the air will be heavy with wreathing colour and scent of burning incense, for incense-burners are generously distributed up and down the chamber.

The stage is now set. The "*zar* possessed" is brought and lies recumbent in the middle of the assembly. The devotees assort themselves in rows about him, seated on the ground, except for the *Umm az Zar*, who occupies a chair. Drums, usually three in number, commence proceedings, and in fact are the mainstay throughout. To a slow rhythm at first, those assembled now gently sway their bodies, clap their hands and nod their heads. The rhythm quickens, and in time their actions become more spirited as they work themselves up. The medium now chants her formulae in some gibberish understood only by the devotees, and these make their proper responses. The night wears on, the drum rhythms are ever changing, the swaying and jerking and bobbing of bodies become more and more vigorous, and the two front rows of spirited females concentrate with closer attention on the patient. As a cobra by the piping of its charmer, the patient himself becomes infected by his surroundings, and sitting up begins to nod his head in harmony with his close neighbours. This is the sign that all are waiting for, evidence that the *zar* within him is on the move and will shortly be susceptible to expulsion.

"Art thou *Zar*?" asks *Umm az Zar*.

"I am *Zar*," comes the reply through the mouth of the possessed one predisposed to answer by the faith that is in him.

"Art thou male or female?"

An answer is given.

"What dost thou want?"

"Blood of the sacrifice," is the reply, for without blood there can be no propitiation.

"Thy name, and thy father's name?"

At this stage the patient's catechism may fail. He breaks down in tears, and is possibly unable to answer at the first time of asking. He must do so before seven nights have passed, however, for that is the term of the ceremony though it is unusual for the third night to go by, even in a debutant, without the *zar* being driven to self-confession.

Meanwhile the orgy of beating drums and gyrating bodies goes on until, one after another, the fair performers fall swooning in an intoxication of voluptuous ecstasy. A similar condition ultimately overtakes the patient, and is regarded as the *zar's* final throw before leaving his body. The vacancy is promptly occupied, however, by the spirit's opposite sexual number, for *zars* are male and female and work in pairs. [38] And now before the second spirit is appeased by similar measures, the coffee-cup goes round and incense-burners are replenished.

Next comes the slaughter. The *zar* has demanded either cow or sheep, and as the knife is whipped across the victim's throat, an empty coffee-cup is held beneath and filled with hot gushing blood, which is promptly handed to the patient, who drinks it. If he has been possessed by a female *zar*, only the blood of the ox or ram will do, if by a male *zar*, then the blood of a cow or ewe. The feast follows. The carcass is roasted whole, and woe to the cook or other who would put a morsel to her own famished lips before the spirit's recent habitation has had its fill. And so it is first brought before the patient, who addresses himself to the head, avoiding what normally would be a delicacy — its eyes —and thereafter the assembly gathers round and partakes of the burnt sacrifice.

I decided to return to Muscat on the morrow. That night the Surites, a stormy brood, celebrated my visit by the wanton murder, just outside the town, of a member of a caravan coming from some hostile Hinawi tribe. Antagonistic elements within the village itself were standing to arms, the innocent afraid of being blamed for the acts of the guilty — if, indeed, the former term had other than an ironical application in Sur — and the war- towers with which the place bristled became hives of activity. The Muscat State would certainly require the murderer, and it was equally certain that he would be withheld by his particular faction. The only measure of hostage possible until he was handed up was to annex and tow one of their dhows to Muscat. A solitary craft swung at anchor in the roads, as I pulled off to *Al Sa'idi*, but she lay within three cables from the beach — that is, well within rifle range — and had, to boot, less water under her bottom than was safe for us to manoeuvre in. Rounding her up would thus be an unpleasant business; but it had to be done.

"Captain Rashid," I said, "I should very much like that dhow taken in tow!"

Captain Rashid raised his eyebrows and ventured on a series of reflections leading to the question, "Are you sure, sir?"

We slowly steamed along to a point as near as we could get to her, about half a cable's distance, placing her in a direct line between us and the dangerous end of the beach, so as to give cover to our boat's crew which must pull over, cut her moorings, and bend on the tow rope.

Our skiff was now alongside her, and the "bow oar" leapt on to her fo'c'sle to get his job over quickly. But we had been spotted from the shore. Armed men on the beach — in Sur no man walked abroad without his rifle — rushed to their towers, and in a few minutes a hail of lead came clattering about us. The hoisting of our skiff, which took but a few minutes, seemed like an hour as the fusillade continued, bullets everywhere splattered around, quite innocuously, however, for though they chipped ironwork and splintered woodwork, they failed, fortunately, to do any bodily hurt. And so we gave Sur a narrow end-on target as we steered for the open sea, screened by their own dhow, which noddingly cleaved our wake as she came briskly after us. But a bullet struck our funnel with the sharp snap of a typewriter key, and told us it was a little early as yet to haul up for Muscat and thus gratuitously present a broadside to the shore. It was, perhaps, just as well that, destined as I was to return by H.M.S. Triad and to land in Sur four days later, I did not return the shore fire with *Al Sa'idi's* machine-gun, though my Arab gunner regarded me in blank astonishment at the time as I placed him at action station but forbade him to open fire.

Now we were safely out of range, and, altering course, passed on to Muscat with our prize; but my personal plans for the Great Southern Desert, at least with the Sur neighbourhood as a starting- point, were scarcely advanced by the episode.

WITH THE BANI BU ALI

THREE MONTHS HAD PASSED BY.

In a calm sea which a light *nashi* left unruffled beneath a sky joyously blue save for vividly white cumulus clouds that heaped themselves along the' southern horizon, *Al Sa'idi* swung peacefully at anchor four cables off the Arabian shore.

Here was Suwaih; here, for me, the beginning of renewed hopes.

A crude mud fort stood on the yellow foreshore; about it were some forty reed huts and an occasional clump of palms, backed in the far distance by the delicately crayoned mountains of Ja'alan, easternmost province of Arabia. Suwaih lay beyond Sur, beyond Khor Jaramah, just a little beyond that point where the great peninsula turns the corner and its shores are no longer washed by the waters of the Gulf of Oman but by the mighty Indian Ocean.

A *houri*, the small dug-out canoe typical of these parts, pushed off from the shore, its two occupants balancing themselves in some uncanny fashion as, standing, they paddled towards us; others like them followed, and soon some thirty swarthy villagers swarmed aboard us. To a natural curiosity to know our business was added the desire to profit. Fish to sell!

for this was their only occupation. But fish without eyes, which had been gouged out, aroused our suspicions. The fishermen pointed to their red gills to reassure us of their freshness, and my apprehensions were soon removed by the discovery that the locals have a partiality for fish eyes, and, incidentally, when out all day at a great distance from the shore satisfy their hunger with raw fish.

My letter to the Amir Muhammad of the Bani bu Ali tribe, living some thirty miles inland, met in due course with its reward, and I found myself on New Year's Eve in the year of grace 1927 leaving sinful razor and tobacco behind me, and donning Badawin kit — for the journey to the village of the Balad Bani bu Ali lay through fanatical Wahhabi country. Twenty odd Badus, camel-mounted, and a half-dozen spare camels, had been brought by the Amir's brother, Shaikh Hamdan, to convey me to their village. My more ambitious plans I dare not as yet betray lest they be prejudiced thereby, though dreams of the south-eastern borderlands, a camel journey extending for six weeks southwards of the setting sun, filled my thoughts — a desert journey at the end of which lay the smiling province of Dhufar, traditional land of Ophir, famed for Solomon's gold and frankincense.

My boxes, containing sextant, - artificial horizon, chronometers, camera, aneroids, compasses, and six bags of Maria Theresa crowns, the Austrian currency of the land, were by reason of their weight scarcely objects of endearment to the spare-camel owners, who naturally would have preferred an easier load, while my unwieldy Bikaner-pattern camel saddle that was to go over the usually exposed hump excited feelings of something between derision and disgust. All was ready at last, however, and so we moved off. The watchful Captain Rashid, complying with secret sailing orders I had given him, gave three farewell blasts on *Al Sa'idi's* siren, weighed, and left for Dhufar.

There he would await me. I had burnt my boats.

The Amir of Bani bu Ali Sheikh Muhammed bin Nasir

Arid sandy hillocks and shell-flecked wadi beds made a desolate ride for the first two hours, the poor scrub supporting only clouds of red locusts, which from time to time enveloped us. Sunset brought us to China, an acacia grove in rolling sand country. And while the Faithful went through the form of preliminary ablutions with sand instead of water before lining up for evening prayers, Ali, my secretary, came to me in trepidation.

"What to do, sir, for I am Shi'ah," said he, "and these men Wahhabi? If I pray with these men they will certainly detect it by my raising my hands according to our different ritual, and thus shall I incur their severe displeasure."

To this I could only reply with a homily on the Vicar of Bray, pointing out that no place could be better suited than the Arabian Desert for an application of his philosophy.

A blazing fire and the call of the *Mu'edhdhin* awoke me with the first pallor of the false dawn, and so — a swig of camels' milk, and into the saddle! Fifteen miles ahead lay our immediate destination, but we were to complete only half that distance when a speck on the skyline grew into a dozen horsemen. This' proved to be the Amir 'Ali, the most eminent kinsman of the Amir Muhammad, who had come out to welcome us. We both drew rein at a distance and advanced on foot to exchange greetings. Anon we proceeded. approaching the village which lay on the near fringes of the date- grove. Before it a thousand welcoming villagers were drawn up in line.

Drums were beating, and the crowd swayed left and right to their rhythm: quivering sword blades flashed in the sun as sword dancers leapt hither and thither, and low chanting grew loud as we approached. Swinging round to form a corridor for us, the tribesmen, holding their rifle butts to their hips for the feu de joie, sent a hail of friendly bullets pinging over our heads. We went on to where the Amir stood for my reception, before the fort, on a carpet placed in the large open square, a favourable position for witnessing the horsemanship and camel-racing that now took place; for, as I have said, such a display is the inevitable feature of an Arab welcome in Oman. A dozen horsemen galloped past, now in this formation, now in that, curveting and firing their rifles at the same time, or racing in pairs down the straight, one rider standing upright on his stirrupless saddle, gripping only with his toes, and maintaining a parlous equilibrium by placing an outstretched arm on the neck of his more comfortably seated fellow-rider. Reforming, the party would move past in close formation at a jog-trot, chanting heroic verse, an ancient Badawin custom deriving from the mighty Antar of antiquity. The leader gabbled his lines, and at the end of each couplet, the rest of the party shouted in chorus *"Allahu Akbar"*.

This is my somewhat free translation:

Leader-. We have filled every quarter with fear till mankind grovels before us.

Chorus: God is great!

We have excelled the Thuraiyya (Pleiades) in its zenith.

God is great!

And whosoever approacheth us seeking trouble shall find us brave as lions.

God is great!

When a boy of ours shall quit his mother's milk, our enemies fall grovelling before him.

God is great!

And on the day of hospitality we give away all that we possess, and fill up the earth with munificence and generosity.

God is great!

And we shoe our horses in the day of battle with bleeding bones and skins.

God is great!

Two old muzzle-loading guns, probably of sixteenth-century Portuguese origin, boomed out a welcome, and the women, veiled of course and crowding the fort roofs, greeted our going in to the feast with their accustomed ululations, a more pleasing variety than the ear-piercing kind I was to hear on the morrow. This latter proclaimed a tribal *fizaa* or standard-raising; for it appeared that during the night the neighbouring hostile tribe of Bani bu Hasan had been on the warpath and had killed a slave belonging to my host in one of the adjoining gardens. This piece of intelligence I came by indirectly, for it would have been shameful for my host to speak of it, and while he was assiduously engaging me with counsel not to prosecute my South Arabian plans, my servant, looking down from the battlements, saw the tribes, men and women alike, hurrying off to the fight, the men carrying their rifles ready at the trail, their women, bowed with the weight of dates and full water-skins, running at their heels in support.

Bani bu Ali Fort

The fort of Balad Bani bu Ali where the Amir lived was large and handsome of its kind; it rose tierlike as a battleship's bridge and gun turrets, and was crowned by two towers. I found myself quartered in the keep that commanded a fine view of a long sweep of date-grove of palms abnormally tall, and lanky war-towers emerging above them. This was lower Wadi Batha, the artery of intramontane Oman, eastwards of that loftiest mass of Arabia, nearly 10,000 feet high, Jabal Akhdhar, whence the wadi comes. Having nourished the province of Sharqiyah from the wells in its bed, it sheds its final bounty here on Balad Bani bu All's palm-grove and passes on a barren course to the coast within sight of Suwaih.

My host exercised paramount influence in this hinterland. His autocratic sway over the Badu Janabah was the requisite means that would enable me to move: alternatively it could prevent my moving at all. Behind an austere and curt manner the Amir possessed a dry sense of humour; he had travelled to India, and was proud of his few words of English; he was enlightened and, would be well disposed to reasonable courses; but alas! his reception of my scheme was unfriendly. His brow became clouded. "No one," he said, amongst his Badus had done the entire journey, for the sea route was the safe and natural means of communication, whereas the desert marches were No-Man's-Land, a land of forced marches between distant and unsure water-holes, and with no sort of protection from the raider. Yes! there were two old greybeards that on past occasions had taken urgent letters to the Sultan of Muscat in Dhufar in summer-time when the south- west monsoon drove every craft from the Indian Ocean, but one of these had died; the other was *hors de combat* with fever. In both cases they had suffered camel casualties en route." The news saddened me, and I found scant pleasure in the reflection that to have got thus far was, by Arabian standards, a privilege, for no European had been allowed to come to this Wahhabi district since the time, a hundred years ago, of Wellsted, a young English naval lieutenant. But I knew my shaikh and I did not despair.

"I have come prepared for hardships," I had said.

"Your honour docs not understand," was the smiling, if patronizing, reply.

The Amir looked in again next morning. "No Badu would dream of risking his camel to the perils of the unknown," said he. "Even if the animals got you through, the risk of the return would be too great, and they would have to be sold for what they would fetch on the spot." Thus was I given to understand that the only hope of getting camels would be for me to buy them outright, and I made a sickly mental calculation of the financial crisis that would be involved.

The third day a fresh obstacle had appeared. To move without a Hinawi *rafiq* would be a suicidal course, and a Hinawi *rafiq* was not to be had. Was Bani bu Ali not at war with Bani bu Hasan?' [39]

I met all these objections as best I could. I pleaded, I cajoled.

"And what if evil befell me! He would then incur the criticisms of every sane Arab for aiding and abetting a reckless enterprise: and would he not be hauled over the coals of authority? even though I travelled, as I said, under no official auspices!"

Four Fishermen of Masirah Island making Nets

The Amir was a difficult man to persuade, but he succumbed at last to my importunities, at least up to a point. He would afford me a party of twelve mounted Badus for the first third of the journey, as far, that is, as the camp of his close ally, the Janabah Shaikh of Masirah Island — a camp that lay on the mainland to the westward. From that point I must return the camels, and make the best arrangements I could, if any, for moving on. But I must give him a letter of absolution from responsibility in case of evil befalling.

While waiting for camels and a Hinawi (Yal Wahiba) *rafiq* I had an opportunity of riding with the Amir about his village, past the gateway and out into the walled lanes and pleasant gardens. Villagers ran out to take hold of our horses' heads and press us to dismount for the hospitable coffee cup, but we waved them aside. Wahhabis these, but their Puritanism was not of an obtrusive kind, unless one observed the absence of tobacco, the use of which, of course, lay under religious stricture. I asked the Amir how an offender would be punished. "Fifteen days' imprisonment," he said, "on short rations, with an occasional beating until the penitent had learnt his lesson." A sad life, indeed, but borne with stoical indifference; and on the occasion of death even outward manifestation of grief is forbidden, for man should have no feelings where the will of God has declared itself.

Turning my back on this oasis of comparative civilization, I rejoiced to find myself with camel caravan fifteen strong, launched out at last into the South Arabian desert previously untrodden by white man.

SOUTHERN BORDERLANDS

FLAT CAMEL-THORN COUNTRY, with easy water-holes at only a day's interval or so, soon gave place to sandy wastes, where on occasion we had to dismount while our camels floundered this way and that over low sand-dunes. Debouching here on to the shores of the Indian Ocean itself, these sands stretched westwards and northwards to the wadi systems of Halfain and Batha respectively, constituting an island triangle cut off from the great central ocean of sands to the west.

Here was the habitat of Yal Wahiba, a nomad tribe of Oman holding Ibadhi tenets and of Hinawi faction, and as such it formed an interesting wedge between a Wahhabi tribe in our rear and a solid bloc of Shafi tribes before us, all owning to the rival Ghafari faction.

A sparse population inhabits these Southern borderlands, where life is supported almost solely by camel- and sheep-breeding, and the spoils of war — a precarious nomadic existence, bloody withal, whose ethics are elemental, practical and cruel. An unwritten law — it could not be otherwise with illiteracy general — governs Badawin conduct, so far as it is governed at all.

Well of Haj in Wadi Halfain

This code has come down out of the unchanging centuries. *Hukm al hauz*, as it is called, conflicts with the *Shar'a*, the Holy law that is practised to the exclusion of any other by non-nomads. Religious leaders living in settled areas of course regard *Hukm al hauz* as a deplorable institution, a secular rival, so to speak, of the sacred sanctions. The Badu it is true, will make, in case of marriage vows and the division of inheritance, a special journey, some- times of more than a hundred miles, to a town in order to enlist the services of a Qadhi for the regularization of these special affairs according to *Shar'a*) but for his own disputes, his wars, his blood feuds, his buying and selling and stealing and straying of camels, only his *Hukm al hauz* is genuinely acceptable. Its interpreter or magistrate is an old wiseacre of the tribe — not always or necessarily the shaikh. When the two roles are not combined, indeed, the shaikh sometimes has to bow to his decision — the decision of one who has acquired the position by the fame of his knowledge and experience, and the traditional rightness of his judgments.

A story is told, true, it is said, of a famous hauz of this very Yal Wahiba tribe. A youth had murdered his maternal uncle — most serious affair, for although it is the paternal side of the family that is privileged in the matters of the hand of a daughter and major inheritance of a dead man's estate (failing male offspring), yet, with those Badawin, the mother's brother is in sentiment rated above a father's brother, and, incidentally, the Badu, unlike the town Arab, will take his mother's name rather than his father's. But that is by the way. The youthful murderer was mortified with grief when it was too late, and, although the family of the murdered man forgave him, [40] he would not be comforted.

"My coat is black," he said. "I am no more acceptable in the assembly than a woman. Life is no longer dear. I must expiate my deed." He disdained forgiveness and an easy requital with the blood-money which *Shar'a* would have decreed. He would betake himself for judgment to the hauz.

The old man listened to the story of the young murderer as he eyed him narrowly. "It is well thou hast come," he said. The tribe, viewing this as no ordinary murder, waited with bated breath a judgment that would not lack in severity.

The moment for its announcement in the open-air assembly had come, the young penitent kneeling in customary suppliant way before the seat of judgment.

"Listen," declaimed the *hauz*, "*Ya fulan*," and he named the young man. "In the bottom of yonder dry' well will be planted some spears with their spikes pointing upwards. My judgment is that thou start from there" — and he indicated with his cane a spot some fifteen paces from the well-mouth — "thou shalt turn thy back upon the well and walk backwards until thou fallest' Murder, according to *Shar'a* law as practised, is not an offence against society, or at least is not judged by this standard. True, between tribes it is a corporate offence, but within a tribe it is one against the family of the murdered man only. The next of kin, a son, and, failing that, a brother, and failing him again, the male paternal cousins, have a right to forgive the offence and take blood-money from the murderer in expiation. *Shar'a* theory' of an eye for an eye is nowhere observed in South-East Arabia. into it. Thus will the stain be removed from thy name. Whether thou diest or livest, the crime thou has committed will then be expiated."

A wave of horror spread through the circle of tribesmen that half-sat, half-knelt, around, and a cold hush fell upon the proceedings.

"*Insha'allah!*" was all the young murderer said in pious acquiescence. He was conscious that this meant certain death, death of a horrible kind, yet was it the only honourable path. To shrink from it before his tribe were unthinkable. He might die. His deed should live.

And so spears were brought, and the well was prepared. The young Badu was taken to the appointed place, and there, facing about, he moved calmly backwards towards his doom, and, reaching the brink, leapt as he was bidden. But ten stalwart Badus, who had been placed there ostensibly to be witness to the immolation, threw their arms about him as he was about to fall within, having been ordered privily to do so if things reached this pass. The old man looked into the young man's eyes as he was brought before him again, "*Ya fulan!* go back to thy tribe," said he, "thy coat is black no longer."

Such is the story told of the days of Saiyid Turki, the grandfather of the present Sultan, and ruler of Muscat and Oman. And the young Badu who unflinchingly had shaken death by the hand was none other than the famous Hamid bin Khalfan, who lived to be paramount shaikh of this Yal Wahiba tribe, and a great man in the land.

A week had passed since I had set out from Balad Bani bu Ali when, breasting a rise, I caught a glimpse of Ghubbat Hashish below us, one of Nature's seaplane bases, and within it the tiny islands of Rig Mahut and Ab, wreathing themselves into odd shapes through the mirage. We descended to the beach, a slippery salt plain that, after recent rain, had become a morass — a regular death-trap for camels prone to fatal splits. Dismounting, we edged our way round the sweep of the bay — the Badus fearful for their animals, '

At last we reached Ras Khaluf — the Ras Abana of Admiralty charts. This latter name, incidentally, is unknown to the Arabs, and would appear to have been produced by one of the Faithful on the spur of the moment to deceive infidel map-makers — a by no means unlikely occurrence. The moral to the traveller, therefore, is to check and recheck every place-name that is ever given to him.

Here was the village of Khaluf and here, for half the year, lived the Shaikh of the Janabah tribe, a tall lean figure of a man with a face of a hawk and aristocratic lineaments that marked him from his ill-looking following. It was fortunate that I found him here, for the chances were even that he would be absent in his island home of Masirah — Ptolemy's Serapis — and it was to him that I had now to look for favours for the onward journey. A favourable factor was that I had arrived under the protection of an escort of Bani bu Ali, his close allies. Yet, as I half expected, he at first blankly negatived my plans, and I had to meet again all the arguments that had been advanced against them at the outset. I had returned my last party, and so was utterly upon the Shaikh's favour to raise me a new' escort and a new relay of camels. A week's virtual imprisonment followed. I was discouraged from leaving my tent, and the treatment of my party, as they innocently walked about the village, left much to be desired. The natives were sullen if not antagonistic. In an indiscreet moment I had asked whether I might sail over and land on the mangrove island of Mahut, a proposal that was construed as having an ulterior motive, and the Shaikh when answering that it was inadvisable, hinted that it was not yet certain whether camels could be raised for my journey westwards, and that, if not, he would gladly arrange for a sea passage to Dhufar for me. That horrible spectre passed, and when, after a week, I found myself with a new camel caravan pushing on through the southern wilderness, it was the Shaikh's brother's own camel that mounted me and a scion of the family who accompanied me as guide.

As we trekked along I made some study of my companions. Daily disputes occurred between them over camel rations, each Badu trying to get a lion's share for his own camel at the expense of his neighbour's, and the oft-repeated drawing of daggers in anger would have taught me, had I not already known it, that the Badu is an inflammable person, requiring firm if understanding treatment.

On ordinary occasions, with little provocation, his voice is capable of becoming suddenly charged with feeling. His emotions lie near to the surface. Fortunately he has a sense of humour in an unsubtle way — cheerfulness would be a better word for it perhaps — but, what is more important to the voyager, he is capable of personal attachment. His manner is one of extreme alertness; his figure is lean and spare, and even the oldest Badu carries himself with boyish gait. He has little sense of time, except as translated into distance; he never learnt what an hour meant, even after days of experience, and as for minutes! they excited his mirth, making him wonder what strange finicky mortals we were to deal in such trifles.

The Three Rabias

Badu conversation exhausts itself in camels, raids, religion, and women. It is interesting to note that in Badawin Arabia scarcely a female of eighteen is to be found unmarried. This is to be accounted for by the religious sanction of polygamy, and also by the fact that in a pastoral society she has an economic value to her husband. Tending flocks, she does the work of a man, and her prospective husband must in consequence pay her father a price for her. Most girls are disposed of on reaching adolescence, which in Arabia is at the age of thirteen or fourteen. These is little flirtation and few genuine love-matches, for an unwritten law prescribes that the son of her paternal uncle has the first claim to the hand of a girl. If he does not avail himself of his privilege, her father disposes of her, often without consulting her inclinations, to the highest bidder — an old, old man, may be, who can be no joy to her. But cousin-marriages are almost an inviolable rule, even though a great disparity of age exists, and in cases where the convention has been infringed I have known of blood being shed, and this with public approbation.

"O Wazir! why don't you take her" (to wife), said one of my Badus one day to me, pointing roguishly at a young veiled Hikmani girl drawing water at a desert well.

"I don't know whether she'll have me," I replied. Then turning to the girl standing by, I exclaimed, "O Shamla! would you marry me?" '

Shamla burked the question laughingly. Still, by the way she hung around I judged the answer to be mere feminine equivocation. Soon, however, she transferred her attention to my more demonstrative servant of dusky hue and unaccented tongue, from whose conversation I learned that she was still unmarried though nearly twenty, an age which Arabia begins to consider *passe*. Asked whether she had not a *bin am* (paternal cousin), she said that that lack, alas! was the reason for her solitary condition. Amongst the Janabah tribe sixty Maria Theresa dollars, say about £5, is a high price for a bride, and if the man is not particular about good birth the equivalent of £1 will suffice for purchase-money, Badawin have seldom more than two wives at one time, and more generally only one. though, if they can buy and feed and clothe them, four are not considered an extravagance distasteful to the angels. Still, I have never met one with the full complement. Divorce is easy for the man. He has only to say *"Talak"* three times, for no better reason than that he is tired of her, give her the purely nominal marriage portion, and the bonds are severed. Three months passing, if she be not found with child, his obligations are at an end. In consequence he enters upon marriage without trepidation, and it is rare indeed for any woman to be left to go to her grave without having tasted domestic bliss: in almost every case, indeed, it has come to her as a girl in the first blush of budding womanhood.

I said to Rashid, a young Badu of my escort, "O Rashid! have you a wife?"

"No," he replied, "but, *Insha'allah*, I'll marry this year."

"Why not before? You told me you were twenty."

"They are costly."

"How much?"

"Sixty dollars." (Five pounds.)

"In my country," I returned, "we don't have to pay a single farthing for a wife."

"*Allahu Akbar*," said he, profoundly moved. "That is a blessed country."

"But," I explained, "Ya Rashid, we can't divorce her. When she gets old and loses her beauty we have to stick to her, and we may not turn her away and marry another young girl as you do." »

"*Allah Karim!*" he ejaculated with much feeling; which, being freely interpreted, meant, "Ah! I thought there was a fly in the ointment somewhere!"

The inconsequence of the Badu spoken word is proverbial, and the following passage amused me vastly. Sitting around the fire one night, I turned to a Harsusi and asked him, "On which does the Badu set most store — his women or his camel?"

"His camel," the Harsusi replied.

"But in your case: if it were fated that you had to lose either your wife or your camel, and you were given your choice, which would it be?"

This was a poser, and needed thinking out.

"If both were dying," he said at last, "and one only could be spared, I would elect for my wife to be left me and the camel taken. But if it were merely a separation from one or the other I would stick to the camel."

"Well done," I approved: "there is mercy in that reply."

A Janabi broke in. "Don't believe him! A Badu prefers his women."

"Why?" I asked.

"The woman is *mal*" (property), the Janabi replied. "Doesn't she produce sons and daughters? and the sons produce sons, and so she is the foundation of your building up a *gom* (a raiding- party) around yourself."

The Harsusi broke in again laconically. "S*udg*" (True), he said, and went on smoking nonchalantly, without considering it necessary to offer the slightest explanation for a complete *volte-face* in the space of five minutes.

Two Yal Wahiba Shaikhs

With the Badawin the camel is more than the ship of the desert. It is *Ata Allah* — the gift of God. To him it is the sustainer of life, providing him with food, transport, and sometimes clothing and shelter. On a raid, and indeed at all times, the camel is his master's first care. In this poor benighted region of the southern borderlands, the brutes seldom got a feed of dates or lucerne as in Northern Oman, where, perhaps, the best camels in Arabia are bred. Here they had to forage for themselves, and often on the march the whole caravan was held up for hours as a result of our coming upon a juicy patch of herbage.

The camel is not always couched to mount, but while on the move she lowers her head for her master to swarm up her neck and half-vault into the saddle, which in this part of Arabia is invariably behind the hump. If couched, the brute gets up as soon as she feels the slightest pressure on her back, so that mounting is not the comparatively leisurely thing that it is with a horse.

A Badu invariably knows the age of his camel, but seldom his own age. He will dispose of his daughter for the half of the sum he asks for his camel. An average cow on the line of my trek would change hands for 200 dollars, and a calf at 60 or 80. My Harsusi guide alleged that he supported a wife, two sons and four daughters on a single cow camel and some twenty sheep. His sixteen-year-old and as yet unmarried daughter, glorying in the name of Aqrab (Scorpion), came tripping along on our arrival close to the camping-ground to greet her father. This she did by lifting her veil and rubbing noses with him. As she demurely went away into the camel-thorn he turned to me jocularly: "o Wazir! for a rifle and sixty dollars she is yours" (to wed). "She is worth infinitely more," said I, by way of disposing of the compliment.

Every two years the camel is covered to keep her in milk, and her pregnancy she delights to announce by flag-wagging her ridiculous tail as you approach to mount her. Her bellowing after dark when she is knee-hobbled and turned out to grass, so to speak, is usually the signal that raiders are about, and false alarms in the dead of night on one or two occasions sot our camp astir, the Badawin leaping from their startled slumbers, seizing their rifles, and scampering in all directions.

The watering of camels varies, of course, with the load carried and the season. In our early stages the rule was every other day, but towards the end we had a six days' trek, a nine hours' ride sometimes with full loads through waterless country and over mountain passes 3,000 feet high, and the animals were pretty well "tucked up" at the end of it. There is always some water in the camel's stomach, and to this fact Badawin in moments of crisis have owed their lives, for, as they have told me, when a water-hole has failed them in the desert and they are faced with death from thirst, they thrust a stick down the animals throat to make it vomit water, and this they drink. If the camel has been watered within a few days the result is tolerably drinkable, but if some long period has elapsed since watering, a green and pretty foul liquid is produced. Still, it is better than death. Vomiting is resorted to for stomach trouble, and this the afflicted Badu induces by drinking a little of the urine of his young cow camel.

I had taken with me a large quantity of quinine and a palanquin of drugs, chiefly of the explosive kind; hence, though I was careful to explain that I was no doctor, the weak and credulous saw in me a glimmer of hope, and I had sick parades wherever there was human habitation. One day, in Yal Wahiba country, a mother had brought along her emaciated youngster with an enormous "tummy" and withered limbs. Although a professing Muslima — and I have no doubt a sincere one — she wished to know whether I was master of the science of *An Najma* (Astrology), and could I tell her whether the child's health would be restored if she changed its name. I turned for enlightenment to the petty shaikh who accompanied her, and what he explained set me wondering whether there was here a survival of the Sabaean star worship of ancient South Arabia. The woman held the belief — presumably a common heritage — that the star under which the child was born was offended by the name it had been given, and she was anxious to discover whether a change of name was likely to appease the wrath with a consequent mending of the body.

Male Badawin, too, have their superstitions. Belief in prophecy and in the interpretation of dreams is universal, and reading the sands has also its exponents. Hamuda, my Janabi *rafiq*, demonstrated to me one day by drawing with his forefinger in the sand a series of straight lines — *shakhut* — and measuring them off into spans and hand-breadths. "Have you heard of Salim bin Fulan?" he asked.

"No," I confessed.

"Not heard of Salim! He was a Harsusi, and famous for his *shakhtu-ing*. W'allahi! his *shakhut* was more truthful than his tongue!" Then he recounted a story, for the truth of which he vouched as an eye-witness. "We were out on a raid, against the Murra," he said. "It was the night before we reached the well where a scout of ours had reported them to be watering. Salim proceeded to make his *shakhut*. After gazing for some minutes in the sand he 'frowned apprehensively, and we feared disaster. Looking up he said, 'Be assured! To-morrow we shall smite the Hinawi and the loot will be rich. But I see blood. It is my blood.' And on the morrow, I call God to witness, we fell upon them and took seventeen camels. Salim was killed. *Wallahi! huwa wa bin amhu"* (he and his cousin).

Yal Wahiba Sand Dune Country

I had made one or two attempts to measure heads for anthropological purposes, but so far with meagre success, as my escort suspected some magical spell. One day an attempt to explain my innocent motives produced from Luwaiti, the Harsusi, the remark: "O Wazir! What are your servants? Are they not of the Baluch?

"I don't know," I replied. "I engaged them in Muscat."

"Are they *Kafirs?* (infidels).

"*Hashak* (God forbid), they are true Muslims."

"What do the *Kafirs* eat?"

"How should I know? I'm not a *Kafir.*"

"Not a *Kafir?* said Luwaiti, looking at me incredulously. "But all the people say 'What do the *Kafirs* want coming amongst us?' And they add, "And you, Luwaiti, Allah will punish you for aiding them."

"Ya Luwaiti," said I, "listen not to ignorant men. I am of the *Nasara* (Christians). We are 'people of the Book' (Quran) and declared to be believers by your Prophet, who, indeed, took a Christian girl to wife."

"Do you pray and fast?" said he.

"Yes."

"Then you must be a Muslim. Bear witness."

I imitated him by drawing my hand down over my face and beard, and added, "*Ashhadu an la illahah ill Allah*" (I bear witness that there is no god but God).

Luwaiti, satisfied in his own mind with this insufficient declaration, was moved into saying, "God be praised! Ya Thomas! You're a Muslim and not an infidel!"

SHARKS AND LOCUSTS

Whizz! crack! and a sudden barking of some six rifles two hundred yards or so ahead of us was followed by the pinging of bullets overhead, and an occasional hiss and snap of foliage, as a round here and there splashed into the acacias desperately close at hand.

I cowered over my saddle, my fellow-rider and *rabia'* Luwaiti excitedly motioning me to halt. Then he himself, like a mad-man, it seemed, galloped forward through the thickets towards our ambushers, waving his head-dress like a piece of ragged bunting high above his head, and shouting his name and tribe re-echoing up the valley.

My relief may be imagined when a few minutes later he emerged again, and dismounted, bringing along with him our would-be murderers, a few wild gollywog Harasis Badawin, his own fellow-tribesmen to boot, who had mistaken us for raiders.

What had happened was that Luwaiti and I, finding ourselves thirsty after long hours in the saddle, and fancying sheep's milk, had trotted a mile or so ahead of the caravan in the hope that this pleasant valley would have attracted a shepherd and his flocks. The thick undergrowth of Wadi Sarab (a verdant jungle pleasantly contrasting with the arid wastes behind us) made perfect ambush. And now, as I exchanged greetings with the newcomers, I scarcely had a right to show the annoyance that I felt, for the blame was really upon my own head. In short, I had been trotting, and trotting is the pace of the raider. Thus to approach a stranger's habitation permits of one construction, and provokes but one reception — possibly the last to be experienced on this earth.

My party now, came up, salaamed the martial Badawin, and reserved their scowls for me — unfairly, I thought, for I had learned my lesson with the maximum of discomfort. Thereafter the caravan kept to their walk, and I kept to the caravan, until, after we had attained the tableland of Al Dhahir that skirted the Jaddat Harasis, where glorious open spaces and sunny and fragrant air, exhilarating as champagne, banished all thoughts of hidden treachery.

Rollers, breaking on to the Indian Ocean beach under the tropical sun, were of luminous transparency, and fish darting through them could be seen with all the clearness of captives in a fish-bowl. Gulls, greyback cormorant, and sea birds of every kind floated listlessly in dark masses off the shore. Beyond them, two young sperm whale sported in the bay and giant crimson flamingos stalked the beach which they shared with diminutive sand-pipers and dense armies of tiny crabs, running hither and thither amongst their innumerable sand-castles. My impressions of such teeming life and of the suppressed roar of wind and ocean mingling along the beaches of Jazir Bay were fancifully heightened, perhaps, after long weeks of the silences of the desert and its largely lifeless void.

Shark for dinner!

Shark for dinner! Attractive solely I'm afraid, as a novel variation in a necessarily humble diet. Not the usual dried cod variety which is salted and sent inland or to Zanzibar, but the red, rank flesh of a young three-footer just out of the water. Sharks are caught in tens of thousands off the coasts of South-East Arabia, where, however, their profit is in their tails and fins, which go to make the notorious epicurean delicacies of China and Malay.

Typical Wadi in Southeastern Borderland

The manner in which they are caught here by the Bautahara fishermen is interesting, in that it recalls the subject of a certain Assyrian bas-relief in the British Museum. The fisherman, too poor to possess a boat, gets out to the scene of his activities swimming on an inflated sheepskin. He takes with him his strong wide-meshed net, casts and anchors it, and returns to the shore. The following morning he again swims off on the monster bladder to examine the net floats that tell him whether he has a catch. If he suspects that the shark has any life at all left, he calls two other fishermen, and they, similarly armed with nothing more than inflated sheepskin, swim off together and bring the netted monster to the shore. Though the sea bristles with sharks, my Bautahari fisherman informant said that he had never heard in his lifetime of a man being taken — this, incidentally, was not my experience along the Gulf Coasts, where wicker craft and small rowing-boats take the place of the inflated skin. An ominous dorsal fin flashing in the sun arrested my attention, and, pointing to it, I asked, "but aren't you afraid of being eaten?" "That is in God's hands," he replied. "If it is not written that I should die young why should I fear? I may swim without danger. And if it is written that I should not reach old age, there is no escape from that which is written."

Chorus of Badawin, fatalistically *"Ai W Allah!"* (Yes, by God!).

Fish, are various and very plentiful. Ranking almost first amongst them is the sardine, caught in vast quantities for use as camel fodder. Here and there catches were laid out in rough square patches to dry in the sun and a vigilant watch was being kept over them by small girls. These, armed with catapults, were frightening off sea-birds that circled noisily around dense as flocking crows, and came swooping down upon their silvery prey. But I was soon to find that gulls were not the only marauders, for, as my caravan passed, two of my Badus slipped off their camels and shamelessly helped themselves, while the fair guardians protested and vainly tugged at their sleeves in angry remonstrance. When I asked a Badu whether this conduct was not shameful he replied that it was 'ada (custom), and jestingly hinted that I must have been disturbed by the beauty of the pretty victims.

In polygamous Arabia where brides are cheap and divorce easy, the Badu, although unable to support more than one or two wives at a time, will, perhaps, have married five or six in the course of his life. And hereby hangs a tale. I had gone shooting one day and on returning to camp spotted at a little distance up the wadi a newly arrived flock of sheep grazing. I dispatched a Badu to investigate, and to buy milk if possible, and he came back in due course bringing with him a young veiled shepherdess. Her flock was the advance guard of a family of Harasis with thirty camels on the move, who were making for the Jaddat whence we had come, and where rain was reported. Miriam, for that was the girl's name, honoured her promise to bring me a delicious bowl of milk. She refused payment. Her only stipulation was that she should be allowed to milk into a receptacle wherein a hot stone had first been placed, a custom I found afterwards to be universal and inviolable in those parts. Later, her menfolk arrived upon the scene. They proved to be friendly, and from them I was able to begin recording one of the four non-Arabic dialects I found current in South Arabia. Next day Hamuda came to me. His mood was confidential.

"What did you think of Miriam?" he asked.

"Passing fair. What did you?"

"Ah!" said he with a sigh, "there is no woman in the country more beautiful than she."

"How do you know?"

"I came near to marrying her once. *Allahu Alim!* (God is the knower!) I took two hundred dollars to her *aulad am* (paternal male cousins). But they refused me. Some enemy of mine had poisoned their minds, and they gave her to a Mahri who is now in Oman buying jewellery." He paused, and after a few minutes, continued; "But last night, after Miriam had brought you the sheep's milk, she and I sat in the shadow of an acacia. *Allahu Alim!*"

"But aren't you satisfied with your present wife?" I asked.

"*Ismi* (Absolutely), for has she not borne me two sons?" A pause. "My daughter is by another wife who is dead — God have mercy upon her."

"Then you were married before? *Bint am* (paternal female cousin), I suppose?"

"No, I had no uncle. My first wife I divorced, not because I did not love her, but because she was barren. Did I not keep her for two years before divorcing her? I saw her yesterday at Lekbi. *Allahu Alim!* and she wanted to send you a sheep as a present, but I told her it was against your religion to take things without pa5dng for them," (here I thought Hamuda had his tongue in his cheek), "and so I gave her four dollars for it, and your servant Muhammad has recompensed me."

"Quite right," I agreed. "But your next wife?"

"Ah! She was a minx: and when I went away grazing, or on a raid, she talked overmuch with neighbours, and I suspected one man, God forgive me, and I struck him with a stick. That night he revenged himself by coming and shooting my own favourite riding camel, and a few days later her brother killed one of my bull camels. But God prevented my shedding their blood. And a truce of one month was made between me and them. At the end of this we made a peace, the man giving me two camels, and her brother a camel and two hundred dollars, and I divorced her."

Wadi Ainan

At the entrance to the Wadi Ainan, I was obliged to change my camels and personnel. And yet once again. This third time my benefactors were the Harasis, a tribe for whose members I learned to have a special affection. Preparatory to the start I dispatched Hamuda to the coast to buy some butter, dates, and rice, but he succeeded in getting dates only, and those at a fabulous price, a failure that was to cause us some hungry marches. The camels had to be taken six miles to the nearest wells to be watered, leaving a new acquaintance, Sharqi, as my only *rabia* with local knowledge. However, the Janabi guide on whom I chiefly relied assured me that the place was absolutely safe, so in the afternoon Sharqi and I took our rifles and tramped over the low hills in search of game. During the last week our line of march through the soft-surfaced plain had from time to time crossed well-beaten tracks, much like a narrow field-path, which my Badawin said were gazelle tracks, and if we followed them up would lead to water, and more than once near by were the ominous spoors of jackal, wolf, or hyena. But this afternoon there were no tell-tale indications, and we went off to take pot luck. It was an ill day. The wind had dropped, to bring a pestilence of flies, and the few distant shots we got drew a blank. In jungle country it is possible to get a close shot by stalking from tree to tree, but in the open the quarry runs off, and you are lucky to get within two hundred yards' range. As our caravan had come along, posses of four and five gazelle were often invisible against a buff background until our passing startled them into flight. This, curiously enough, was not directly away from us, but often at a tangent to, or even parallel with the course we were taking. When, however, gazelle happen to be down wind of you, and get your scent betimes, off they go in single file in a direction conducive to their maximum well being. Suddenly in mid-career and without rhyme or reason they bound into the air, off all feet at once, as though from a spring-board, and, alighting, carry on their impetuous course. Their speed is marvellous, and in action and grace they seem to me to excel any other of God's creatures. We had no long-dogs with us, and I doubt whether, if we had had, they would have served us much. I had experimented in Mesopotamia in pursuing gazelle in a car — but not as a sport, let me add. After doing 40 m.p.h. for some minutes, the dogs had been put down fresh, but these never once succeeded in coming up with the gazelle. And now the local Arabs I questioned agreed that they had never heard of a long-dog bringing a gazelle down. When I told them of the contrary claims of other men I had met, the answer was that the gazelle must have been very young and weak, or else was an old doe heavy with young.

But if we went short of venison in Wadi Ainan we had many a feed of locusts. Just before getting into camp we had passed through a barrage of a large red species, miles deep. They darkened the sky and smothered the acacia jungle, the tamarisk and camel thorn, and anything that was green. My servant overnight collected bundle handkerchiefs of them that recalled mushrooms, and roasting them occupied a large part of the mornings. A Badu squatted, presiding over the wood fire. Flattening the ash with his riding cane he would plunge his hand into the bundle, draw out a handful of locusts, their dry wings cracking under the pressure, and heartlessly throw them alive on to the fire, at the same time sweeping his cane backwards and forwards to bury them under the hot ash. One wretched locust, perhaps at the edge and only half submerged, would attempt to waddle out to freedom, only to be swept back into the middle, with no mistake this time. After a couple of minutes, the ash would be turned back, and the roasted locusts picked out and added to the fast-growing heap at the fireside. To eat them, you shake off the ash, avoiding over fastidiousness if you would be in the fashion, pluck the wings and tail off, pull away the head and with it the internal digestive apparatus — my Badus, however, sometimes waved this latter formality as representing a waste of food — and what is left is good to eat. It is not a dish on which to write lyrics. But the Arab considers locusts a delicacy, and, weight for weight, they fetch a higher price than chicken in the Arab booth.

THE UNKNOWN INTERIOR

I WAS GLAD INDEED WHEN, after a few days, we could leave the coast and strike once more into the unknown interior, [41] the Badawin habitat. In the early stages I had enjoyed the protection of powerful shaikhs, and even then my party was held up on three different occasions, one of which, that in Wadi Sarab, I have related. But the last stage of the journey lay for more than a hundred miles through mountainous, comparatively waterless country, a belt inside the populated coastal mountains, acknowledging no paramount shaikh, and used only by raiders. Here, indeed, it was necessary to run the gauntlet of terra incognita.

"It is a cold day, Abdullah."

"God will lighten the heaviness," he replied.

"And what of the way?" I asked.

"There is no habitation between here and the Qara Mountains, and any man that should be upon the road would be seeking evil and not good."

By day we moved cautiously, and by night lit no fires. Water now was too precious to permit of the luxury of washing. The temperature fell to

44° Fahr. by night, and sleeping out in Badawin kit, unchanged for eight days, was not ideally comfortable. However, apart from the excitement of the unknown, of what lay beyond the skyline, the good' humour of the Badawin was a mental tonic, and helped to support the effects of slight dysentery — inevitable towards the end of a six weeks' journey. One had eaten no green food, the diet for the most part consisting of dates, rice, and camels' milk.

On Trek in The Mahara Country

Hamuda beguiled the hours chanting, and his chants as usual told chiefly of love and war; others were improvisations on themes provided by the incidents of the day's march. I wrote down as many of the old camel chants as I could; that is, so far as European notation would allow, for it is almost impossible, since the Arab uses the old- Greek Pythagorean scale of quarter tones. Chants there are for every activity and pace of camels: loading, unloading, walking, trotting, over water, calling to water, and the rest, reminiscent of the methods of our old sea-chanties. The features of desert music were its fondness for sequences and grace-notes, the absence of any interval greater than a third, and preference of ascent to descent in the melody. The time defies one, and I could record it only by using different time signatures for alternate bars, *a la Ravel*. But the chants are quite short, and are endlessly repeated, the rhythm being subordinated completely to the stress of the words. It all sounds very much out of tune to a European ear, and dull in the extreme. Riding along one day after the conclusion of some Badu chanting, the Harsusi asked me for one of our songs. Nothing loath, I obliged with;

Kind, kind and gentle is she.

Kind is my Mary.

He declared it awful. I, who had thought mine had his beaten to a frazzle, now felt constrained to say that it wasn't really a man's song at all, but what our girls sing. I then tried "Three Blind Mice", and said in anticipation of hostile reception, that it was a boy's song. The tune of "Three Blind Mice" caused him to laugh, but he didn't want it again. He wanted "Kind, kind," possibly, I thought, because he might have relented and felt his original judgment to have been a trifle severe, but this was not so, for he afterwards confessed, with merry twinkle in his eyes, that Shumla, his camel, had misbehaved and wanted to run off, and a repetition of the provocative tune would, he thought, put him in the proper frame of mind for dealing with her. I then made the experiment of humming some Gregorian chants, and these, as I anticipated, won his immediate approval — they were not so very far removed from some of his own melodies. The *piece de resistance* in the Badu repertoire seemed to be a *raghazait* of the Mahra. In it the Badu conception that the camel is altogether beautiful is so well exemplified that the words of its refrain seemed worth recording.

The fairness of beautiful girls

Is as that of Banat Safair.[42]

Sa'id's daughter approaching a camp-fire

Is as the descent [43] of a difficult pass.

Her fresh face is like camel's flesh

Which the dew has not struck, nor the cold.

Chanting is done in & high voice, impassioned but never sentimental. Virility is the keynote of 'the Badu's character. His adulation and flattery are of the open, honest kind, too extravagant ever to deceive. He does not cringe, and though he will shamelessly ask for money or anything he sees, he suffers no rebuff by being refused. His mood is quixotic. Having sworn that parting with you is like parting with his own soul, when the time -comes he takes his dues and departs laughing, conscious only of the inexorable will of God.

The law of sanctuary is sacred. A fugitive from another's wrath, whatever the acts that have occasioned it, has only to escape to a distant tribe and make his *dakhala* (appeal for sanctuary), henceforward to be protected, and asylum once conceded, only an act of treachery could betray him. Should he be a criminal and the arm of Government sufficiently long to bring pressure, his protectors would be in honour bound to pass him on to a remoter shaikh, where the process would be repeated.

Liberty is the Badu's darling passion, and this, though it involves a hungry and thirsty existence, he prefers to the comfort and material rewards that go with servitude. But he has to preserve that liberty with his own right arm. Feuds, family, tribal, and factional, are without beginning and without end. No man dare go abroad unarmed, and to travel through country used by hostile elements is to court death and the confiscation of his camels, except during the intermittent periods of truce, and then it is necessary for him to be accompanied by a *rafiq* (member of the opposing faction). A small boy will suffice, and one constantly meets with this humorous side of it, but he must be of tribal blood and not a slave, for in only one tribe in South Arabia — the Qara — are slaves accepted as *rafiqs*. Slaves taken in the raid everywhere escape the death that is meted out to their freeborn companions. In fact, they, like the camels rounded up at the same time, are of course loot, and both pass into some convenient market to be exchanged for rifle ammunition or, possibly, rice.

Tribal peace is ephemeral; so is tribal war. Alternating war and peace between rival neighbours is the normal condition, and must have been so for hundreds, nay, perhaps thousands of years.

During my journey an armistice between two such tribes that I passed through came to an end, and my two *rabias*, representing, respectively, 'the two hostile factions, became in theory mortal enemies, so that I found myself in the anomalous role of protecting my protectors. I asked Muhammad bin Khamis, the Wahibi, what sense there was in keeping up this feud. "Surely it is against your religion, and besides, what good does it do? No good, but only evil. To-day your tribe raids the Janabah and kills four men and takes twenty camels. Next year the Janabah counter raid and inflict similar losses on you,, and during the interval you are each living in terror of the other."

"True," he said, "but a permanent peace is not possible. Mutual hatred is too strong. A man who has lost a father or brother or son killed would never consent to peace until he had avenged him. To advocate peace would be to lose caste and influence in a war-minded tribe."

Al Mahara Country

And Hamuda, to whom I then put the question, was also "anti", though he lived in dread of the Manahil, two of whose tribesmen he had killed in avenging his father's death. He was prepared to condemn violence in the abstract, but justified it in the particular. Raiding to him was "the spice of life", and he was doubtless a fair representative of his kind. His talk and his poetry both eulogized the warrior valiant in battle. Yet he was deeply religious and prayed for himself five times a day. In fact, his contempt for people who neither prayed nor fasted was as strong as his admiration for those who slew their enemies. Economic necessity cannot here be tempered by ideals of rationalization. In a pastoral country where water, the source of life, is not plentiful nor even a constant factor, men may arrive in days of drought at a well that is already occupied, and the means of life may not be sufficient for both parties.

"What do you think of the Bautahara?" I asked Hamuda, referring to a *declasse* tribe that speaks a "language of birds".[44]

"Nothing," he replied. "*Hashak!* You know the slaves? Well, one degree better." Then apparently having considered that he had gone too far. he added a rider: "But they have men among them, men who can slaughter."

"But surely," I said, "you don't judge men by their ability to fight?"

"Yes, I do; and you do; and all men do," said he. "Don't you Inglaiz fight?"

"Yes, but only our enemies," I added weakly.

"*Billahi*" (Tell me in God's name), he continued, "is it true that men have a woman to rule them?"

"I believe it is," said I, hedging, knowing the Arab view of women and wondering how he could have come by this knowledge.

"Well, then, who?"

"We English had a Queen," I confessed, "a very great Queen, but she died many years ago, and then her son succeeded, and now her son's son rules in her place."

"*Alhamdu I'illah!*" said Hamuda with a sigh of satisfaction. In view of the conditions of life in this hungry and thirsty land, it is not unnatural that a kind of communism should flourish. Beggary in a squalid sense does not exist. Poverty there is, perhaps, a general poverty according to European standards; but if one man has food and another none, it would be unthinkable for the better-off not to give to the less fortunate. A stranger coming upon the scene is never allowed to depart without being invited to sit down and share the common dish, however poor the host, and though it be the meagrest crust; and with a well-to- do host there is a three days' law of hospitality. In this poor and famished land, generosity is the supreme quality.

Folk-lore stories, which are legion, not unnaturally labour the everlasting moral that it is blessed to give and that miserliness is of the devil. These simple stories, usually animal stories, have often a legendary religious background. Luwaiti asked me om day whether I knew how it was that the sand lizard (*dabba*), which every Badu considers a most succulent dish, came to be good for human food, and did I know the origin of Adam's apple? I displayed an eager ignorance. And so he fell to telling me in his entrancing nuances begotten of the sands of the desert.

The Pass of Maut Bikhun

"One day the Prophet Muhammad was travelling with a companion. And when the evening fell they couched their camels close to some tents. Now these tents belonged to a rich man who. besides possessing flocks and herds, was a great merchant. And the rich man heard of the arrival of strangers, but he knew not who they were. Needs must he send word and invite, them to dinner; but he was a mean man, and instead of killing for them the fatted calf, he put in its place an old cat. And this was not hidden from the 'Sent One of God'. So when the dish arrived, the Prophet warned his companion not to eat of it, and calling upon the cat to come forth alive out of the dish, it did so, mewing, and ran away. Then the Prophet prayed to God that the rich man might be rewarded according to his acts, and God turned him into a *dabba* and made the *dabba* to be *hallal*, i.e. lawful for all men to eat.

"On the following day the Prophet moved on, and at sundown halted near the habitation of a poor man. And the poor man also knew not the quality of his guests, but loving-kindness dwelt in his heart. So, taking a knife, he slaughtered the fattest of his few sheep, and set his wife to cook it for the strangers' evening meal. Now this man had two young children, and the elder, picking up the knife, said to his brother, 'Lift up your head that we play at slaughtering, even as our father slaughtered the sheep.' And his young brother did as he was bid, and so fell down dead in a pool of blood with his throat cut. The mother, entering upon the scene, was about to scream to relieve her distress, but the poor husband stopped her, saying, 'No, lest our guests hear of what has happened and so be not minded to take of our food. First let them eat, and then you may weep afterwards.' So the meal was prepared and the poor man brought in the dishes and set them before his guests, saying, 'Take, eat.' Now the Prophet had been told of God all that had come to pass. And he turned to the poor man and said, 'First bring your sons with you so that we may all eat together.' But the poor man, overcome with grief which he was scarce able to conceal, had perforce to make excuses. 'Better,' said he, 'that you eat first, and we eat afterwards.' Then the Prophet required of him the names of his two sons. Now the name of the dead one was Musellim. Thereupon the Prophet prayed to God that he would raise Musellim, and, crying aloud his name, the boy became alive again, albeit with this lump (Adam's apple) in his throat. And all joyously partook of the evening meal. And the Prophet prayed to God that he would reward the poor man after his acts. Then turning to him, said: "To-morrow when you awake all that you see around you shall be yours'!' And when the morrow dawned the man went forth to tend his tiny flock, and lo! there in their place he found innumerable camels and horses, and flocks of sheep and goats, and herds of cattle, and he rejoiced, for they were all his."

ENDNOTES

1 It was while flying over this area that Sir Alan Cobham, on his momentous flight to Australia in 1926, was shot at from the ground, and had his mechanic killed outright at his side.

2 *Jihad*, or Holy War. This is one of the five tenets of Islam, the other four being Prayer, Fasting, Almsgiving, and the Pilgrimage to Mecca. In theory Jihad is a call to arms for the protection of the true faith. But the weapon in the hands of the Turks, before the Sultan abrogated the role of Caliph, could be turned to political account. This was done in Mesopotamia, when on the outbreak of the Great War the tribes rose at the Turks' behest on a religious issue. In his translation of the Quran, Maulvi Muhammad Ali renders the word Jihad as "Striving" (the view, doubtless, of the small Ahmadi sect) and denies any warlike significance for it. Etymologically this may be so, but in practice amongst Arab tribes themselves the word has the connotation I have given.

Note in this edition

The claim that Jihad is a tenant of Islam is incorrect. The five tenants are i/ Profession of Faith (*shahada*). The belief that "There is no god but God, and Muhammad is the Messenger of God" is central to Islam.

ii/ Prayer (*salat*).

iii/ Fasting (*sawm*).

iv/ Alms (*zakat*).

v/ Pilgrimage (*haj*).

The meaning of the word '*jihad*' is to strive or struggle.

3 At this time Major, now Lieutenant-Colonel, H. R. P. Dickson, C.T.E., Political Agent, Kuwait, Persian Gulf.

4 This form of nickname, *laqab*, as the Arabic has it, is by no means unflattering, and the truly eminent rarely escape. Sir Richard, then Captain Burton, on his Secret Journey to Mecca was known to his old Badawi as *Abu Shawarib*, i.e. "The father of moustachios", owing to his failure to clip his moustache in the universal Shaf'i manner. I was amused on one occasion in South Arabia to bear of a distinguished British officer who had visited the place many years before remembered only as *Abu Khartum*, i.e. "The father of the trunk" — a reference to his conspicuous and masterful nose.

5 During the latter end of the War and the immediate post- War period the present term, "High Commissioner for Iraq," was not in use. The Supreme Civil Authority was known as "Civil Commissioner of Mesopotamia", a post held first by Sir Percy Cox and later by Sir Arnold Wilson.

6 The tribal shaikhs of Mesopotamia seem in this respect to outrun the shaikhs of any other part of the Peninsula. Fifteen or twenty women (all manual workers and economically profitable) belonging to one man was by no means rare among the Muntafiq, though cohabitation was generally reserved to three or four, the experience of the others being limited to the brief duration of their early arrival, that is, when they were about fourteen or fifteen years old. In theory Muslims are allowed four legal wives only. Additional women are, however, permissible as

concubines or slaves. But it is the institution of *Muta'* that is the explanation of Badr's extravagant plurality, an institution peculiar to the Shi'ahs, the sect of the vast majority of Iraq tribesmen south of Baghdad. It constitutes a contractual relationship with free women, which in tribal practice can be indistinguishable from marriage; the *Muta'* unlike the concubine, being a legal heiress to the man's estate in the same degree as his four prescribed wives. The system is conveniently elastic, however, for during the pilgrimage to the Holy Places of Karbala and Najaf a tribesman would obtain on the spot a *Muta'* wife, taking her for one night, or for a week, or for the period of his stay. Such short-term contracts, though still not contravening Shi'ah religious rules, are, I understand, at present frowned on even in Persia.

7 At the time of which I write, burial at the Holy Place of Najaf was an invariable rule for the Shi'ah tribesmen, and seldom a day passed but one saw donkeys with their mummy-like burdens starting off on their hundred-mile journey northwards. Even from far-distant Muscat to-day the corpses of those Shi'ahs who can afford it; are dug up after six months' desiccation in their local resting-place and sent by dhow to Basrah, and thence transhipped to Najaf — all this in the faith that the body that is carried seven times round the shrine of Ali, and buried in the same soil he was buried in, is transported straight to Paradise.

8 Abbas, son of Ali, the Hothead and terrible Avenger. His shrine at Karbala is to the Shi*ah a place of great sanctity, and an oath upon it, if falsely made, will bring terrible consequences. Hence this oath upon Abbas at his shrine is, to the Shi'ah tribesmen of Iraq, the greatest oath a man may take, the oath from which he will most shrink. A counterpart is found in South Arabia in the name of Abu Hud, a pre-Islam saint. To a majority of the people of Dhufar, swearing by God or His Prophet, or on the Quran, has not the same awful significance as an oath on the shrine of Abu Hud, and the guilty suspect proclaiming his innocence will generally be found to confess his guilt rather than face the consequences of false swearing when brought to this shrine.

9 The *subha* (rosary) in common use throughout these marshlands consisted of ninety-nine beads, more or less, a difference being observed between that used for prayer and that carried and toyed with as a

general habit. The superstitious tribesmen had grown to believe in the *subha* possessing magical powers, as an instrument through which the Divine Will would express itself. Perhaps the most common method — a method now employed by Shaikh Muhammad, who sought Divine guidance in the proposition I had put to him— was as follows: Taking his string of beads he isolated a section of them haphazardly between finger and thumb of both hands. The beads thus divided off he named from right to left with the formula, "Allah, Muhammad, Ali, Abu Jahl", assigning Allah to the first and succeeding names to successive beads, the formula being repeated until the last bead was reached. If this bead coincided with one of the names, Allah, Muhammad, or Ali, it was a propitious omen; if with Abu Jahl, the contrary. (Abu Jahl, a contemporary of the Prophet, and a fellow-member of the Quraish tribe, was an enemy of Islam and is cursed by every Muslim to this day.)

10 The stand-up fight is unpopular with the tribal Arab. During the War the successes he had were the result of his mobility. Slipping round the flanks, especially after dark, and getting away perhaps unseen were made possible by his light equipment and his being so admirably mounted. The Arab pony of the country was a stranger to dandy-brush and curry- comb, had been brought up to irregular feeding, and watering, and could do thirty miles a day for days on end without turning a hair. Add to that the knowledge of the country, making it unnecessary for him to carry rations, and it becomes clear that only a force locally raised and similarly equipped and mounted was likely to be able to come to grips.

11 The site of Nisin may, however, be Bahriyat, mounds seventeen miles south of Nippur. The late Professor A. T. Clay, to whom I made known the discovery of a Libit Ishtar Cone, in *situ*, by Colonel K. Stevenson, R.E., a companion amateur archaeologist, considered that the provenance of the cone probably determines the site of this ancient city.

12 Major A. H. Ditchbum, O.B.E., Administrative Inspector, Iraq.

13 By permission of Truth from its issue of January 19, 1921.

14 Three Brigadiers on G.H.Q. Staff, respectively the Deputy Q.M.G., the Director of Medical Services, and the Director of Railways.

15 Ibadhism is another considerable dissenting sect: in origin the Separatists or Khuwarij, which now flourishes only in Oman and parts of North Africa. It also stands for a Theocracy, but the Imamate is not hereditary nor exclusively restricted to any family, the Prophet's or other, but is elective. The Imamate may be suspended for considerable periods in the absence of suitable candidate — whence the Ibadhis deny the Caliphates of Uthman and AH. The memory of the latter, indeed, is execrated by them.

16 Taqiya as understood by the tribesmen is not a conspicuously helpful belief and practice any more than it was an inspiring moral ideal. Baldly put, it implies that there is no sin in lying to an unbeliever.

17 The notion I have heard expressed in European circles that syphilis is likely to follow a camel bite is scouted by the local.

18 There is a delightful fort at Fulaij which lies well out under the Hajar, square with Barkah, and was used as a shooting-box by former Sultans. It was built by Sultan bin Hamad, the second ruler of the present Dynasty, who lived at the end of the eighteenth century. I found it in much better preservation than the Batinah forts, perhaps because its foundations rest in solid limestone instead of sand. Nearby is the important Wadi Ma'awil (*pace* Palgrave there is no name *Ma'wah* known in the neighbourhood of Sahar) whence caravans pass to and from its port of Barkah. Its falaj sometimes dries up, and the inhabitants had a custom of going up to the mountain whence it springs, and saying: 'Give us water! give us water! We have a corpse I We have a guest ! Give us water!"

19 On a previous visit here I had taken the same road in company with the Heir Apparent and its owner, Saiyid Hamad bin Ibrahim bin Iman Azan, to ride across the plain to Hazm, a fort and oasis under the mountains a few miles short of Rostaq, the ancient capital of the land. The fort at Hazm is the noblest monument I have seen in South-East Arabia. It dates from the last of the Ya'araba Imams, and it shares with Bir 'Ain and Nazwa the reputation of being one of the three finest forts in Oman. A truly magnificent building it is, which for strength and size leave the Portuguese efforts at Muscat a long way behind, though it lacks

their external beauty of line. The entrance is by a most gorgeously ornamented doorway (brass studded as though for defence purposes against elephants) with an inscription that it came from Surat in the days of Saif bin Sultan. A *falaj* runs beneath it as by natural rule. The interior reminded me of parts of the Saladin-cum-Crusader fort of Kerak (in Trans- Jordan), though it is on a much smaller plan. The walls, in places six feet thick, are built of locally hewn stone and cement. Lofty rooms and corridors grace its interior. Its upper storeys are accessible by four flights of slippery stone steps, besides a secret stairway that threads one of its massive walls.

20 This term, or its even commoner alternative, *Hashak*, means "God exalts you". In Badu conversation it is invariably used before a word representing a degraded object — presumably to flatter the person addressed that Allah has cast him in nobler mould. Thus the words "dog", "pig", "cow", "woman", "wife", "daughter", "virgin", "Jew", "Banian", and sometimes "Christian" must carry the prefix. But the Badu, no hypocrite, emphatically exempts the words "horse" and "camel".

21 Every tribe in South-East Arabia is either Hinawi or Ghafari. Superficially these terms appear to date from a dynastic squabble over succession in Oman in the early eighteenth century, but they are of much deeper significance, for generally speaking the Hinawi label coincides with tribes of Qahtani descent, the Ghafari label with those of Maadic or Nizari. Within limits, therefore, the division is racial in origin.

22 The extent of this type of archaeological remain is widespread throughout Oman, and each locality seems to have a different name for it. At Sahar it is *Bait al Jahal* in Wadi Sama'il, *Uga* or *rijjam al Jahal*; -in the Hajar, *buma* (s.), *buam* (pi.); in the Ja'alan, *Uquq al Jahal*.

23 The names of those main wadi gorges which give access from the interior to the Batinah are, in order from south to north. Sama'il, Ma'awil, Hawasinah, Bani 'Umr Ahin, Jizzi, Hatta, Qaur, and Ham. Where they debouch on to the plain they each split up into many shallow beds, and thus carry on to the sea. These shallow wadi beds in the plain are dry except for a day or two following rains, when they are

in spate. Each has a different and separate name from the main mountain wadi, and where they make a break in the date-grove to reach the sea are known as *bathas*.

24 A discovery that lends colour to this theory is that Sumerian copper has been found to contain a certain percentage of nickel; and the analysis of copper ores brought respectively from Asia Minor, Western Persia, Sinai, and Oman, the possible sources of Sumerian supply, shows that it is only the copper of Oman which contains nickel in the same proportion.

25 Shaikh Salim, my host, was destined to be murdered two years later. The murderer was his brother Ma'adhid, and the motive, the shaikhship of the Bani Ka'ab tribe to which the murderer then succeeded. In the courtyard of the mosque at Mahadha, as Salim prepared for prayers, he was shot dead while his son at his side was mortally wounded. Other sons promptly escaped and will now live for revenge. This is the bloody rule. Fratricide is the normal method of succession, hallowed by precedent, in many of these Oman tribes, notably the Bani Ali (Yunqil) and Bani Yas (Abu Dhabi). It is predestined!

26 The nature and position of Ukdat has for long years exercised the minds of Arabian explorers — a squabble which I was able now to set at rest. Wellsted first mentioned Jabal Ukdat in 1820 as a mountain range existing to the south of Baraimi. Palgrave in 1867 confirms its existence. Miles travelling to Baraimi in 1885 declares that Wellsted's Okdat is purely mythical. Samuel Zwemer, who travelled that way twenty years later, followed the older authorities and put the name in his map. Sir Percy Cox, who travelled a year or two after Zwemer, follows Miles, but hazarded that the name may be used by local Arabs synonymously for Jabal Hafit. In point of fact Uqdat exists not as a mountain range but as a district, a thick acacia jungle in a sandstone plain. There are two such separate areas, Uqdat al Hafit and Uqdat al Baraimi. The word Uqdat itself meaning "knot" may be suggested by the knotted branches of the acacia, which here is the characteristic vegetation.

27 It was my privilege three years later to explore the Southern Rub'al Khali. See "A Journey into Rub' al Khali, the Southern Arabian Desert", communicated to the Royal Geographical Society.

28 For a full discussion of this phenomenon in Arabia elsewhere, see Curzon, *Tales of Travel*.

29 My reading in the halts of our journey had not unnaturally been about these peoples. One author, Sir John Malcolm, who was in these parts over a hundred years ago, had said: "Their occupation is piracy and their delight murder; they are monsters."

30 The "Reader" blows a hot breath on the victim, and then strokes his arm, reciting at the same time from four Suras of the Quran, i.e. The Dawn, The Men, The Allies, and The Pen.

31 The cult in wartime Iraq was, I remember, widespread. The special efficacy of turquoise is believed in there to keep off the evil. Few men or women or children will not have a turquoise ring or other ornament, and almost every little wayside caravanserai shows a small blue piece of pottery iet into the rude plaster above the doorway in the simple faith of its repelling virtue.

32 This Riyaisa tribe have a unique practice of disinheriting their women- kind — an absolute contravention of the religious rules of inheritance, of almost universal application in Arabia, by which a daughter's share is half that of a son's and a widow's is an eighth of the estate. Men say of the Riyaisa that they are of Baluchi origin, too, for what Arab tribe names its sons Shanba and the like ?

33 It was my duty, alas! to remove Muhammad two years later from the Waliship. He had usurped my functions, for powers of life and death vested in the Sultan, and, in his absence, in the Council of Ministers, and Muhammad had seen fit to carry out an execution without reference, and in a manner utterly reprehensible. The victim was a notorious camel - thief who had long eluded capture and his last brazen act was to force an entrance into the Wall's fort by night and attempt to remove a child from its mother's arms to carry it away and sell it into bondage. The Wali roped the thief with his stomach facing close the

mouth of the old muzzle-loading Portuguese gun, and he himself fired the touch-hole which sent the wretch flying into a dozen bloody pieces.

34 I later saw some rough boulder inscriptions equally crude in Wadi Ghaf, an affluent of Wadi Qaur, two hours' ride from Abu Baqara. These seem to be primitive pictorial representations of mounted camels, but one of the glazed red boulders so inscribed bears the words "There is no God but God, Muhammad is the Prophet of God", in angular, almost Cufic character.

35 A dozen of the old British clipper ships thus passed into Muscat owner- ship, and ended their days in the Calcutta trade — chiefly a date cargo "out" and rice "home". Muscat at one time almost completely monopolized the entrepot trade of the Persian Gulf, the coasting trade being carried on in small Arab dhows: the old eighteenth-century prints of Muscat Harbour show it to be a forest of tall masts and spars. To-day the modern steamship serves a dozen Persian and Arab ports. Muscat's former clients have gone and her commerce has declined to an insignificant share of that of the Gulf.

36 See also reference to cave-dwellers in Job xxx. 6,

37 Jesus -- 'Isa is not an uncommon name among the Arabs. The use of a surname as employed in Europe is not often found among tribal folk at all. Their names follow the New Testament model of Simon, son of Jonas (father's name). These names, too, often have a religious meaning (though no religious significance), and recall the vogue of our old Roundheads,

Thus, to take the meaning of the names occurring in these pages:

'Isa bin Abdul Latif

Jesus, son of the Servant of the Subtle One

Hasan bin Muhammad

Beauteous, son of the Praised One

Salih bin Muhammad

Restorer, son of the Praised One

Rashid

Rightly guided

Muhammad bin Sulaiman

Praised One, son of Solomon

Nasir bin Khalfan

Ally, son of the Bequeather

Ibrahim bin Muhammad bin Juma

Abraham, son of the Praised One, son of the Assembly

38 *Zars*, though they are conceived of as male or female, slave or free, and as having kinship with one another, yet possess, each as an entity, the property of omnipresence. Thus *Saif Shungar, Bursait, Nuray*, and *Dira*, the more popular of them, frequently possess several people in different places at the same time. Instances of working pairs of male and female *zars* are *Warar* and *Mug, Saif Shungar* and *Of.Mamid* (sometimes called *Tulubizan*) *Alim Sejjed* and either *Mug* or *Ingalul*—the polygamist. Other male spirits are *Dumjur, Al Qust, Dair Sejjed, Am Bessu, Fasil*; female ones, *Suriq, Iskander, Dai Katu, Taizar*, and *Wilaj*. A devotee of the cult who is periodically possessed by one of these will probably have had his (her) finger-ring washed in the blood of the sacrifice.

39 The Amir was killed in a skirmish a year later.

40 A description of the geography of the entire journey is given in my paper, "The South-Eastern Borderlands of Rub 'al Khali", read before the Royal Geographical Society and published in its Journal, vol. lxxiii, no. 3. March 1929.

41 A famous Mahri breed of camels.

42 A simile of the supercilious air with which a camel turns her head from side to side when descending a hillside.

43 Anthropological aspects of the last stage of the journey formed the subject of my paper, "Among some Non-Arab Tribes of South Arabia", read to the congress of Orientalists at Oxford in 1928, and published in the Journal of the Royal Anthropological Institute, 1929, vol. lix, January-June.

IMAGES

ALARMS

Bertram Thomas:
24;44;82;109;136;140;162;164;166;168;171;184;187;193; 204;207;214;217;218;220;221;234;237;243;256;262;279; 289;294;298;302;305;308;313;316;320;323;325;

Paul Dober:

58;70

unknown photographers:

Dedication; preface xxi; 107;253;258;

Arabesque: 112;134;167;169;175;180;188;190;230;249;280;292

Maps – Bertram Thomas some adapted by Arabesque 4;226;228;278;

INDEX

Arab first name, European family name first

INDEX INTRODUCTORY PAGES

Al Jabal Al Akhdar-x

Alarms & Excursions in Arabia (Book) -v, viii, ix, xii, xiii, xv, xvii

Arabia Felix (book) -vi, xvii

Baghdad-viii, ix, xii

Bombay-xi

Britain-vi, viii, ix, x, xvii

British Political Agent-x, xi, xii, xv

British Political Agents

Crosthwaite, Charles Gilbert-xi, xii

Hinde, Reginald Graham-x

Alban , Reginald George Evelyn William-xii

Council of Ministers of Oman-xi, xiii, xv, xx

Dehra Dun (Indian town) -x, xi

Dhufar-xx

English East India Company-ix

Gwadar (Omani exclave in Pakistan) -ix

India-vii, viii, x, xi, xiii

Iraq-v, vi, viii, ix, x, xiv, xv

Iraq/Mesopotamia-vii, viii, xx

Jordan-vi, xi, xx

Kut (town and military battle in Iraq) -viii

London-viii, xi, xvi, xvii

Muscat-vi, xi, xii, xiii, xiv, xv, xvi, xvii, xx

Mutrah-xii

Nasir bin Murshid Al Yarubi (Imam of Oman) -ix

Oman-v, vi, ix, x, xi, xii, xiv, xvi, xvii, xx

Ottoman-viii

Persian Gulf Resident-vii, viii, x, xi, xii, xiii, xv

Persian Gulf Residents

Prideaux, Francis Bellville-xiii

Pill (English village - Thomas's birthplace) -vii, xvii

Powell, Sir Thomas (British ambassador for King James I) - ix

Ramsay MacDonald (British Prime Minister) -vii

Ras al Had-xx

Rub al Khali-xx

Rub Al Khali-vi, vii, xiv, xv, xvi, xvii

Said bin Sultan Al Said (Sultan of Oman) -ix

Salim ibn Rashid al-Kharusi (Imam Oman) -ix

Shatrah (town in Iraq) -viii

Somerset Light Infantry (Army battalion of Thomas) - vii, viii

Taimur bin Faisal Al Said (Sultan of Oman) - iii, vi, ix, x, xi, xii, xiv, xv, xvii, xx

Thomas, Bertram-v, vi, vii, vii, viii, ix, x, xi, xii, xiii, xiv, xv, xvi, xvii

Thomas, Bessie (nee Hoile wife of Bertram Thomas) -xvii

Thomas, Elizabeth (daughter) -xvii

Thomas, Eliza (mother) -vii

Thomas, William (father) -vii, xvi

Treaty of Seeb (internal Oman treaty) -ix, x

Trevor, Arthur Prescott-x

Willingdon, Earl of (Viceroy of India) -vii

Wilson, Arnold (administrator of Iraq) -viii, xii, xvii, xxii

Wingate, Ronald-x

Wylde, Philip (ambassador for English East India Company) - ix

Zanzibar-ix

MAIN TEXT

afarit (demon spirit), 167, 171

Agha Khan, 131

Al Fathi (Iraqi government fort southeast of Shatrah), 27, 28, 30, 41, 44

Al Sa'idi (Oman government boat), 233, 234, 239, 242, 243, 250, 251, 257, 258, 259, 261, 263, 269, 273, 279, 284, 285, 287, 288

INDEX

Ali (Amir at Bani Bu Ali), 290, 293, 294, 295

Ali (secretary of Bertram Thomas), 290

Ali Al Khalili, Shaikh (governor of region near Muscat), 116, 149, 151

Amarah (Iraqi town northeast of Shatrah), 29, 34, 36, 37

Amr bin Al'As (representative to Oman from Prophet Mohammed), 169

Arab Bureau (British Cairo based approach to the Arab world), 51

Arabian leopard (noted as panther), 181

Auhi (oasis near Sahar), 163, 168

azwa (traditional Omani dance and chant), 181, 182

Badr bin Rumaiyidh (shaikh in Iraq), 3, 4, 6, 7, 8, 9, 11, 12, 13, 14, 18, 19, 20, 21, 22, 23, 27, 28, 29, 30, 35, 36, 37, 38, 39, 40, 43, 44, 45, 46, 331

Baghdad, 3, 8, 46, 49, 52, 54, 57, 67, 71, 72, 74, 81, 82, 84, 87, 91, 94, 95, 100, 102, 103, 170, 331

Bait al Falaj fort (military fort near Muscat), 221

Bait al Jalil (man made structures in Oman), 165, 166, 167

Balfour Declaration, 53, 57

Baluchis (tribe in Oman originally from Pakistan), 108, 131, 135, 137, 144, 148, 203

Bani bu Ali (town and tribe in eastern Oman), 155, 245, 288, 289, 292, 294, 300, 301

Bani bu Hasan (tribe and town near Bani bu Ali in eastern Oman), 155, 218, 291, 294

Bani Ka'ab (tribe in northern Oman), 161, 163, 164, 176, 177, 180, 183, 201, 210, 335

Bani Qitab (tribe in northern Oman), 183, 184, 201, 217

Banian (person of Indian origin), 123, 124, 125, 126, 334

Baraimi (Oasis on the north-eastern edge of the Rub Al Khali), 173, 174, 175, 177, 179, 182, 183, 335

barasti (Omani building made from date palm leaves), 164

Barkah (town with major fort west of Muscat), 129, 130, 133, 134, 219, 333

Basrah (Iraqi town southeast of Shatrah), 3, 30, 52, 81, 87, 90, 91, 331

Batinah (region of Oman extending northwest of Muscat to Trucial Oman), 117, 122, 129, 134, 137, 138, 139, 140, 145, 158, 161, 163, 172, 177, 180, 181, 189, 190, 203, 207, 213, 215, 218, 237, 333, 334

Bautahara / Bautahari (tribe or member of that tribe in southern Oman), 313, 324

Bell, Gertrude (British administrator and archaeologist in Iraq), 57

Biblical Book of Job and Musandam's tribes, 244, 246

Bikaner (Indian style camel saddle), 288

Biyasara Omani (population group), 148, 149

Bombay, 131, 236

Boshar (village near the mountains west of Muscat), 116, 117, 119

Britain / British, 3, 6, 11, 12, 14, 21, 24, 34, 44, 45, 49, 50, 51, 52, 53, 54, 55, 56, 61, 62, 64, 65, 66, 67, 69, 72, 75, 85, 89, 90, 91, 97, 101, 103, 104, 113, 145, 207, 221, 232, 235, 248, 252, 258, 261, 330, 337

burza (public reception in Oman), 110, 111, 123, 136, 157, 178, 189, 219

camel, 34, 39, 107, 108, 109, 110, 113, 117, 118, 119, 126, 127, 128, 129, 131, 133, 134, 135, 137, 138, 139, 141, 142, 143, 147, 151, 153, 154, 155, 156, 162, 165, 166, 170, 172, 179, 181, 183, 189, 193, 195, 196, 198, 199, 200, 208, 209, 211, 214, 215, 221, 222, 241, 245, 279, 281, 288, 290, 293, 294, 295, 297, 298, 300, 301, 302, 304, 305, 306,

307, 308, 314, 315, 316, 317, 320, 321, 322, 323, 326, 327, 333, 334, 336, 337, 338, 339

coffee, 32, 64, 78, 110, 111, 130, 196, 216, 217, 218, 284

Cox, Percy (British Political representative), 162, 180, 330, 335

Daba (village and area in Musandam), 204, 205, 207, 231, 232, 239, 250, 259, 269, 271, 272

Davidson, F.D. (British army officer), 30

Dawaiyah (town in Iraq north east of Shatrah), 31, 34, 41, 83

Dhahirah (region in northwest Oman), 163, 165, 176, 177, 182, 189, 202, 203, 205, 218

Dhufar (southern Oman), 122, 129, 195, 219, 288, 293, 301, 331

Dickson, Major Harold (British military officer in Iraq), 6, 7, 8, 9, 13, 18, 19, 30, 36, 39, 43, 330

Ditchburn, Major A.H. (British military officer in Iraq), 43, 45

Dubai, 126, 182, 189, 202, 211, 217, 220, 272

Elphinstone (sea inlet east of Khasab Musandam), 249, 252, 263

Faisal, (Amir of Sharif family in Hijaz), 56, 57

falaj (man made water channel in Oman, 131, 165, 166, 168, 173, 175, 209, 213, 214, 333, 334

Firefly, (British ship in Iraq), 11, 12, 13, 20, 21

French, 52, 53, 56, 57, 108, 233

Fujaira (town on east coast of Trucial Oman), 205, 206, 207, 208

fuwala (Omani light refreshment), 110, 178, 199

gazelle, 108, 118, 143, 162, 164, 173, 214, 316, 317

German, 50, 57, 62

Gharraf (man-made canal, town and area in Iraq south of Shatrah), 23, 61, 65, 66, 71, 77, 79, 85, 86, 87, 88, 90, 93, 94, 95, 99, 102, 104

Greenfly (ship in Iraq), 11, 12, 13, 20, 21, 81, 88, 96

Grieg, D'Arcy (British pilot in Iraq), 94

Lupin, H.M.S. (British ship in Musandam) 242, 250, 251, 253, 257, 258, 261, 263, 265, 268, 269, 273

Cyclamen H.M.S. (British ship in Musandam), 253, 258, 263, 269

Haji Almas (Iraqi associate of Thomas), 96, 97, 98

Hall, Captain F. W. Hall (British officer in Iraq), 27, 36, 40, 41, 99, 100, 101, 102, 103

Hamad bin Faisal, Sayyid (Brother of the Sultan Taimur), 190

Hamdan, Shaikh (in Bani bu Ali Oman), 288

Harasis / Harsusi (tribe or member of that tribe in central Oman), 311, 312, 314, 316

Hasan (Badr bin Rumaiyidh's son), 18, 19, 44, 45

Hasan (Shaikh in Musandam Oman), 225, 229, 231, 232, 240, 241, 244, 247, 248, 249, 250, 251, 255, 259, 261, 262, 263, 269, 270, 271, 272, 273, 337

Haura Burgha (hill fortification west of Sahar Oman), 164, 168, 169

Haysom, Captain R. R. (British officer in Iraq), 13

hukm al hauz (tribal law in Oman), 298, 299

Ibadhi (Islamic school of thought), 116, 126, 130, 134, 150, 181, 182, 202, 205, 216, 297

Ibn Sa'ud (Abdulaziz, Sultan of Nejd), 52, 129, 146, 150, 174, 175, 176

India, 44, 50, 51, 64, 65, 90, 113, 122, 138, 205, 207, 227, 246, 277, 293

350   INDEX

Indian School (Indian Raj approach to Iraq rule), 51, 52

Iraq / Mesopotamia / Mesopotamian, 3, 29, 49, 50, 51, 52, 53, 54, 55, 56, 63, 65, 69, 70, 71, 72, 80, 87, 89, 104, 124, 150, 216, 245, 317, 329, 330

Isa bin Salih, Shaikh (major regional Shaikh from eastern Oman), 218

Ja'alan (region of eastern Oman), 218, 287

Janabah (tribe in eastern Oman), 293, 294, 300, 303, 323

Jayakar, Dr (19th century surgeon and British Agent in Muscat), 158

jinn (genie), 139, 171, 179, 192, 203, 279, 280, 281, 282

Kalba (village on east coast of Trucial Oman), 205, 206, 207, 208, 209

Karam (Omani Baluch slave-trader), 144, 145, 217

Khabura (Oman town on Batinah coast), 147, 152, 156, 193, 214, 215

Khaiyyun al 'Ubaid, Shaikh (and battle leader), 67, 80, 82, 85, 86, 87, 88, 90, 92, 93, 94, 99, 100, 101, 102, 103

Khaluf (village on coast of eastern Oman), 300

Khan Bahadur (secretary to the Sultan of Muscat & Oman), 114

Khasab (important town in Musandam), 225, 230, 231, 232, 240, 242, 245, 248, 249, 250, 251, 255, 259, 260, 261, 262, 263, 265, 271, 272, 273

Khor Fakkan (village on east coast of Trucial Oman), 204, 206, 207

Khor Jaramah (sea inlet in eastern Oman), 277, 279, 280, 287

Khutma Malaha (border settlement between Trucial Oman and the sultanate), 117, 204, 209

Khuwair (village west of Muscat), 219, 221

Khuwara (Camel owned by Thomas), 108, 109, 161, 198

Kitchener, General (British officer), 44, 50

INDEX

Kitnah (village in northern Oman), 177, 179, 180

Kumzar (northernmost town in Musandam), 242, 256, 260, 273

Kut (Iraqi town and Battle north of Shatrah), 3, 61, 65, 66, 81, 82, 88, 94, 96

Leachman, Colonel Gerard (British military and intelligence officer Iraq) 58

Liwa (fort and town in northern Oman), 199

Luxmore, Colonel C. de J. (British officer in Iraq), 13, 20, 40

Ma'adan (Iraqi marsh men), 25

Mabruk (butcher for the Oman Batinah journey), 191, 192, 194, 195, 196, 197, 198, 219

madhif (Iraqi reed building), 25, 31, 32, 33, 58, 78, 84

Magan (previous historic name for northern Oman), 174

Mahadha (northern Oman town), 180, 181, 183, 335

Mahra / Mahri (tribe or member of that tribe in southern Oman), 321, 338

Mahut, island, 300, 301

Malak bin Faisal, Saiyid (Sultan Taimur's brother), 250, 269

Marrs (British official at Amarah), 36

mash-hufs (Iraqi canoe), 25, 70

Masirah Island (Oman), 294, 301

Matrah (town in Oman west of Muscat), 108, 121, 148, 219, 221

Mazun (previous historic name for northern Oman), 174

Mesopotamia / Mesopotamian / Iraq, 3, 29, 49, 50, 51, 52, 53, 54, 55, 56, 63, 65, 69, 70, 71, 72, 80, 87, 89, 104, 124, 150, 216, 245, 317, 329, 330

Miles, Samuel Barrett (19thc British Political Agent in Muscat), 169

Mosul (northern Iraqi town), 3, 57

Muhammed, Shaikh (Iraqi sheikh), 31, 32, 33

Muhammad bin Nasir (Amir of Bani bu Ali Oman), 288, 289

Muhammad bin Mahdi (Shaikh of Kumzar Oman), 259, 260

Muhammad bin Sulaiman (Shaikh of Qada Oman), 248, 338

Mulla Mishrif (Badr bin Rumaiyidh's religious advisor), 18, 19

Muntafiq (major tribe in southern Iraq), 23, 24, 27, 29, 30, 36, 41, 65, 66, 70, 71, 76, 90, 92, 99, 104, 330

Muqbali (person of the Muqabil tribe in northern Oman), 179

Musana'a (coastal town in Batinah Oman), 130, 131, 135, 136

Musandam (northern exclave of Oman), 225, 226, 228, 232, 243, 244, 245, 246, 251, 255, 259

Muscat, 51, 107, 108, 110, 117, 121, 122, 125, 131, 144, 145, 153, 161, 172, 182, 187, 191, 192, 205, 219, 221, 226, 231, 232, 233, 234, 235, 239, 240, 241, 245, 251, 252, 258, 261, 262, 269, 272, 273, 284, 285, 293, 300, 308, 331, 333, 337

Naif, Shaikh (of region near Shatrah), 33, 83, 84

Na'im (tribe of northern Oman & Trucial Oman), 155, 173, 174, 177, 182, 245

Najaf (Iraqi town northwest of Shatrah), 26, 73, 90, 100, 169, 331

Nasir bin Khalfan (Governor of Khasab Oman), 231, 338

Nasiriyah (Iraqi town south of Shatrah), 3, 7, 8, 11, 13, 19, 27, 29, 30, 40, 46, 62, 66, 67, 76, 81, 82, 87, 90, 93, 95, 96, 99, 101, 102, 103

Ormonde, H.M.S. (British Royal Navy ship), 225, 229, 231

Ottoman / Turkish / Turks/, 3, 4, 6, 21, 34, 49, 50, 51, 52, 53, 54, 57, 65, 66, 67, 69, 71, 72, 73, 77, 78, 79, 84, 97, 124, 177, 194, 227, 329

Palgrave (British explorer), 122, 140, 189, 333, 335

Persian/s, 24, 26, 35, 39, 51, 58, 59, 73, 83, 108, 165, 167, 168, 169, 171, 174, 187, 194, 202, 203, 239, 243, 244, 245, 280, 330, 337

Platts, A. (British officer in Iraq), 45

Pliny (Greek historian), 239, 245

Qada (coastal village west of Khasab Musandam), 247, 248, 250, 261, 263, 265, 266, 268, 269, 270, 271, 272

Qalat Sikar (Iraqi town north of Shatrah), 65, 76, 88, 91, 92, 94, 95, 96, 99, 100, 104

Qara Mountain (southern Oman mountains), 319

Qawasim / Qasimi (tribe and member of ruling family in Trucial Oman), 204, 205, 207, 232

239, 241

Qusbiyat as Sultan (coastal fort Batinah Oman), 156

rafiq (tribal escort or guide in Oman), 294, 307, 322

rabia (tribal escort and protector in Oman), 302, 311, 316, 323

Rashid (Captain of Oman's Al Sa'idi boat), 147, 234, 235, 236, 237, 239, 242, 250, 259, 260, 261, 273, 284, 288

Rivett-Carnac (British officer in Iraq), 36

Rub' al Khali (desert), 113, 183, 277, 336

Rumaitha (Iraqi town west of Shatrah), 89, 91, 96

Sa'dun (Arab aristocratic family in southern Iraq), 65, 66, 80

Sa'id bin Maktum, (Shaikh of Dubai), 272

sablas (meeting location in Oman), 129, 217

Saham (Oman coastal town), 156, 157, 213

INDEX

Sahar (major Oman town, 157, 158, 161, 163, 169, 170, 175, 176, 185, 187, 188, 189, 195, 196, 199, 211, 333, 334

Saif bin Ya'rab (accompanied Thomas in the Batinah), 109, 137, 151, 192, 194, 195, 199

Sa'id bin Sultan, Saiyid (heir apparent of Oman), 107, 108, 119, 122, 123, 143, 182, 204, 205, 207, 210, 333

Salih bin Muhammad (Sheikh of Daba area in Musandam), 231, 240, 272, 337

Salim, Shaikh (northern Oman Muqabil shaikh), 166, 167, 182, 183, 307, 335

Salim bin Thuwaini (Omani Mid 19thc Sultan), 189

Samawah (Iraqi city), 81, 84, 91, 95, 96

Sha'ar (court jester to Sultan Taimur), 155, 156, 158, 159, 195

Sikar al Na'ama, Shaikh (Iraqi Shaikh) 36, 37

Shamailiyah (northern Oman region), 135, 165, 198, 200, 202

Sharifan (family or supporters of the Sharif of Mecca), 52, 53, 56

Sharjah (town in Trucial Oman), 182, 185, 205

Shatrah (the Iraq town that Thomas was Political Administrator for), 23, 29, 31, 41, 61, 62, 63, 64, 65, 66, 67, 75, 77, 78, 79, 80, 81, 82, 83, 84, 86, 87, 89, 91, 92, 93, 94, 95, 96, 97, 98, 99, 100, 101, 102, 103, 104

Shihuh / Shihi (tribe or member of that tribe in Musandam Oman), 208, 218, 225, 226, 227, 229, 231, 232, 234, 237, 239, 240, 241, 242, 244, 245, 247, 250, 255, 258, 260, 270, 272, 273

Shinas (Oman town on northern Batinah coast), 163, 197, 199, 200, 209, 211

Sib (coastal town west of Muscat), 121, 122, 124, 127, 219

Soane, Ely Bannister (British administrator in northern Iraq), 58

INDEX

Sowars (Indian soldiers), 30, 36, 101

Strait of Hormuz, 243, 261

Suq ash Shuyukh, 13, 21, 23, 30, 45, 67, 77, 78

Sur (town in eastern Oman), 279, 280, 281, 284, 285, 287

Suwaih (village in central Oman east coast), 287, 292

Suwaiq (coastal town in Batinah), 130, 142, 143

Sykes-Picot Agreement, 53, 56, 57

Taimur bin Faisal, Sultan of Oman, 108, 110, 111, 113, 114, 115, 116, 118, 121, 123, 125, 126, 127, 130, 131, 136, 137, 140, 141, 143, 144, 145, 147, 150, 151, 153, 154, 155, 157, 158, 159, 160, 189, 190, 191, 192, 195, 196, 198, 199, 201, 204, 205, 207, 208, 209, 211, 214, 215, 216, 218, 219, 220, 231, 252, 260, 293, 329, 336

Thomas, Bertram (mentioned by name only), 24, 61, 62, 81, 109, 262, 266, 278, 309, 341

Thuwaini bin Said (Omani mid 19thc Sultan), 189

Townshend, General, (British general involved in several major Iraqi battles in WW1) 66

Trucial Oman (the modern United Arab Emirates, 204, 229, 252, 254

Turkish / Turks / Ottoman, 3, 4, 6, 21, 34, 49, 50, 51, 52, 53, 54, 57, 65, 66, 67, 69, 71, 72, 73, 77, 78, 79, 84, 97, 124, 177, 194, 227, 329

Ubaid, Shaikh (travelled with Thomas in Batinah), 195

Ubaidha (coastal settlement west of Muscat), 118, 219

Wadi Adai (valley near Muscat), 116

Wadi Ainan (Wadi in southern Oman), 316, 317

Wadi Halfain (major wadi descending from the northern mountains to the coast near Mahut), 298

Wadi Jizzi (valley from desert to coast near Sahar), 170, 171

Wadi Sama'il (major valley west of Muscat), 120, 334

Wahhabi (Sunni school of thought, originating in central Arabia), 297

Wataiyah (village near to Muscat), 109, 110, 112, 221

Wilson, Arnold (British civil commissioner in Iraq), 57, 61, 330

Wilson, President (USA), 54, 56

Yal Sa'ad (Omani tribe in Batinah), 142, 145, 148, 217

Yal Wahiba (tribe in eastern Oman), 294, 297, 298, 300, 305, 307, 308

Yiti (coastal village east of Muscat), 117

zar (spirit that can posses a person), 282, 283, 284

zatut (population group in Oman), 148, 149

Zubair, Shaikh (member of the Council of Oman), 242, 250

Zwemer, Samuel (medical practitioner in Oman from USA), 162, 335

CPSIA information can be obtained
at www.ICGtesting.com
Printed in the USA
BVHW040015060421
604237BV00015B/2241